POVERTY IN A LAND OF PLENTY

MARYLAND BICENTENNIAL STUDIES

Sponsored by the Maryland Bicentennial Commission
The Honorable Louise Gore, Chairman

MONOGRAPHS
A Spirit of Dissension: Economics, Politics, and the Revolution in Maryland, by Ronald Hoffman

In Pursuit of Profit: The Annapolis Merchants in the Era of the American Revolution, 1763–1805, by Edward C. Papenfuse

Poverty in a Land of Plenty: Tenancy in Eighteenth-Century Maryland, by Gregory A. Stiverson

DOCUMENTARY EDITIONS
Maryland and the Empire, 1773: The Antilon–First Citizen Letters, by Peter S. Onuf

Representative Government and the Revolution: The Maryland Constitutional Crisis of 1787, by Melvin Yazawa

GREGORY A. STIVERSON

Poverty
in a Land of Plenty

TENANCY
IN EIGHTEENTH-CENTURY
MARYLAND

THE JOHNS HOPKINS UNIVERSITY
PRESS

Baltimore and London

Publication of this volume was assisted by
the Maryland Bicentennial Commission.

Manufactured in the United States of America
The Johns Hopkins University Press, Baltimore, Maryland 21218
The Johns Hopkins Press Ltd., London

Library of Congress Catalog Card Number 77–4554
ISBN 0-8018-1966-0
Library of Congress Cataloging in Publication data will be found
on the last printed page of this book.

FOR
Cynthia Zignego Stiverson
Felicity Ann Zignego Stiverson

CONTENTS

TABLES

FIGURES

PREFACE

The literature on tenancy in the Chesapeake region during the seventeenth and eighteenth centuries is meager, but until recently the general consensus has been that there were relatively few tenants and that tenancy was usually only a temporary status for persons who soon moved into the landowning class.[1] Assessment records reveal, however, that by 1783 nonlandowners comprised at least half of the heads of households in the older settled counties of Maryland and that a large proportion of the householders were tenants in all sections of the province.[2] Other studies of both Maryland and Virginia completed in the last few years suggest that the economic mobility of tenants in the two colonies, defined as their ability to accumulate real and personal property, was exceedingly limited throughout the eighteenth century, with the constriction of opportunity beginning with the decline of tobacco prices in the late seventeenth century and increasing throughout the remainder of the colonial period.[3]

Although the numerical importance of tenants in Maryland has been established and plausible economic causes have been advanced to explain the rise in the number of nonlandowners, little is known about the tenants themselves. Documentary evidence concerning tenants is disproportionately small compared to their number in the total population, and the historian frequently cannot even identify who the tenants were in any given geographical area.

Several factors account for the paucity of evidence concerning tenants in colonial Maryland. Leases were frequently oral agreements that were not systematically recorded. In addition, tenant farmers and planters[4] were not prominent in commerce or politics and many were illiterate. As a result, relatively few private papers were generated by tenants, and references to them in public records are infrequent.

One large body of papers concerning a particular group of tenants in colonial Maryland has survived. These are the proprietary manor papers, and they provide what is essential for any study of tenants—a list of names of leaseholders. Although most of the information on the proprietary tenants was compiled in 1767 and 1768, the possession of manor tenements can be traced backward and forward from those dates. Furthermore, the proprietary papers include data on lease terms, tenement size, natural resources, and the improvements on each leasehold, all of which shed additional light on the life of the tenants.

The proprietary manor papers comprise the core of data for this study, although probate records, land records, assessment lists, and court records were also searched for supplemental information. For some tenants the records were barren, but the data were sufficiently full for others so that the lifestyles and economic conditions of tenants in different parts of the province can be discussed.

Proprietary tenants cannot be exactly equated with the more numerous class of tenants who rented land from private landlords, although most generalizations about the former undoubtedly applied to the latter. On the average, proprietary tenants were better off economically than private tenants, because they paid a much lower rent for their land and they held long-term leases. But an inability to accumulate the capital or to obtain the credit necessary to acquire land and labor characterized both proprietary and private tenants, and the reasons accounting for the lack of economic mobility of members of the one group have validity for the other.

A study of the proprietary tenants reveals factors that affected the lives of the large number of householders in the province who were nonlandowners, but the conclusions that are reached may not be directly applicable to any of the other American colonies. Tenancy in the northern colonies, for example, was undoubtedly dissimilar to that in Maryland. The northern colonies, characterized by numerous urban centers and diversified agriculture conducted on small farms, lacked the pervasive plantation psychology that was fundamental in shaping the character and extent of tenancy in Maryland. Available evidence even casts doubt on the possibility of generalizing from Maryland to Virginia, though the two colonies shared similar staple crops, labor supplies, and commercial networks. The presence of a much larger frontier region in Virginia seems to have resulted in a smaller proportion of tenants in the total population, though even there the opportunity for economic mobility for persons in the lower economic ranks was severely restricted by the mid-eighteenth century.[5]

Although the applicability of the findings of this study to the remainder of the American colonies must await further research, the plethora of recent publications concerning rural populations in England provides some basis for comparing tenancy in Britain and Maryland.[6] The differences between the mother country and the colony are striking, because the feudal customs and obligations that were so important in regulating the lives and protecting the rights of English tenants were completely lacking in Maryland. The divergence of Maryland from the feudal tradition is readily apparent in the proprietary manors, which were not manors at all in the feudal sense, but merely tracts of land reserved for the private use of the proprietor.

Another important difference between English and Maryland tenancy resulted from the method of granting land in the latter. The Maryland land system encouraged the development of spatially dispersed agricultural units, rather than the common fields and farm plots surrounding a central village typical in much of England. As a result, the average tenant in Maryland rented more acreage than his English counterpart, but the greater geographical separation between leaseholds impaired the tenant's ability to band with others to bargain for better terms from the landlord or to launch mutually beneficial programs.

The crop and labor base were also important factors causing Maryland tenancy to develop into a different type of institution than tenancy in England. Tobacco was the universal staple in Maryland in the first decades of settlement, and the necessity of transporting crops long distances to market impeded the adoption of alternative agricultural commodities. The labor-intensive nature of tobacco cultivation nurtured the growth of slavery, and the possession of slaves became an important mark of status, as well as a prerequisite for economic success, in the eighteenth century. Since Maryland tenants could rarely obtain credit to purchase slaves, they were consigned to a relatively lower social status than English tenants. They were also faced with the difficult task of competing in a market dominated by large slaveowners, who almost always had a lower ratio of dependents to laborers than tenants, who rarely owned, or could afford to hire, extrafamilial laborers.

Perhaps the most important difference between tenancy in England and Maryland was that Maryland tenants were in a more ambiguous social position that their English counterparts. The English feudal tradition provided a rationale for tenancy by assigning the tenant an integral role in the social structure. The Maryland tenant lived in a society still dominated by the freehold ideal, but in reality, population and economic pressures had prevented some members of society from ever acquiring land as early as the late seventeenth century. As tenancy became a permanent condition for an ever-increasing number of Maryland householders, the ambiguity of being trapped in what had once been no more than a transitional stage in the progression to freehold status generated a high degree of insecurity. The tenants of private landlords, who by the mid-eighteenth century were often forced to pay rents that exceeded the annual income from their cash crops, moved from place to place in search of land and economic opportunity, but the number who attained those goals constantly declined. By the end of the colonial period, some tenants may have resigned themselves to their condition. The great surge of population into the West after the War for Independence, however, suggests that acquiring land always remained a compelling aspiration for most tenants in Maryland.

The factors accounting for the dissimilarity of English and Maryland tenancy did not result in a uniformity of experience for tenants on Lord Baltimore's manors in the colony. Although tenants on the different proprietary manors paid similar rents and had approximately the same size leaseholds, other factors profoundly affected their lifestyles and opportunities for economic mobility. The natural resources on a tenant's leasehold were the key to his being able to produce surplus crops, but the tenant had little control over the quality of his soil or whether he had adequate supplies of wood or water. The tenant had more control over other factors affecting his life, but social norms, rather than economic considerations, frequently dictated his choice or severely limited his options. Even though he was a member of a lower social and economic class, the tenant was subject to the same social pressures as the wealthier members of society. Just as the most affluent planter could be ruined by conspicuous consumption, so the tenant, on a much smaller scale, could accumulate debts too large for him to pay or could be induced by social values dictated by his economic betters to divert capital into nonproductive consumption. The tenant forced to flee the colony because he could not pay so much as ten shillings sterling per year in rent, the tenant with a single slave worth many times the value of the remainder of his estate, and the tenant whose inventory at death was dominated by a set of silver teaspoons indicate how powerfully the social imperatives of the plantation society bore on even the poorest of its inhabitants.

This study suggests that much can be learned by identifying the variables that affected the lives of tenants. Lower class behavior can reveal as much about the conditions of colonial life as the activities of the social elites, who have received most attention from scholars. Furthermore, variations in the lifestyles of tenants in different geographical regions of the province probably are a more accurate barometer of the local social and economic forces acting on individuals than the behavior patterns of the elite, who were subject to interregional stimuli. Studying tenants, in short, can provide a new perspective on the economic and social history of colonial America, a perspective that is particularly useful for elucidating the differences between groups of people within relatively small geographical areas.

ACKNOWLEDGMENTS

An author invariably accumulates a host of obligations in researching and writing a book, and with the present volume the list of such obligations is perhaps longer than usual. Morris L. Radoff and his staff at the Maryland Hall of Records and P. William Filby and his staff at the Maryland Historical Society always gave freely of their time and professional expertise. Phebe R. Jacobsen deserves special mention for her cheerful encouragement. Edward C. Papenfuse first suggested the topic of this volume, and he has remained a valued adviser and friend. Jack P. Greene, Russel R. Menard, and Paul G. E. Clemens each read the manuscript carefully and provided useful criticisms. I am grateful to Alyce Libby, Donna McDonald, and Stephanie Tooles for assistance in preparing the manuscript, and to Mary Donaldson and Sheila Steinberg for their editing skills.

I had intended to dedicate this book to my parents, Mr. and Mrs. Harold A. Stiverson, and they unquestionably deserve recognition for the support they unfailingly provided whenever it was needed. The final, frantic work on this volume began just as our first child was born, however, and the postman bearing additional edited manuscript that required immediate attention seemed almost maliciously intent on keeping me separated from wife and daughter. Thus, I cannot resist the impulse to celebrate the conclusion of this work and the commencement of real fatherhood by lovingly dedicating this book to them.

POVERTY IN A LAND OF PLENTY

CHAPTER ONE

"A Valuable Augmentation of Riches": The Proprietary Manor System

Throughout much of the seventeenth century, a major problem faced by the Calverts was devising means to populate their province of Maryland in the New World. They adopted a scheme of headright allotments similar to that used in Virginia, and it proved to be effective. By the 1680s, the Calverts were able to discontinue granting headrights, thereafter charging a purchase price for land taken up in the colony. By the end of the century population growth and settlement on the most desirable tracts along the Chesapeake Bay, the rivers that flowed into it, and other transportation routes had caused the price of land to rise.

The Calverts made provisions for sharing in the increase in land values by setting aside specific tracts of land known as the proprietary manors. Although proprietary manors differed from private manors and freeholds in the province, they were not manors in the feudal sense. In essence, the proprietary manors were no more than tracts of land upon which private freeholds could not be granted unless specifically approved by the proprietor.

The proprietor had the option either to sell the manors as the price of land increased or to lease land on them to persons who were unable to acquire a freehold. Although some land was sold as freeholds within a few decades of the establishment of every manor, the Calverts were primarily interested in the long-term revenue potential of the manors. To increase the value of their manor holdings, the proprietors adopted a plan of developmental leasing that involved deferring current income in exchange for improvements intended to increase the value of the manor tenements. Despite a host of managerial problems, developmental leasing did attract hundreds of tenants to the manors, and by the end of the colonial period the proprietor was the largest landlord in the province.

In an effort to encourage settlers to move to their colony in America, the Calverts permitted every immigrant who paid his own passage to claim a specific amount of land for himself and for each person he brought with him. Called headright allotments, these allowances varied from a high of 2,000 acres for every five persons imported in 1633 to only 50 acres for every person imported after June 20, 1652.[1] Although anyone could claim a headright, the Calverts attempted to attract adventurers who would transport large numbers of persons by providing for the erection of private manors in the colony. The owner of a private manor was allowed special privileges as lord of the manor, including the right to enjoy "within the said Mannor a Court Leet and Court Baron, with all things thereunto belonging. . . ."[2] In 1634, a private manor was defined as a tract of 1,000, 2,000, or 3,000 acres, with a 1,000-acre grant requiring the headrights of just five persons. After 1649, 3,000 acres was the smallest tract that could qualify as a private manor, and a grant of that size required the headrights of thirty persons. In 1652, the number of headrights required for a 3,000-acre private manor was increased to sixty. The Calverts continued to grant private manors until 1684. Up to that time they had made sixty-two manorial grants to private individuals.[3]

Although the lure of manorial privileges encouraged a few wealthy immigrants to sail for the colony, most land grants in Maryland prior to 1684 were for parcels containing less acreage than that required for a private manor. The size of these smaller grants was also determined by headrights, but the landowner did not have the right to exercise manorial privileges on his land.[4] Both private manors and freeholds were held in common socage, with the grants conditional only upon the payment of an annual fee, or quitrent, to the proprietor. The amount of the quitrent varied in the early years of settlement, but by 1671 four shillings sterling per 100 acres had become the standard annual rate.[5]

Charles, third Lord Baltimore, abolished the headright system in 1683. Thereafter, land grants in Maryland could be secured only through the payment of a sum of cash called "caution money." Originally amounting to only 200 pounds of tobacco per 100 acres, the proprietor soon raised the caution money to 240 pounds of tobacco, then to forty shillings sterling, and finally, in 1738, to five pounds sterling for each 100 acres of unimproved and uncultivated land patented. Caution money remained the basis for freehold acquisition in Maryland until the end of the colonial period. As with private manors and headright freeholds, the proprietor retained the right to an annual quitrent on all freeholds obtained through the payment of caution money.[6]

A major inducement for attracting settlers to Maryland during the seventeenth century was the low cost of acquiring a freehold, but

Cecilius, second Lord Baltimore, realized that as the population of the province increased the value of land would also rise. The proprietor sought to ensure that he and his descendants would profit by the increase in the price of land by ordering manors to be surveyed for him in all Maryland counties. Proprietary manors were a special type of land grant, consisting of "such parcels of Land as the Lord Proprietor had elected to make his own peculiar private Property."[7] The Calverts owned all vacant land in Maryland, so establishing proprietary manors involved nothing more than prohibiting the erection of private manors and freeholds within specified geographical areas.[8]

When Cecilius, Lord Baltimore, first conceived of setting aside large tracts of vacant land for himself is uncertain, but the decision had been reached by the 1660s when several manors were surveyed for him in the colony.[9] In 1673, the proprietor noted in his instructions to Gov. Charles Calvert that he had previously ordered that at least two proprietary manors of not less than 6,000 acres each be set aside for him in each county. His orders, Lord Baltimore reported, had not been executed.[10] In 1679, the new proprietor, Charles, third Lord Baltimore, sent additional instructions for the erection of two manors in each county to William Talbot, chief secretary of the province.[11] In response to these orders, several manors were surveyed in the 1660s and 1670s, and a few privately owned tracts that had reverted to the proprietor by escheat were also set aside as manors.[12] This initial core of manors was augmented during the eighteenth century as the successive Lords Baltimore issued additional instructions for the establishment of manors in new counties that were erected as well as for reserves around Annapolis and later around Baltimore.[13]

By establishing the first proprietary manors and continuing to order the erection of new manors as the area of settlement in the colony expanded, the Calverts demonstrated their conviction that a lucrative income could be derived from leasing or selling land once population pressure had decreased the quantity of vacant and inexpensive land in the province.[14] The price of land began to rise in the last two decades of the seventeenth century, and the Calverts were able to sell or lease some of their manor lands.[15] Most sales were to favorites, however, and the Calverts appear always to have preferred a policy of leasing manor tracts rather than of selling them. With so much vacant land in the province, the proprietors were unable to attract many tenants to the manors in the seventeenth century. As a result, for the first few decades after proprietary manors were established in Maryland most of the tracts remained uninhabited. Thus, the proprietary manors represented a form of land speculation, one that could eventually pay handsome dividends if the Calverts' heirs exercised patience and judiciously utilized the land that

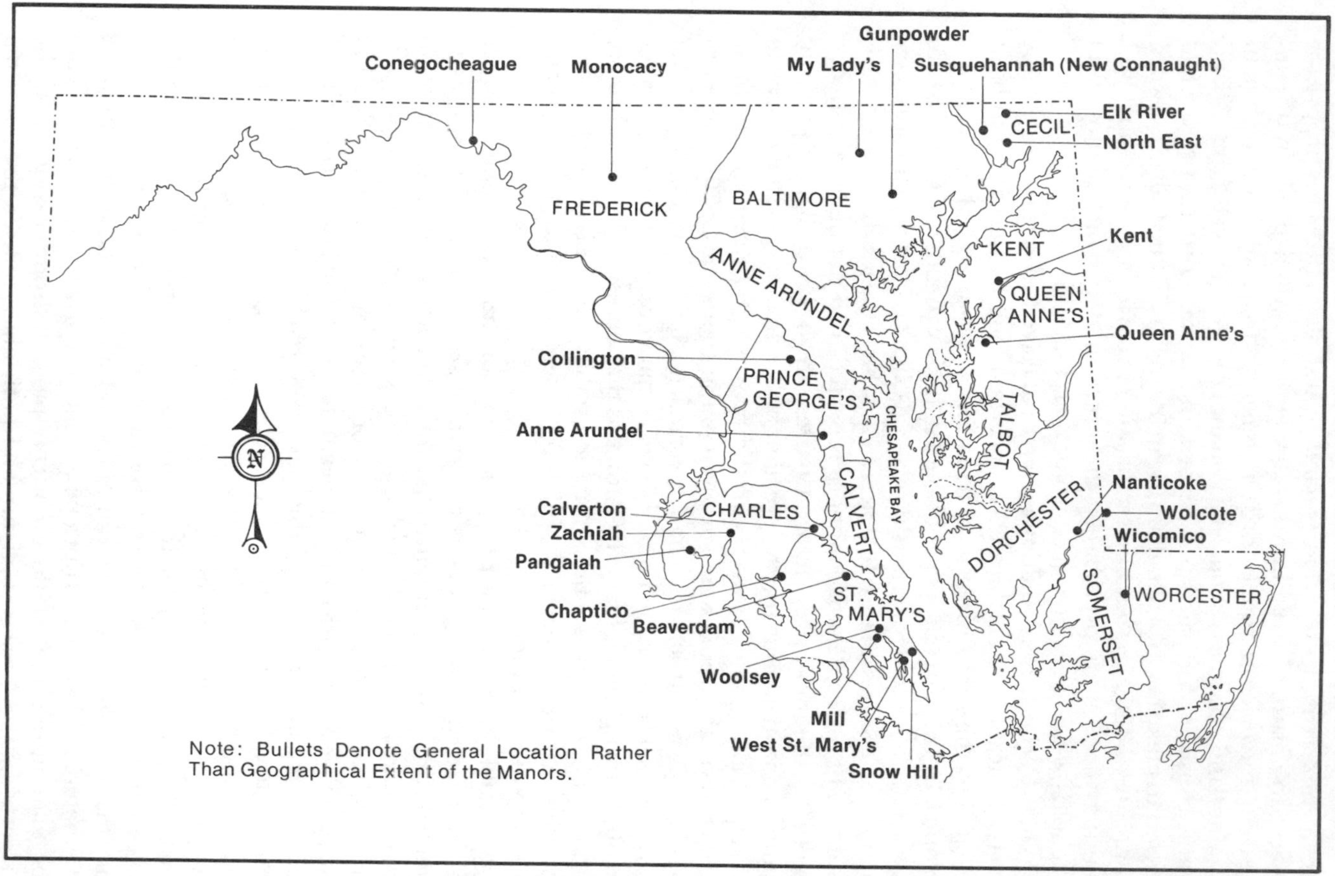

FIGURE 1. Proprietary Manors in Maryland, 1767–1768

Gunpowder

Susquehannah (New Connaught)
Elk River
North East
CECIL
Kent
KENT
QUEEN ANNE'S
Queen Anne's
TALBOT
DORCHESTER
Nanticoke
Wolcote
Wicomico
SOMERSET
WORCESTER

My Lady's
BALTIMORE
ANNE ARUNDEL
PRINCE GEORGE'S
CALVERT
CHESAPEAKE BAY
ST. MARY'S
Mill
Snow Hill
West St. Mary's

Monocacy
FREDERICK
Collington
Anne Arundel
CHARLES
Calverton
Zachiah
Pangaiah
Chaptico
Beaverdam
Woolsey

Conegocheague

Note: Bullets Denote General Location Rather
Than Geographical Extent of the Manors.

had been set aside for them. Cecilius Calvert, secretary to Frederick, sixth Lord Baltimore, summarized the family's reasons for establishing and expanding the manor system in Maryland in a letter written in 1752 to Benjamin Tasker, the proprietor's agent in the colony. According to Calvert the manors were "planned by the first Proprietary to inform his successors, that by reserving Judicially particular Parcels of Lands in and about the Province, such properties in time would be a valuable Augmentation of Riches to them, as the increase of People settling about such Premises would in time make the Demand of them Lands very valuable, and one of the chiefest Recompence for his and their great Expense and Labour for the Enlargement of the Empire and Dominion of Great Britain."[16]

The orders for reserving two manors in each Maryland county were never fully executed, but at various times in the 100 years after 1660 tracts were set aside as proprietary manors. Because the manors were the private property of the Calvert family, the public records of the colony contain few references to them; the manors were never patented, and manor leases were retained by the proprietary agent rather than being recorded in county or provincial deed books. Because of the private nature of the proprietary manor system, identifying the names, locations, and dates the various manors were surveyed would be difficult or impossible if Frederick, sixth and last Lord Baltimore, had not attempted to sell the manors in the mid-1760s. Frederick's decision to divest himself of his manor holdings necessitated a complete survey of each proprietary tract.[17] Papers relating to the sale of the proprietary manors have survived. They include not only the names and locations of all proprietary manors in existence in 1767 and 1768 when the resurveys were made, but also a wide variety of information concerning the occupants of manor leaseholds, the quality of natural resources and improvements on individual manor tracts, and the terms for leasing land on the proprietor's land.[18]

In 1767, the proprietor had twenty-three manors in Maryland, encompassing approximately 190 thousand acres (*see* figure 1).[19] Eleven of the manors, all of which had been erected in the seventeenth century, were located on the lower Western Shore. Four of the eleven were small manors situated in the southern half of St. Mary's County. These manors—West St. Mary's, Snow Hill, Mill, and Woolsey—all contained 2,000 acres or less. Snow Hill was established in 1640, followed by West St. Mary's in 1642, and Mill and Woolsey in the 1660s. In addition to these four manors, two larger proprietary tracts were also located in St. Mary's County. Beaverdam Manor, situated in the west-central portion of the county, contained 7,180 acres when it was first surveyed in 1666.

Chaptico Manor, located on the northern border of the county and extending slightly into Charles County, was surveyed five years later. The original survey for Chaptico Manor has not survived, but the tract contained over 18 thousand acres when it was resurveyed in 1767.

Three of the five remaining manors on the lower Western Shore were located in Charles County. Calverton Manor was surveyed in 1666, followed by Zachiah and Pangaiah manors a year later. Calverton Manor contained 6,000 acres and was situated inland from the Patuxent River on the western border of the county. Zachiah Manor, also surveyed for 6,000 acres, was located at the head of Allen's Fresh Run on the west side of Zachiah Swamp. Located on a tributary of the Port Tobacco River, Pangaiah Manor originally contained only 1,200 acres. The boundaries of the manor became confused during the eighteenth century, however, and when it was resurveyed in 1768, Pangaiah encompassed 10,240 1/2 acres, much of which was freehold land.

Only one proprietary manor was located in Anne Arundel County. Named Anne Arundel, the tract was one of the larger manors reserved for the Calverts. Originally surveyed in 1669 for 10,000 acres, the size of the manor was increased to 12,634 acres in a resurvey made in 1698. The final proprietary tract on the lower Western Shore, Collington Manor, was in Prince George's County. Situated on a tributary of the Patuxent River in the western section of the county, Collington contained 1,100 acres when it was surveyed for the proprietor in 1684.

Just three proprietary manors were erected on the lower Eastern Shore. Nanticoke Manor, situated on the north side of the Nanticoke River in Dorchester County, contained 6,000 acres according to the original survey of 1664. The other two manors were both surveyed in 1674. Wicomico Manor, located on the border between Wicomico and Somerset counties, originally contained 6,000 acres, although encroachments from adjacent freeholds had reduced the acreage to less than 4,000 acres by 1756. Wolcote Manor, originally called "a mannour in Somersett," was situated on the south side of the Nanticoke River, upstream from Nanticoke Manor. Although the manor was surveyed for 6,000 acres, a survey in the 1760s revealed that all but 200 acres of it lay in Delaware.

The first manors erected on the upper Eastern Shore were located in the extreme northern part of the province near the head of the Chesapeake Bay. North East Manor was surveyed for 6,000 acres in 1667, and Elk, or Elk River, Manor, which adjoined North East Manor, appears to have been surveyed at about the same time. To the west of Elk and North East manors was Susquehannah Manor, also called New Connaught Manor. Surveyed in 1683 for George Talbot, an Irish cousin of the second Lord Baltimore, Susquehannah Manor contained 32,000 acres and extended east from Elk and North East manors to the Susquehanna River and north into the present state of Pennsylvania. Following his conviction for murder, Talbot's manor reverted to the proprietor, but conflicting claims to ownership of Susquehannah Manor persisted almost to the end of the colonial period.

The two remaining manors on the upper Eastern Shore were located on the Chester River. The northernmost was Kent Manor, lying in Kent County, which was surveyed in 1675 for 8,000 acres. Queen Anne's Manor, located in the county of the same name, was surveyed in 1681 for 6,000 acres, although the manor was probably the same as the one first surveyed in 1666 and then known as Talbot's Manor.

Three of the four upper Western Shore manors were surveyed in the eighteenth century. The only seventeenth-century manor in the area was Gunpowder, established for the proprietor in 1683 and surveyed for 7,031 acres. Gunpowder Manor was located in the fork between the north and south branches of the Gunpowder River in Baltimore County. Situated upriver from Gunpowder Manor, My Lady's Manor was a 10,000-acre tract surveyed in 1713 for the wife of the proprietor. At her death, Lady Baltimore devised the manor to her relatives, the Brerewoods. Legal ownership of the manor remained a subject of dispute as late as 1768, with both the proprietor and the heirs of the Brerewood family claiming possession.

Located in central Frederick County on the Monocacy River, the 10,000-acre Monocacy Manor was not surveyed until 1724. Even farther west was Conegocheague Manor, surveyed for the proprietor in 1734 for 10,594 1/4 acres. Conegocheague's status as a proprietary manor terminated in 1768 when the proprietor gave the manor to a friend, John Morton Jordan.

In addition to these manors, three other tracts were reserved for the proprietor on the upper Western Shore. In 1768, two proprietary manors containing more than 120 thousand acres were laid out on the extreme western frontier of the province. Little is known about these manors, but with the exception of a few squatters they were not settled during the colonial period. In addition, over 33 thousand acres of extremely poor land in Baltimore County was set aside for the proprietor. Called the Baltimore Reserves, or the Baltimore Reserved Lands, the land was never organized into a coherent tract.[20]

Although a few leases for land on the proprietary manors were issued in the late seventeenth century, there was little demand for manor land until the second and third decades of the eighteenth century.[21] The ability of the proprietor to lease manor tenements was directly related to the growth of population in the province and to the rise in the cost of acquiring a freehold. The number of inhabitants in Maryland more than tripled between 1700 and 1730, and by 1750 there were nearly five times as many residents as there had been at the beginning of the century. Reflecting the increase in population pressure, both improved and un-improved tracts rose in value. Since the lower Western Shore was the first settled area of the colony, population density and a shortage of land caused tenements on manors in that section of the province to be in demand earlier than elsewhere in the colony. Although few original leases have survived, several tenements on the manors in St. Mary's and Charles counties are known to have been rented in the first decade of the eighteenth century, and the number of proprietary tenants in the area slowly increased during the next twenty years. At about the same time, the proprietor's agent was able to begin leasing tracts on manors in the older settled sections of the Eastern Shore.[22]

The first list of proprietary tenants that is at all complete was compiled in 1733, the year that Charles, fifth Lord Baltimore, visited the colony.[23] This list is somewhat deficient, because it omits returns from several manors that are known to have been at least partly tenanted by that date. Leases on Gunpowder Manor, for example, were issued as early as 1720, and yet no account is given of tenants or rents for that manor.[24] In addition, Anne Arundel Manor was so close to the capital, Annapolis, that it must have been tenanted by 1733.[25] Manor stewards were fre-quently remiss in their duties, however, and they were probably respon-sible for the 1733 list being less than comprehensive.

Although the 1733 list does not include information for every tene-ment leased by that date, it does provide an indication of early settlement patterns on the manors.[26] By 1733, the manors in St. Mary's and Charles counties on the lower Western Shore were all well tenanted, and a few leases had been issued for land on the lower Eastern Shore (*see* table 1–1). Tenement size averaged over 200 acres on all of the Eastern Shore manors except Nanticoke, but it was closer to 150 acres on the more heavily populated Western Shore manors. The manors on the upper Western and Eastern shores were untenanted, with the exception of a lease to the Principio Iron Works for land on Susquehannah and North East manors in Cecil County. The lease had been issued to the ironworks to provide it with a source of woodland and probably involved the set-tlement of few households in addition to those of the men employed at the works.[27]

Subsequent to 1733, no comprehensive list of proprietary tenants was compiled until the years 1767 and 1768. But proprietary financial ac-counts show that manor revenues rose from £170.13.11 1/2 sterling in

TABLE 1-1
Tenants on the Proprietary Manors, 1733

Manor	County	Number of Tenants	Acres Leased	Average Acres per Leaseholder
Western Shore:				
Mill				
Woolsey				
West St. Mary's				
St. John's	St. Mary's	29	3,566½	123.0
Beaverdam	St. Mary's	33	4,956	150.2
Chaptico	St. Mary's	22	3,745	170.2
Calverton	Charles	30	3,454	115.1
Zachiah	Charles	14	2,665	190.4
Pangaiah	Charles	2	1,737½	868.7
Collington	Prince George's	4	1,760½	440.1
Eastern Shore:				
Kent	Kent	5	1,351½	270.3
Queen Anne's	Queen Anne's	2	436¼	218.1
Nanticoke	Dorchester	6	697	116.2
Susquehannah and North East	Cecil	1	—	—
		148	24,369¼ +	

SOURCE: Calvert Papers, no. 914, Maryland Historical Society, Baltimore, Maryland.

1733 to £740.19.8 sterling in 1748, indicating both a rapid rise in the demand for leasehold land and in the number of tenants on the manors.[28]

The most important reason for the rise in the number of tenants on the proprietary manors was that after 1733 the terms of acquiring a lease were changed, making it less expensive to become a tenant.[29] Only a few leases issued prior to 1733 have survived, but they reveal that between 1701 and 1726 a consideration fee of four pounds sterling was charged upon the delivery of a lease to a tenant.[30] The consideration fee was a large sum in the early eighteenth century and it greatly restricted the number of people who could afford to become proprietary tenants.

The consideration fee was dropped in 1734 and thereafter the number of leases for land on the proprietary manors increased rapidly. The annual rent for manor land remained unchanged, however, which raises the question of why the proprietor would voluntarily relinquish the revenue he derived from the consideration fee. A Kent Manor lease, issued in 1731, carried a consideration fee of only two pounds sterling, half the amount charged on all earlier leases that have survived. The proprietor may have been attempting to encourage leasing of the manors by lowering the consideration fee, and if so, he must have determined that even two pounds sterling was too much for most nonlandowners in the colony to pay.[31] Since Charles, fifth Lord Baltimore, visited Maryland in 1733, he must have decided at that time that by attracting more tenants to his manors the increase in annual rents and the improvements that they would make on their tenements would more than offset the loss in revenue caused by the elimination of the consideration fee. By dropping the consideration payment to encourage the leasing of the manors, the proprietor fully embraced a policy of developmental leasing.[32]

The principal object of developmental leasing was to encourage tenants to develop previously uncultivated land into working farms and plantations so that the rental or sale value of the tract would be increased. Ideally, developmental leasing benefited both landlord and tenant. The tenant received a tract of land for a low annual rent, and the landlord could charge much higher rates when the first lease expired, counterbalancing the years of small income from the developmental lease.

Leases issued prior to 1734 were developmental to a limited extent, because the proprietor's tenants were required to plant an apple orchard and to refrain from wasting woodlands. Although the proprietor was not adopting a completely new policy when he relinquished the consideration fee, his actions did signal a new program designed to attract tenants to the manors. The proprietor believed that developmental leasing could succeed only if most of the land on each manor was leased to tenants who would improve their tenements. The principal difference between leases that included the consideration fee and leases issued after 1734 was that the latter relied on improvements to increase the value of the leasehold in preference to the immediate monetary return of a consideration fee.

Developmental leases issued by the proprietor varied from one manor to another, but all contained several standard provisions.[33] The proprietor customarily reserved his right to mines of gold, silver, copper, lead, tin, and iron discovered on any tenement. Furthermore, a forfeiture clause was included in every lease allowing the proprietor to reclaim the property if the rent was overdue for a specified period of time, usually thirty days, and the proprietor reserved the right to cancel a lease if the tenant wasted wood or failed to pay an alienation fine upon conveying his lease to a third party. Leases issued after 1734 included more stringent restrictions against wasting timber than earlier leases had, suggesting that promiscuous timber cutting had occurred on tenements leased earlier in the century. After 1734, tenants were forbidden to cut more wood than was necessary for constructing improvements on their lots or for clearing land for cultivation. Finally, all leases required that at the expiration of the agreement the property be surrendered in "tenantable Repair and order," the anticipated end product of the developmental lease.[34]

In addition to the standard provisions that appeared in all developmental leases, tenants on most manors were required to construct specific improvements at their own expense (*see* table 1–2). On most of the proprietary manors, leaseholders were required to build a "substantial dwelling house" thirty feet long by twenty feet wide with a brick chimney. Surviving leases for land on the Baltimore Reserves and on Wicomico and Zachiah manors omitted the house requirement, probably because the land on each of the tracts was so poor that tenants would have been deterred from accepting leases if they had been forced to build such large dwellings.[35] Furthermore, tenants on all proprietary manors were required to plant an orchard, generally consisting of 100 trees. The orchard had to be planted within five years of the execution of the lease, the tenant had to protect it with a strong fence, and he was required to replant trees that died or were destroyed. The only exceptions to the usual number of trees required in developmental leases was that tenants on Queen Anne's Manor had to plant 1 tree for each acre of land they leased, and tenants on Zachiach Manor were required to plant 200 trees regardless of the size of their tract.[36]

TABLE 1-2
Terms of Leasing Tenements on Proprietary Manors for
Which Original Leases Survive, ca. 1734–1755

Manor	Tenure	Rent per 100 Acres (sterling)	Alienation Fine (sterling)	House Required	Orchard Required
Anne Arundel	21 years	£3.15.0 to 5.0.0	£7.0.0 to 10.0.0	yes	yes
Baltimore Reserves	99 years	0.10.0	0.10.0	no	no
Chaptico	3 lives	0.10.0	0.20.0	yes	yes
Zachiah	3 lives	0.10.0	0.20.0	no	yes
Gunpowder	3 lives	0.10.0	0.20.0	yes	yes
Wicomico	3 lives	0.10.0	0.20.0	no	yes
Nanticoke	3 lives	0.10.0	0.20.0	yes	yes
Kent	3 lives	0.10.0	0.10.0	yes	yes
Queen Anne's	3 lives	0.10.0 + 2 capons	0.20.0 + 4 capons	yes	yes
Susquehannah (New Connaught)	3 lives	0.20.0	0.40.0	yes	yes
Elk River	3 lives	0.10.0	0.10.0	yes	yes
North East	3 lives	0.10.0	0.20.0	yes	yes

SOURCE: Proprietary Leases A–C, Hall of Records, Annapolis, Maryland; Original Proprietary Leases, Scharf Papers, Maryland Historical Society, Baltimore, Maryland.

Developmental leases never required a tenant to clear a specific amount of land for cultivation, although some leases stipulated that one-fourth of the tenement was to remain uncleared.[37] The proprietor assumed that tenants would clear land without being forced to do so, because they could not produce an income from crops unless they did. Dwelling houses and orchards were specifically mentioned in leases because otherwise neighboring landowners could have rented manor land as extensions to their freeholds without making any improvements. Merely clearing the land would not necessarily add to the value of a leasehold, but building a house and planting an orchard transformed the land into a habitable tenement.[38]

Although the provisions of developmental leases varied slightly from one manor to another, all tenants on the same manor were usually required to construct similar improvements to fulfill their obligations to the proprietor. In special cases, however, the proprietary agent or the governor of the province did alter the requirements for leasing a particular tract of manor land. The most frequent change in lease terms was the deletion of the dwelling and orchard clauses. Exemption from making these improvements was usually given when the tenement was very small or when the lease was a renewal on a previously developed tract.[39] Most leases that exempted the tenant from customary obligations were issued after 1760, but as early as 1737 John Parnham, Jr.'s lease for a tract on Chaptico Manor concluded with the statement that "no advantage shall be taken of the within Lessee in case he does not Comply with [the] requirements of the Orchard & house."[40] Other minor variations found in some leases were an omission of the obligation to pay capons in addition to the monetary rent and a reduction in the dimensions of the house that was to be built.[41]

The proprietor would have benefited if his agents had insisted that a lessee perform substitute labor when there was no need for the usual improvements on a leasehold. Only one lease has been found, however, where an alternative type of improvement was substituted for the customary tenant obligations. Gerrit McKenney's lease for fourteen acres of marsh land on Elk River Manor required that he "well and faithfully Ditch and secure the aforesaid marsh so as to make a Good meadow thereof" and maintain the meadow until the lease expired.[42] In other cases where the usual requirements for improvements were deleted from a lease, no additional obligations were imposed on the tenant.

Since developmental leases generally required the tenant to construct specific improvements at his own expense, the proprietor had to compensate by providing the tenant with favorable lease terms. Tenants usually benefited from developmental leases in one of two ways: they paid a very small annual rent, or the tenure of their lease was much longer than that of conventional leases. Tenants on the Maryland proprietary manors received both benefits.[43]

Except for land on Anne Arundel Manor and some tenements on Susquehannah Manor, developmental leases on the proprietor's land generally cost only ten shillings sterling per 100 acres,[44] far less than the rents charged by large private landlords in the colony.[45] Furthermore, land on every manor except Anne Arundel and the Baltimore Reserves was leased for three lives. In three-life leases, the lessee named three persons as the "lives," and the lease did not expire until the last of the three had died. Because the term of three-life leases was dependent upon the longevity of the persons named in the lease, tenure was uncertain. Tenants customarily named two of their children in three-life leases in the hope that at least one would survive to adulthood, thus extending the tenure of the lease to several decades. Tenants took a risk when they named young children in their leases, but evidence from the proprietary manors indicates that such leases frequently remained valid for forty or more years.[46] The two manors that were leased on terms other than for three lives were both exceptional. The proximity of Anne Arundel Manor to Annapolis and the high quality of its soil enabled the proprietor to charge double the usual rent on the first developmental leases and to make them valid for only twenty-one years. The Baltimore Reserves, on the other hand, was a vast expanse of extremely poor land, descriptively called the "Barrens,"[47] and to induce settlement in the area the proprietor was compelled to offer especially favorable lease terms and to allow a ninety-nine-year tenure.[48]

The success of developmental leasing on the Maryland proprietary manors depended on several factors. First, tenants had to be enticed to rent all or most of the manor leaseholds, but this posed little problem because three-life leases at ten shillings sterling per 100 acres were better terms than could be obtained from private landlords. Second, tenants had to make the improvements specified in their leases, or the proprietor could not raise rents at the expiration of the first lease. Finally, the manors had to be closely supervised to ensure that the conditions of the developmental leases were carried out, that rents were collected, and that all leases were renewed at a higher rate to reflect the value of the improvements that had been made on the leaseholds.

Anne Arundel Manor provides an example of successful developmental leasing. The location of the manor was excellent, since it was near the capital, Annapolis, and its western boundary was a navigable river. Furthermore, the manor had exceptionally fertile soil that was particularly well suited to the cultivation of high-quality tobacco.[49] Because of the manor's location and the quality of its soil, the proprietor was able from the beginning to extract double the usual rent, or twenty shillings sterling per 100 acres, on twenty-one-year leases.[50]

Despite the less favorable lease terms, Anne Arundel Manor was quickly populated by tenants. The leaseholders built houses, cleared fields, and made other improvements on their tenements, which, combined with the intrinsic worth of the land, enabled the proprietor to raise the rents when the developmental leases began to expire. By 1746, the cost of renting 100 acres on Anne Arundel Manor had risen from £0.20.0 sterling to £3.15.0 sterling.[51] Rents were increased again in 1754, and thereafter a twenty-one-year lease on 100 acres cost £5.0.0 sterling.[52] The proprietor undoubtedly hoped that his other manors would yield increasing revenues similar to those of Anne Arundel Manor, but this was not the case. Developmental leasing was a failure everywhere in the colony except on Anne Arundel Manor. The reasons for the failure of the proprietor's developmental leasing plan are instructive for what they reveal about the management of the manors as well as for the light they shed on the administration of the province as a whole.

Managing the farflung network of proprietary manors would have been difficult under the best of circumstances, but a number of obstacles impeded their efficient administration. One serious problem resulted from a defect built into the whole land system of the colony. Ideally, each manor should have been surveyed in the shape of a rectangle with individual lots being formed from equal subdivisions. A rectangular manor of 1,000 acres, for example, could have been laid out into ten 100-acre tenements following a simple gridwork pattern. Several of the proprietary manors were approximately rectangular in shape, but individual lots on every manor were surveyed without regard to a systematic plan.[53]

Neither freeholds nor manor leaselots were surveyed prior to the application of a potential purchaser or lessee. In the case of freeholds, the prospective purchaser obtained a land warrant for a specific number of acres of vacant land, took the warrant to the county surveyor, and showed him where he wanted the tract located. The best land was inevitably surveyed first, leaving poorer land vacant.[54] Frequently, land excluded from earlier surveys was in such small strips and irregular pieces that it was of little value to anyone except persons owning land on either side. Most vacancies were too small to support separate families, and yet purchasers could not be coerced into including poor land in their surveys. By the mid-eighteenth century, planters resurveying their land were required to incorporate surrounding vacancies, but the waste caused by small tracts of unpatented land remained a persistent problem throughout the colonial period.[55]

Manor tenements were laid out in the same manner as freeholds. When a tenant applied for a lease on one of the proprietary manors, the manor steward surveyed the lot, beginning at a point and following a course indicated by the lessee.[56] Poor soil, land without adequate water, and thinly timbered sections of the manors were avoided by lessees. As with freeholders, tenants were eventually required to incorporate vacancies whenever their leaselots were resurveyed, but as late as the mid-1760s many vacancies were still to be found on every manor.[57]

The practice of laying out lots wherever a tenant desired created several problems. First, a considerable amount of manor land could not be leased because vacancies between tenements were usually too small for separate leaseholds. Second, because leaselots could be laid out in an endless variety of shapes, calculating the acreage contained in each tenement was difficult.[58] Third, manor stewards could not do an efficient job leasing manor tenements, nor could they prevent tenants from exploiting vacancies, unless they had accurate plats of the manors.[59] Charles, fifth Lord Baltimore, and Frederick, sixth Lord Baltimore, repeatedly requested that the manors be surveyed, but the complexity of manor leaseholds made the job difficult and their instructions were usually ignored.[60] Finally, colonial surveyors frequently used perishable boundary markers, such as trees and fenceposts. If each manor tenement had been surveyed according to a standard size and shape, the problem of disappearing boundary markers would not have been so great. But many leaselots had dozens of lines, and boundary markers were inevitably lost, resulting in conflicting claims regarding what portions of the manors were leased.

The way in which manor leaselots were surveyed was only one factor complicating the management of the proprietary tracts. Another was the presence of patented land within the boundaries of manors. Occasionally, patented land was intentionally encompassed within the boundaries of a new manor, because no other sizable tract of vacant land was available in the area.[61] In other instances, patented tracts were inadvertently laid out on manor land, especially when the surveyor was uncertain where the boundaries of the manor were located. Pangaiah Manor, for example, was severely encroached upon by patented lands, allegedly because no one knew where the boundaries of the manor lay.[62] Most patented tracts within the manors, however, resulted from proprietary grants to favorites.[63] The proprietor had the right to permit individuals to survey freeholds on the manors, but the practice made the job of the steward much more difficult. When leaselots were separated by large tracts of private land, the manor steward was impeded in his effort to oversee all the tenements for which he was responsible.[64] Furthermore, freeholds given to favorites were usually surveyed from the best land on

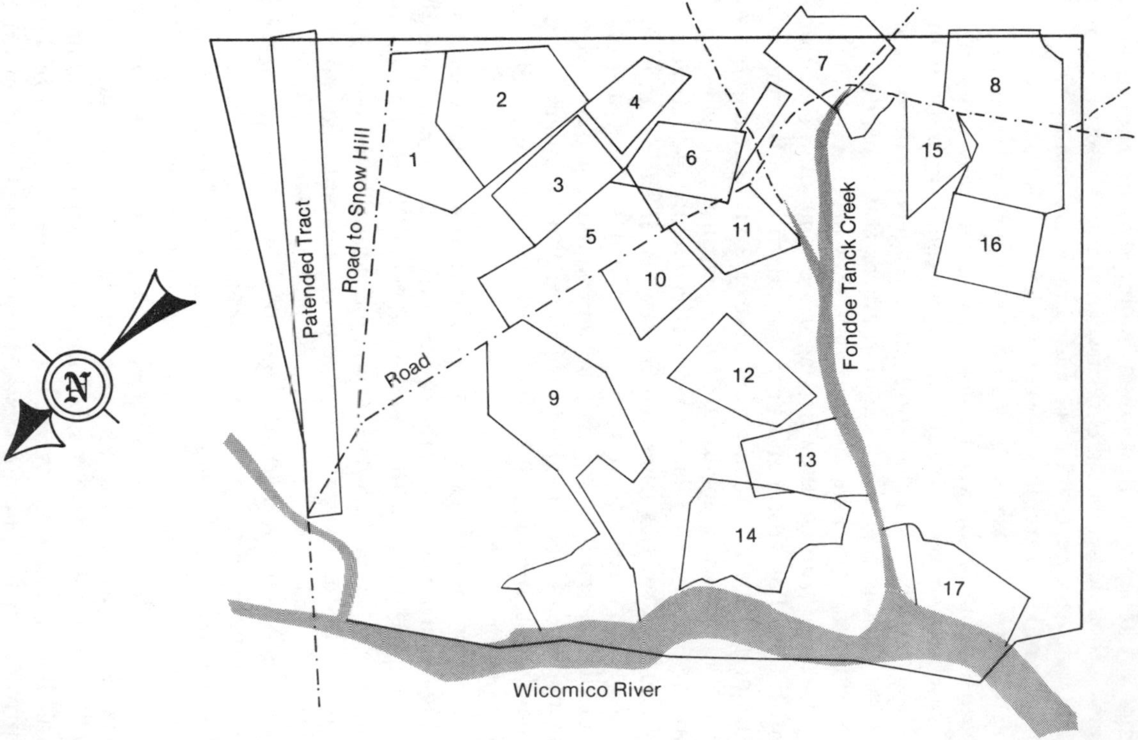

FIGURE 2. Wicomico Manor, 1756

Source: Plats, Division 4, No. 1, Hall of Records, Annapolis, Maryland.

the manor, which meant that the steward was left with the less desirable tracts to rent.[65]

A plat of Wicomico Manor, dated December 20, 1756, illustrates the haphazard development of manor leaseholds (see figure 2).[66] About half of the manor was still vacant in 1756, and the existing tenements had been laid out in fairly simple shapes. To lease the remaining land on the manor, however, the steward would have been compelled to execute some highly complex surveys. Only one small patented tract had been laid out on the manor, and as yet it did not separate any of the manor tenements. The vacant land to the east of the patented tract, however, might have been difficult to lease, and the freehold tract did encompass a section of the main road that passed through the manor.

The Wicomico plat shows that one consideration important to early leaseholders on the manor was having access to transportation routes. Lots 9, 12, 13, 14, and 17 bordered the river, and lots 1, 5, 6, 7, 8, 9, 10, 11, and 15 adjoined a road. Lot 9 was bounded by both a road and the Wicomico River, a highly desirable situation that was achieved by connecting two large tracts by a narrow corridor of land. Even though much of the manor was still unleased in 1756, a number of small vacancies could be found, particularly the interstices between lots 2, 3, 4, 5, and 6. Finally, the Wicomico plat reveals several examples of inaccurate surveying. Some lots overlapped each other, especially lots 13 and 14, and others protruded outside the manor, especially lot 7.

Poor surveying and the haphazard method of laying out tenements complicated the management of the proprietary manors, but they alone could not have caused the failure of developmental leasing. Administrative problems were far more important and damaging. Perhaps the most important reason for the inefficient management of the manors was the absentee status of the proprietor. If the proprietor had resided in the colony, the manors would certainly have received more attention from provincial officials. The fact that a list of tenants and their annual rents was compiled in 1733, immediately after the visit to the colony of Charles, fifth Lord Baltimore, indicates that the presence of the proprietor made a decided difference.[67] But with the proprietor residing in England, sending only occasional instructions to the colony, his manor system inevitably suffered from neglect.[68]

Another reason for the failure of developmental leasing was the insufficient remuneration provided manor stewards.[69] Stewards received a rent-free tenement plus a commission on rents collected, but the commission was inadequate to induce them to be diligent.[70] When a tenant failed to deliver his annual rent to the manor steward's house as required by his lease, the steward had little monetary incentive to seek him out.[71] Furthermore, stewards were frequently responsible for far more land

than they could effectively manage. Young Parren, for example, was the
steward for all the manors in St. Mary's and Charles counties, a total of
more than 35,000 acres of land (*see* table 1–3). Although his respon-
sibilities were great, Parren's annual commission could not have exceeded £18 sterling prior to the late 1750s.[72] Despite the low pay, Parren
was a conscientious steward, collecting an average of £123 sterling, or
nearly 70 percent of the maximum amount due, from the proprietor's
tenants for the years 1752 to 1761.[73]

TABLE 1-3
Average Annual Revenue from Proprietary Manors and Reserves, 1752–1761

Manor	Acres	Average Revenue Per Annum (sterling)	Average Maximum Revenue[a] (sterling)
Anne Arundel	10,680⅞	£266	£534
West St. Mary's			
Snowhill			
Woolsey			
St. John's			
St. Barbara's			
Mill	35,172½	123	176
Beaverdam			
Chaptico			
Calverton			
Zachiah			
Pangaiah			
Gunpowder	7,265¼	30	36
My Lady's	10,000	38	50
Collington	3,001½	4	15
Monocacy and Conegocheague	21,586	19	108
Susquehannah (New Connaught)	32,000	103	160
Kent	8,000	23	40
Queen Anne's	6,000	10	30
Nanticoke	6,000	5	30
Wicomico	3,957	5	20
North East and Elk River	22,000	12	110
Baltimore Reserves	33,036	112	165
	198,699⅛	£750	£1,474

SOURCE: Executive Papers, portfolio 3, folder 19; Prince George's County Unpatented
Certificates, no. 91, both at the Hall of Records, Annapolis, Maryland; Claim of Henry
Harford, Public Record Office, Audit Office 12/79, f. 127, London (microfilm copy
available at the Hall of Records, Annapolis, Maryland); Calvert Papers, nos. 927, 932, 935,
939, 943, 955, 956, 960, and 977, Maryland Historical Society, Baltimore, Maryland.

[a]The estimate for maximum possible revenue assumes that rents were collected for the
total acreage on every manor. For Anne Arundel Manor, the estimate is based on five
pounds sterling per 100 acres. All other estimates are based on ten shillings sterling per
100 acres. Estimates and actual revenue figures are rounded off to the nearest pound.

Other stewards did not consider the commission adequate to warrant a strenuous effort to collect the rents due from their tenants. The steward for Monocacy and Conegocheague manors, for example, was responsible for 21,586 acres and returned an average of only nineteen pounds sterling per year to the proprietor between 1752 and 1761.[74] The steward for Nanticoke Manor returned only one-sixth the amount of money that the land he was responsible for should have produced during the same decade, and North East and Elk River manors yielded less than one-ninth of the sum they could have produced. As table 1–3 shows, these examples are not exceptional. Not all manors were completely leased, of course, but the data in the table do not include additions to manor revenues from alienation fines. The difference between the annual receipts received from the stewards during the decade from 1752 to 1761 and the maximum possible revenue that could have been derived from the manors clearly suggests widespread negligence on the part of manor stewards.[75]

In addition to the absence of the proprietor and the laxity of the manor stewards, the effective management of the manors was hindered by certain high-placed provincial officials. Edward Lloyd, a wealthy Talbot County planter who was the proprietor's agent and receiver general from 1753 to 1768, was directly responsible for much mismanagement of the proprietary land revenues. Despite repeated pleas and admonitions from the proprietor, the proprietor's secretary, and Gov. Horatio Sharpe, Lloyd refused to transact the duties of his office promptly or adequately. As early as 1755, Lloyd was nearly two years behind in settling his accounts with the proprietor, and later in 1755 Cecilius Calvert wrote to Governor Sharpe that the proprietor was so distressed with Lloyd's conduct that he intended to remove him from office if he did not improve immediately. The proprietor did not dismiss Lloyd, however, and in 1760 Governor Sharpe explained to Lord Baltimore that the reorganization of the manors had been delayed because Lloyd "seldom spends a Day in Annapolis and his Attention & Thoughts are so engrossed by his own affairs I have long despaired seeing any Plan for their better Regulation carried into Excecution. . . ." Insulted because Sharpe had ordered an audit of his accounts, Lloyd finally resigned in 1768, only to be replaced by an equally inept man, the Rev. Bennett Allen.[76]

Having defended the proprietor against a rape charge, Allen was one of Frederick, Lord Baltimore's, favorites, and he made conspicuous and offensive use of his proprietary influence. Allen quickly alienated many influential citizens of the colony, including Samuel Chase, who threw Allen out of his house while flailing at him with a stick, and the powerful Dulanys, one of whom, Lloyd Dulany, Allen later shot to death in a duel.[77] Allen, like Lloyd, had neither the perseverance nor the dedication necessary to institute a comprehensive reform of the proprietary land system, let alone to develop a rational procedure for managing the proprietary manors.

Although administrative inefficiency was the primary cause for the failure of developmental leasing on the proprietary manors, the tenants must also bear a large part of the blame. John Anstey, the Loyalist claims commissioner who investigated the case of Henry Harford, the natural son and heir of the last Lord Baltimore, analyzed the problems that afflicted the proprietary manor system. Anstey concentrated on managerial deficiencies, explaining that the "rents reserved upon the Leases were ill collected though as amply assured as the Quitrents . . . partly owing to the laxness of the Steward[s], the smallness of the commission to the collector and the Indulgence and remissness of the Agent. . . ." In addition to general "bad management," however, Anstey commented on the problem of "Tenants running away and selling their leases fraudulently."[78] If developmental leasing was to succeed, tenants had to make the improvements required by their leases. But given the neglect of the provincial officials responsible for the manors, the fact that many tenants failed to abide by their lease agreements is not surprising. Lists drawn up in 1767 and 1768 describing each proprietary tenement show that many tenants had made no improvements on their lots.[79] In other cases, leaseholders had stripped all the timber from their land, rendering the tenements nearly worthless.[80] The man who surveyed the tenements on Nanticoke Manor in November 1767, for example, concluded his report by noting that "the whole Manor is much Pillaged of Timber."[81] Other lots, which had not so much as a single building on them, had been cultivated until the land was completely exhausted.[82]

In addition to failing to abide by the provisions of their leases, tenants were guilty of other practices detrimental to developmental leasing. Some people lived on manor land without ever procuring a lease. Squatters occasionally paid rent as though they held a lease, but usually they paid nothing.[83] A plat of Kent Manor, dated 1709, shows four tenants holding leases and five others "settled on their own account."[84] Squatters were still a problem in the 1760s, when Governor Sharpe made a concerted effort to force them to take out leases. But as late as the Revolution some people were still living on the manors who had no other right than possession.[85]

Not only did some people live on the manors as squatters, but many others who did hold valid leases were unable to pay the small annual rent due to the proprietor. A comparison of rents collected on Monocacy Manor in 1757 with the number of lots leased reveals that rents were due on a minimum of thirty-seven lots, totaling 4,864 acres, but rents were received on only twenty-one lots, encompassing 3,009 acres.[86] Jonathan

Hall, steward for Queen Anne's Manor, reported in 1767 that rents and arrears due from his tenants amounted to £73.12.0 3/4 sterling, but he had only been able to collect £28.12.10 1/4 sterling. Young Parren's accounts for the manors in St. Mary's County show that rents totaling £136.17.2 sterling were due for the year 1765. Arrears of rents more than equaled that amount, however, and although Parren's account does not reveal how much he could collect of the £291.0.0 3/4 sterling that was due, nonpayment by his tenants was obviously a serious problem.[87]

In addition to an annual rent, proprietary tenants were required to pay an alienation fine equal to not less than one year's rent whenever they renewed their lease or sold it to a third party. Alienation fines were rarely collected before the 1760s, however, even though tenants were guilty of "selling their leases fraudulently" when they failed to pay the fine.[88] In 1760, Lord Baltimore complained about the small revenue produced by alienation fines, and thereafter Governor Sharpe attempted to increase that part of the proprietor's income.[89] Each leaseholder was assessed for the arrears of fines due on his tenement, and in some cases the accumulated fines amounted to several times the annual rent.[90] The proprietor's income from fines did increase in the 1760s, but the size of the arrears indicates widespread noncompliance by tenants in paying the alienation fee before that decade.[91]

Twenty years after the proprietor had adopted developmental leasing in the early 1730s as a means for tenanting his Maryland lands, the manor system was in total disarray. The successive Lords Baltimore occasionally admonished their provincial officials concerning the mismanagement of the manors, but no serious attempt at reform was initiated until Frederick, sixth Lord Baltimore, named Horatio Sharpe governor of the colony in 1753.[92] Sharpe served as the colony's chief executive until 1769, and the record of his administration reveals a man who was for the most part both responsible and competent.[93] From the time Sharpe was inducted as governor, his correspondence with the proprietor reveals that Baltimore's main concern was that Sharpe increase the revenue produced by the colony in every way possible. On May 14, 1755, for example, Baltimore wrote Sharpe that he was "well satisfied" with his "zeal and capacity for the service of his majesty & myself," and with particular reference to himself added, "I desire you will see the collection of my Revenues established on the best footing, the completion of which as I have some time expected I beg may no longer be delayed."[94] Sharpe's efforts to satisfy his employer's pecuniary desires centered on four measures: lowering the commission paid to the collectors of the quitrent, improving the quality and accessibility of land records, increasing the returns from alienation fines, and reorganizing the proprietary manor system.

Sharpe's attempts to improve the management of the proprietor's affairs met with constant resistance and impediments. People were loath to pay more than they already did to the proprietor; all efforts at reform were hindered by the French and Indian War; and Lord Baltimore indirectly interfered by appointing incompetent men to high office and by continuing to support them longer than he should. Despite the obstacles, Sharpe proposed various measures designed to regularize and rationalize the proprietary manor system, and his efforts were at least partly successful.

Sharpe immediately recognized that nothing could be done about reforming the manor system until accurate plats of each manor were made, and during his first year as governor he ordered all the manors resurveyed.[95] Cecilius Calvert, Lord Baltimore's uncle and secretary, applauded Sharpe's determination to have the manors platted, but warned that he should "take care how they do them, otherways they will be sadly executed. . . ." Calvert further requested that the plats be "all of a size Large & Booked with the Particularys relating to the premises [of each tenement] fairly & with accuracy incerted. . . ."[96]

On October 20, 1755, Sharpe reported to Calvert that the plats were still not completed, although he had "left Nothing undone" to expedite the task.[97] Not until early 1757 was Sharpe finally able to transmit a book containing plats of most of the manors in the province. The plats were less than satisfactory, however, because some were of poor quality and none included descriptions of the improvements on individual leaseholds.[98] Sharpe explained that the deficiencies in the plats were due to the "Neglect of those who have heretofore had the Care & Management of these Lands, None of whom have recorded or Kept Copies of the Leases that they granted, & as many Tenants have lost their Leases & know not how their Lands are situated or bounded the Surveyors have scarcely any thing to direct them in running out the Tenements. . . ."[99] Furthermore, Sharpe noted that the boundaries of individual lots on some manors "greatly interfere with & intersect each other," a situation that could only be rectified by completely resurveying each tract.[100] In short, Sharpe's labors of over three years had produced a book of manor plats that was incomplete, deficient in detail, and of little use to the proprietor, the governor, or the manor stewards.[101]

But the difficulty Sharpe experienced in making even inferior plats of some of the proprietary manors produced one positive result. The main obstacle confronting the surveyors who had attempted to resurvey the manors was that the boundaries of individual tenements could not be located because the original leases had been lost and the proprietary agent had failed to retain copies. This convinced Sharpe that a general reorganization of the proprietary manor system was necessary and that the major emphasis should be placed on both stimulating the individual manor stewards to perform their jobs more effectively and on collecting and preserving all relevant documents pertaining to the manors.[102]

On July 30, 1757, Sharpe wrote to Secretary Calvert proposing several major changes in the management of the manors. He reiterated that the disorganization of the manor system was due to inadequate administration in the past and the loss of original leases. Stewards, the keystone in the system, had been "heretofore extremely negligent," and in addition, some "resided at so great a Distance from the Mannours which they were appointed to take Care of that perhaps they never or very seldom saw them." The problem with the stewards, Sharpe believed, was that "the Sallaries allowed were too small to encourage a Person of Credit to undertake that Duty or to induce any one to execute it with Dilligence."[103]

Sharpe suggested that the proprietor invest a small percentage of his revenue from the manors to raise the commissions of the stewards. Rather than providing them rent-free tenements and small commissions on rents collected, commissions should be offered that would be sufficiently large to induce the stewards to work actively toward improving the management of the manors. Although the initial investment in higher commissions would decrease proprietary revenues, Sharpe contended that "his Lordship would in the End be a Gainer seeing it might be expected that the mannours would be better managed & in all probability better tenanted."[104]

According to Sharpe's plan, each steward would be required to keep a book in which all leases as well as a description of every leasehold were recorded. The stewards would also be provided with plats of their manors, which would enable prospective tenants to locate vacant land and to provide a ready means for provincial officials to determine the state of the manors and the revenue to be anticipated from them. In addition, Sharpe proposed that stewards be allowed to advertise for tenants, reporting in public announcements the terms upon which leases could be obtained. Finally, Sharpe insisted that stewards should not be allowed to let tenants who were negligent in paying their rents remain on the manors. Sharpe believed that "nothing is so detrimental as giving them long Credit," although he was willing to permit stewards to carry a tenant for a short period if he seemed to be industrious and dependable.[105]

In another move to increase the efficiency of managing the proprietor's affairs in the colony, Sharpe wrote to Secretary Calvert later in 1757 recommending that a central revenue office be built in Annapolis.[106] Sharpe's proposal was approved, and Calvert directed that the office also be used to house all proprietary manor leases.[107] Unfortunately, the construction of the building was entrusted to the receiver general, Edward Lloyd. As in the performance of his other duties, Lloyd was extremely dilatory and construction did not begin until 1766.[108]

In addition to suggesting reforms for the administration of the manors, Governor Sharpe attempted to increase the proprietor's revenue from the manors by raising rents and lowering the tenure on new leases. Despite the proprietor's objections, his provincial officials had continued to lease most manor land on developmental terms, even after the first lease had expired. As late as the mid-1750s, most proprietary leases were granted for three lives at ten shillings sterling per 100 acres. Baltimore specifically prohibited Sharpe from issuing three-life leases, and in 1754 the governor reported that he had ordered the rents doubled and the tenure reduced to twenty-one years on all new leases issued for land on the proprietary manors in Frederick and Baltimore counties.[109] Despite Sharpe's instructions, as late as 1759 some leases for land in Frederick County were still issued under the old developmental terms.[110] Tenants resisted the attempt to double their rents and lower the length of tenure on their leases, and the stewards supported them. Thomas Prather, the steward for Conegocheague Manor, explained that the typical tenant on his manor "Generally thinks [it is] hard ... to lease rough Land for Twenty One Years at Twenty Shillings Sterling. . . ." Prather contended that uncultivated tracts on the manor should be leased at the former rent of ten shillings sterling, because such terms encouraged the development of the manor. If the new rents were imposed, Prather was afraid that tenants would "relinquish and not be concerned with it, [and] by that Means most part of the manor will lay uncultivated."[111]

Despite objections from tenants and stewards, Sharpe made a determined effort to double rents and to reduce the tenure on new leases to twenty-one years.[112] If the terms of the developmental leases had been fulfilled, Sharpe should have had little difficulty extracting higher rents from the proprietary tenants when they renewed their leases, because even at twenty shillings sterling per 100 acres proprietary manor land was a bargain compared to leaseholds on private land. But developmental leasing had failed, and when an established tenant could not pay the higher rent the improvements on his tenement were frequently so poor that no one else was willing to assume his lease. Furthermore, although Sharpe attempted to improve the efficiency of the manor stewards so that the proprietor's land would produce more revenue, Edward Lloyd, the agent and receiver general, was the person directly responsible for implementing reforms in the collection of manor rents. As a result, raising the rents on manor tenements often resulted in nothing more than an increase in the amount of arrears due from the tenants.

By the mid-1760s, Sharpe's reforms had brought an unprecedented measure of order and rationality to the proprietary manor system. Much work still needed to be done, but at least the proprietor should have had reason to hope that the manors would produce an increasing amount of revenue each year. Instead, on January 16, 1765, Frederick, Lord Baltimore, sent instructions ordering the sale of five manors that he understood were untenanted.[113] Sharpe replied on July 10, 1765, that a considerable portion of each of the manors he had designated for sale were leased to tenants. Furthermore, Sharpe argued against selling any of the manors, noting that "if it is worth the while of Gentlemen here to purchase Lands at this time at a pretty high price with no other View than to lease them out hereafter when Patent Land is not to be obtained, It must I think answer as well for His Lordship to keep what Mannours he has especially if he can now get Tenants for them. . . ." Sharpe assured the proprietor that tenants could be obtained and that manor rents "would soon amount to a considerable Sum & hereafter become the most valuable Part of the Lord Proprietary's Estate. . . ."[114] But Sharpe's arguments were futile. The proprietor issued new instructions on February 23, 1766, ordering the sale of all his manors and reserved lands in the colony.[115]

The proprietor never explained to Sharpe why he disregarded the governor's advice concerning the sale of the manors. Frederick, Lord Baltimore, was a man who loved money and what it could buy, however, and he had no direct male heir to assume his land and title after his death, only an illegitimate son. Perhaps the proprietor simply wanted to enjoy as much of his fortune as he could before his death, and he saw the sale of the manors as an immediate source of cash.[116]

If the proprietor was motivated by the desire to extract as much money as possible from the colony, a letter he received from Daniel Dulany, one of the leading citizens of Maryland, was probably decisive in convincing him to liquidate his manor holdings. Dulany wrote to Lord Baltimore on September 10, 1764, in response to a letter he had received from the proprietor dated February 28 of that year. Lord Baltimore's letter has not been discovered, but it must have been long, perhaps even rambling, because Dulany's response required many pages to answer all the questions posed by the proprietor. Lord Baltimore must certainly have been considering selling his manors by early 1764, because he asked Dulany's opinion on the profitability of leasing land in Maryland. Dulany owned vast quantities of land in the province and had many tenants, but like so many other landlords in the Chesapeake region he must have experienced difficulty in attracting dependable tenants who could produce sufficient cash crops to pay their rents regularly. In his response to Baltimore, Dulany noted that resident landlords in the colony made very little profit from land they leased out and that they found it nearly impossible to receive an annual rent "equal to half the interest which would arise from the money, for which the Land would sell." Dulany also noted that even when a landlord lived near his tenements it was difficult to prevent "the Abuses of Tenants in the Commission of waste." Dulany concluded that if "Landlords on the Spot find little profit, & suffer much from waste & Destruction of Timber, it may be easily imagined, that his Lordship finds less, & suffers more."[117]

Nearly every large landowner in the Chesapeake region who leased out a portion of his surplus acreage would have agreed with the points made by Dulany in his letter to Lord Baltimore, particularly with the statement that the rents actually received were far less than the legal interest on the value of the land. In reality, however, large landowners who attempted to sell excess land frequently found that there was no one willing to purchase the property, especially at the price they expected. Wealthy Marylanders and Virginians bought land on the frontier as an investment, but by the time the area of settlement had expanded to where the land could be sold at a profit, the value of the tract had increased so much that few people had enough capital to purchase the whole tract. Those affluent men who could afford to buy large amounts of land usually preferred to invest in tracts farther west where the potential for speculative increases in value were greater. As a result, planters like Dulany were often faced with the alternative of leaving their tracts uncultivated or renting them to tenants in an effort to recover at least the taxes or quitrents on the property. Thus, while Dulany's statements to the proprietor were accurate and reflected the views of most large landowners in the province, neither he nor they were likely to receive what they considered the full value of the land if they attempted to sell it all at once.

The proprietor was probably unaware of the difficulties faced by Chesapeake planters who attempted to dispose of large tracts of land, however, and Dulany's letter undoubtedly convinced him that liquidation of his manor holdings would be a profitable venture. Furthermore, the proprietor could confirm much of what Dulany had written concerning the low returns received by Maryland landlords by looking in his own account books. Baltimore had never seen a detailed description of his manor tenements, so he may not have known just how accurate Dulany's description of tenant depredations was, but he certainly knew that the manors had not become the major source of proprietary revenue that his ancestors had anticipated.[118] The proprietor's own accounts showed that rents from the manors and reserves had amounted to only 2.1 percent of the gross proprietary revenue from the colony in 1733, the year in which the decision had been made to adopt the policy of developmental leasing. Beneficial lease terms had attracted many new tenants to the manors, and by 1748 income from the manors and reserves accounted for 6.4 percent of the gross proprietary revenue from the colony. But in 1754 and 1760, income from the manors had dropped to 5.2 and 5.5 percent respectively of the gross proprietary receipts.[119] Manor revenues may have begun increasing after 1760 because of better administration and the doubling of the rents on new leases, but problems with collecting the rents undoubtedly kept the income from the manors far short of what the proprietor considered reasonable.[120] Furthermore, developmental leasing had been an unqualified success only on Anne Arundel Manor, and although Sharpe had begun doubling the rent for tenements on other manors, there was little probability that rents could be raised again in the near future.[121]

Finally, selling the manors and reserved lands offered the important administrative advantage of permitting their integration into the general land system of the colony. Once sold, the manor lands would be subject to the same quitrent as other freeholds in the colony. The need for stewards, special rent books, and manor plats would be eliminated, and the collectors of the quitrent would have the responsibility for all land revenue in the province.

Although Lord Baltimore could cite compelling reasons for selling his manors in the province, including the opinion of one of the colony's leading citizens and landlords, the decision to do so had important implications for the proprietor's tenants. The sale of the manors offered tenants an opportunity to purchase their leaseholds, but if they could not do so they were faced with the possibility of having their tenements sold away from them. Before the effect of the proprietary manor sales can be appreciated, however, we must examine who the tenants were and how they made a living on their manor tenements.

CHAPTER TWO

The Proprietary Tenants

Examining the tenants on each of the twenty-three proprietary manors proved futile, because comparable information was not available for each of them. Consequently, a sample of eight manors was selected for closer study. The data required for inclusion in the sample were a list of the leaseholders with the dates and terms of their leases, a record of the tenants in possession of manor tenements at the time of the proprietary surveys in the years 1767 and 1768, a plat of the manor, a description of the natural resources and improvements on individual leaselots, and records for the proprietary sales and the subsequent state sales of the manor tracts. Plats could not be found for three of the sample manors, but maps could be reconstructed from existing surveys of individual tenements. The names of the original leaseholders on Queen Anne's Manor are not known, nor was a list of improvements or natural resources discovered for the manor, but it was nevertheless included in the sample because of the desire to consider more than one Eastern Shore manor. The eight manors finally selected were located in all regions of the province, they had been settled at different dates, and the tenant populations represented various ethnic combinations. As a result, the sample manors provide an opportunity to examine the life experiences of tenants living under diverse economic, social, and cultural conditions.

Lower Western Shore manors selected for the sample include Beaverdam and Chaptico in St. Mary's County and Zachiah and Calverton in Charles County. The Eastern Shore is represented by Kent Manor in Kent County and Queen Anne's Manor in Queen Anne's County. Upper Western Shore manors are Gunpowder Manor in Baltimore County and Monocacy Manor in Frederick County (*see* figure 3).[1] The sample manors ranged in size from 7,230 to 18,546 acres and encompassed a total of 73,589 1/2 acres of land. Nearly one-third of the land on the manors was unleased due to patented tracts and vacancies within the manor boundaries.[2] Most vacancies were confined to small interstices between leaseholds, however, with only Monocacy containing a considerable amount of land that had never been tenanted.[3]

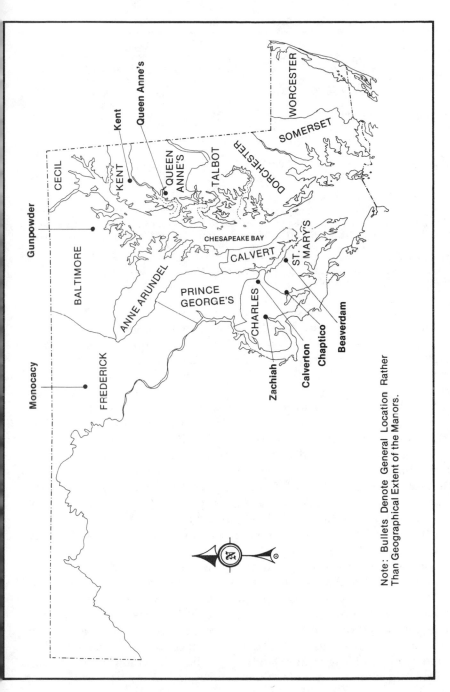

Note: Bullets Denote General Location Rather Than Geographical Extent of the Manors.

FIGURE 3. Selected Proprietary Manors in Maryland, 1767–1768

TABLE 2-1
Leaselots on Selected Proprietary Manors, 1767–1768

Manor	Total Acres	Acres Leased	Leaselots			
			Number	Average	Median	Range
Beaverdam	7,680	7,034¼	68	103.4	92¾	6–357¼
Chaptico	18,546	6,581	51	129.0	106	7–376¾
Zachiah	9,637	3,930½	48	81.9	80¾	12–290
Calverton	7,230	4,167	30	138.9	116½	36–383
Kent	8,000	7,070¼	64	110.5	93	5–450
Queen Anne's[a]	6,000	4,392	50	89.8	62½	40–281
Gunpowder	7,265½	7,001¼	64	109.4	100	13–295
Monocacy	9,231	7,414¾	69	107.5	100½	7½–252
	73,589½	47,591	444			

SOURCE: Gaius Marcus Brumbaugh, *Maryland Records, Colonial, Revolutionary, County and Church*, 2 vols. (1915–28; reprinted, Baltimore, 1967), 2:4–73; Claim of Henry Harford, Public Record Office, Audit Office 12/79, f. 129, London (microfilm copy available at the Hall of Records, Annapolis, Maryland).

[a]Lists of leases are not extant for Queen Anne's Manor. These figures are based on the holdings of tenants in 1767.

The number of individual leaseholds on the eight sample manors ranged from a low of thirty on Calverton Manor to sixty-nine on Monocacy Manor (*see* table 2–1), and the dates leases had been granted spanned the entire first six decades of the eighteenth century. The size of leaseholds ranged from 5 to 450 acres, with the average being 107 1/5 acres. The smallest lots were generally leased by persons who held contiguous tracts, but the number of very large leaseholds was small. Thus, most lots on every manor barely exceeded 100 acres.[4]

The average leasehold on the sample manors contained about 100 acres, but some tenants on every manor leased more than one tract. Because of multiple tract holdings, the 308 leaseholders on the eight manors actually possessed an average of 140 1/3 acres each (*see* table 2–2). Despite multiple tract holdings and the presence of a few men who had large leaseholds, the preponderance of tenants on all the manors held less than 150 acres of land.

Some concentration of family groups is evident on each of the sample manors, a factor that is significant for evaluating how tenants viewed their manor leaseholds.[5] If a proprietary lease was considered the last resort for a person who could not make a living elsewhere, or if a manor tenement was thought of as only a temporary residence for newly freed servants or immigrants, the incidence of more than one member of the same family holding manor land should have been low. But if tenants considered manor leaseholds their permanent family seat, or if tenants

TABLE 2-2
Acreage Held by Leaseholders on Selected Proprietary Manors to 1767–1768

Manor	Acres Leased	Leaseholders	Family Names	Acres Held by Leaseholders			
				Average	Median	Range	Average per Family
Beaverdam	7,034¼	49	35	143.6	129	6–422½	201.0
Chaptico	6,581	45	36	146.2	132¼	19–427½	182.8
Zachiah	3,930½	34	22	115.6	92¼	12–426¼	178.7
Calverton	4,167	27	19	155.6	132	36–494	219.3
Kent	7,070¼	49	39	144.3	130	15–450	181.3
Queen Anne's[a]	—	—	—	—	—	—	—
Gunpowder	7,001¼	45	37	155.6	140	14–755	189.2
Monocacy	7,414¾	59	47	125.7	114¼	7½–352	157.8
	43,199	308	235				

SOURCE: Gaius Marcus Brumbaugh, *Maryland Records, Colonial, Revolutionary, County and Church*, 2 vols. (1915–28; reprinted, Baltimore, 1967), 2:4–73.
[a]There is no record of leaseholders on Queen Anne's Manor.

TABLE 2-3

Acreage Held by Tenants on Selected Proprietary Manors, 1767–1768

Manor	Acres Tenanted[a]	Tenants	Family Names	Acres Held By Tenants			
				Average	Median	Range	Average per Family
Beaverdam	7,078¼	45	27	157.3	129½	28-549	262.2
Chaptico	7,134¾	39	31	182.9	121½	19-1,043¼	230.2
Zachiah	3,930½	29	21	135.5	92¾	12-619½	187.3
Calverton	4,189	18	16	232.7	231	57-494	261.8
Kent	7,070¼	46	40	153.7	125	18-450	176.8
Queen Anne's	4,392	39	28	112.7	100	25-341	156.9
Gunpowder	7,001¼	36	33	194.5	154½	73-832	212.2
Monocacy	7,414¾	55	35	134.8	115¾	7½-380¾	211.9
	48,210¾	307	231				

SOURCE: Gaius Marcus Brumbaugh, *Maryland Records, Colonial, Revolutionary, County and Church*, 2 vols. (1915–28; reprinted, Baltimore, 1967), 2:4–73; Claim of Henry Harford, Public Record Office, Audit Office 12/79, f. 129, London (microfilm copy available at the Hall of Records, Annapolis, Maryland).

[a]The increase in acreage tenanted over acres leased on some manors (*see* table 2-2) is due to the inclusion of tracts possessed by tenants who did not have valid leases for their land.

were economically unable to move off the manors, then sons, brothers, and daughters could also be expected to settle on the same manor. As table 2–2 shows, family groups were important on each of the sample manors, and in addition, the number of acres held by leaseholders who had other members of their family on the same manor was consistently higher than the average acreage held by all leaseholders. Therefore, the concentration of land among members of family groups suggests that the manors were not primarily populated by transients who quickly moved on to freeholds or other tenements, but rather by people who considered the manor their permanent home.

Following the proprietor's decision to sell the manors, lists were compiled in 1767 and 1768 giving the names of every tenant who held land on the proprietary manors. The people in possession of manor tenements in those years were frequently the original leaseholders or their direct descendants, but some tenements had been sold by the original leaseholder to another tenant on the manor or to an outsider.

Tenants on the eight sample manors in 1767 and 1768 held an average of 157 acres of land, or nearly 17 acres more than the average leaseholder (see tables 2–3 and 2–4). Several factors may account for the increased acreage held by these tenants. Soil depletion could have caused the minimum number of acres necessary for a self-sustaining agricultural unit to rise, especially on the earliest settled manors on the lower Western Shore, thereby forcing tenants to augment their holdings. More important, some original leaseholders failed to retain possession of

TABLE 2-4
Summary of Average Acreage Held by Leaseholders and Tenants
on Selected Proprietary Manors to 1767–1768

Manor	Size of Leaselots	Leaseholders	Tenants	Leaseholding Families	Tenant Families
Beaverdam	103.4	143.6	157.3	201.0	262.2
Chaptico	129.0	146.2	182.9	182.8	230.2
Zachiah	81.9	115.6	135.5	178.7	187.2
Calverton	138.9	155.6	232.7	219.3	261.8
Kent	110.5	144.3	153.7	181.3	176.8
Queen Anne's	89.8	—	112.7	—	156.9
Gunpowder	109.4	155.6	194.5	189.2	212.2
Monacacy	107.5	125.7	134.8	157.8	211.9

SOURCE: Gaius Marcus Brumbaugh, *Maryland Records, Colonial, Revolutionary, County and Church,* 2 vols. (1915–28; reprinted, Baltimore, 1967), 2:4–73; Claim of Henry Harford, Public Record Office, Audit Office 12/79, f. 129, London (microfilm copy available at the Hall of Records, Annapolis, Maryland).

TABLE 2-5

Population Stability on Selected Proprietary Manors: Leaseholders before 1767–1768

Manor	Total Leaseholders	Number Who Disappeared	Percentage	Total Leaseholder Families	Number Who Disappeared	Percentage
Beaverdam	49	13	26.5	35	13	37.1
Chaptico	45	14	31.1	36	13	36.1
Zachiah	34	9	26.5	22	6	27.3
Calverton	27	9	33.3	19	6	31.6
Kent	49	13	26.5	39	12	30.8
Queen Anne's	—	—	—	—	—	—
Gunpowder	45	11	24.4	37	11	29.7
Monocacy	59	19	32.2	47	19	40.4
	308	88		235	80	

Source: Gaius Marcus Brumbaugh, *Maryland Records, Colonial, Revolutionary, County and Church*, 2 vols. (1915–28; reprinted, Baltimore, 1967), 2:4–73.

their land. When a leaseholder died without heirs, his tenement was sold by the executor or administrator of his estate. Such tenements were frequently purchased by another tenant on the same manor, resulting in a decrease in the number of tenants and a rise in the average size of holdings on the manor.[6] In other cases, indebtedness forced a leaseholder to sell his tenement. Tenants could sell their right to manor land—legally only by paying an alienation fine to the proprietor—and a proprietary lease, especially if it was for lives, was frequently a poor tenant's most valuable asset. After the mid-eighteenth century, proprietary leases were often worth as much as ten to twenty shillings Maryland currency per acre, and if a tenant had to satisfy his creditors, he often had little else to sell except his leasehold.[7]

When a tenant was forced by indebtedness to sell his lease and move off the manor, he found few places to resettle in Maryland. Proprietary manor rents were considerably lower than the rates charged by large private landlords, and freehold land was far too expensive for destitute tenants. Because Maryland offered few opportunities for people who were poor, many tenants who had to sell their manor leaseholds had little choice but to leave the colony. The lists of tenants compiled in 1767 and 1768 note the destination of some leaseholders who left the province. Most migrated to "Carolina," meaning the frontier region of western North or South Carolina, although a few settled on the Virginia frontier.[8]

Eighty-eight original leaseholders representing eighty family names had relinquished their right to manor land before the proprietary surveys in 1767 and 1768 (see table 2–5). The close correlation between the number of leaseholders who left the manors and the family names that were eliminated by their departure suggests that many of the leaseholders who moved may have been recent arrivals in the colony or newly freed servants. This suggestion is strengthened by the fact that the incidence of outmigration was highest among those who had no known family connections on the manor.[9]

Persons who either died without heirs or sold the right to their manor tract represented 28.6 percent of the original leaseholders on the sample manors. Leases had been issued as early as the first decade of the eighteenth century on the manors, however, and most of the land on them had been tenanted by the 1750s. Thus, the number of leaseholders who relinquished their land was actually quite small. No leaseholder is known to have sold his tenement to move onto a freehold, and only two have been found who moved from one proprietary manor to another.[10] In short, except for sales forced by indebtedness or the death of a leaseholder without heirs, the proprietary tenants clung tenaciously to

TABLE 2-6
Population Stability on Selected Proprietary Manors: Tenants, 1767–1768

Manor	Total Tenants	New Entrants	Percentage	Total Tenant Families	New Entrants	Percentage
Beaverdam	45	5	11.1	27	5	18.5
Chaptico	39	13	33.3	31	10	32.3
Zachiah	29	5	17.2	21	5	23.8
Calverton	18	4	22.2	16	4	25.0
Kent	46	12	26.1	40	12	30.0
Queen Anne's	—	—	—	—	—	—
Gunpowder	36	7	19.4	33	7	21.2
Monocacy	55	9	16.4	35	8	22.9
	268	55		203	51	

SOURCE: Gaius Marcus Brumbaugh, *Maryland Records, Colonial, Revolutionary, County and Church,* 2 vols. (1915–28; reprinted, Baltimore, 1967), 2:4–73.

their manor lots, and when the original leaseholder died his tract almost invariably passed on to another member of his family.

Although other tenants on the manors frequently purchased tracts that were relinquished by the original leaseholder, on other occasions the tract was purchased by a person who had not previously held a proprietary lease. New entrants—those men who acquired land by buying it from the leaseholder rather than by renting it directly from the proprietor—accounted for 20.5 percent of the tenants on the seven sample manors in 1767 and 1768 for which the original lessees are known (*see* table 2–6). The reasons why new entrants purchased land on the manors are not always known, but some took up residence and farmed their tracts, others were merchants who acquired the land in settlement for debts, and a few purchased manor land as extensions to nearby freeholds or as speculative investments.[11]

Because fewer new entrants purchased land on the manors than the number of lessees who relinquished their tenements, concentrations of landholding had occurred on every manor by 1767 and 1768. The number of tenants on the sample manors in those years was from four to nine fewer than the number of original leaseholders, with the average decrease in the tenant populations amounting to nearly 13 percent. Furthermore, since most of the leaseholders who died without heirs or moved elsewhere had no other family member on the manor, the tenants in 1767 and 1768 represented fewer family names than did the original leaseholders on every manor except Kent. A net increase of one family was recorded on Kent Manor, with the other seven manors registering a decrease of from one to twelve families (*see* table 2–7).

TABLE 2-7

Net Change in Possession of Manor Tracts from Settlement to 1767–1768

Manor	Leaseholders	Tenants	Net Change	Percentage	Leaseholder Families	Tenant Families	Net Change	Percentage
Beaverdam	49	45	−4	−8.2	35	27	−8	−22.9
Chaptico	45	39	−6	−13.3	36	31	−5	−13.9
Zachiah	34	29	−5	−14.7	22	21	−1	−4.5
Calverton	27	18	−9	−33.3	19	16	−3	−15.8
Kent	49	46	−3	−6.1	39	40	+1	+2.6
Queen Anne's	—	—	—	—	—	—	—	—
Gunpowder	45	36	−9	−20.0	37	33	−4	−10.8
Monocacy	59	55	−4	−6.8	47	35	−12	−25.5
	308	268			235	203		

SOURCE: Gaius Marcus Brumbaugh, Maryland Records, Colonial, Revolutionary, County and Church, 2 vols. (1915–28; reprinted, Baltimore, 1967), 2:4–73.

TABLE 2-8
Proprietary Leaseholders and Tenants Who Owned Freehold Land

Manor	Total Leaseholders	Number with Freeholds	Percentage	Total Tenants	Number with Freeholds	Percentage
Beaverdam	49	15	30.6	45	16	35.6
Chaptico	45	20	44.4	39	22	56.4
Zachiah	34	5	14.7	29	10	34.5
Calverton	27	6	22.2	18	7	38.9
Kent	49	27	55.1	46	25	54.4
Queen Anne's	—	—	—	39	14	35.9
Gunpowder	45	8	17.8	36	7	19.4
Monocacy	59	15	25.4	55	14	25.5
	308	96		307	115	

SOURCE: County Debt Books; Prerogative Court and County Court Probate Records, all at the Hall of Records, Annapolis, Maryland; Claim of Henry Harford, Public Record Office, Audit Office 12/79, ff. 129–43, London (microfilm copy available at the Hall of Records, Annapolis, Maryland).

Some leaseholders on each of the eight sample manors owned freehold land in addition to their manor tenements. Leaseholders who were able to acquire a freehold after living on the manor for many years frequently continued to live on their manor tracts, and none is known to have sold his manor lot after becoming a freeholder. Other tenants, especially new entrants who owned land before they acquired manor leases, never resided on the manors, preferring either to sublet the tracts or let them lie uncultivated until they could be rented or resold at a profit.

As table 2–8 shows, the number of leaseholders who owned freehold land ranged from a low of 14.7 percent on Zachiah Manor to a high of 55.1 percent of Kent Manor. By 1767 and 1768, the percentage of tenants who owned freeholds had increased on every manor except Kent, where the percentage of freeholders had dropped slightly. The percentage of original leaseholders and tenants in 1767 and 1768 who owned freeholds was highest on Chaptico and Kent manors and lowest on the two upper Western Shore manors, Gunpowder and Monocacy.

Except on Monocacy Manor, the majority of tenants with freeholds did not reside on their manor tracts (*see* table 2–9). Nonresident freeholders were almost always more well-to-do than resident tenants, but they did not engross a disproportionate share of the land on any manor. As

TABLE 2-9
Nonresidents Who Leased Land on the Proprietary Manors, 1767–1768

Manor	Total Tenants	Number with Freeholds	Number of Nonresidents	Percentage of Nonresidents
Beaverdam	45	16	10	22.2
Chaptico	39	22	19	48.7
Zachiah	29	10	11[a]	37.9
Calverton	18	7	4	22.2
Kent	46	25	23	50.0
Queen Anne's	39	14	10	25.6
Gunpowder	36	7	5	13.9
Monocacy	55	14	6	10.9
	307	115	88	

SOURCE: County Debt Books; Prerogative Court and County Court Wills, all at the Hall of Records, Annapolis, Maryland; Claim of Henry Harford, Public Record Office, Audit Office 12/79, ff. 129–43, London (microfilm copy available at the Hall of Records, Annapolis, Maryland).
[a]One known nonresident apparently did not own freehold land.

TABLE 2-10
Manor Holdings of Nonresident Tenants, 1767–1768

Manor	Number of Nonresident Tenants	Percentage of all Tenants	Acres Leased	Percentage of all Acres Leased
Beaverdam	10	22.2	1,712½	24.2
Chaptico	19	48.7	1,868¾	26.2
Zachiah	11	37.9	1,417¾	36.1
Calverton	4	22.2	1,106	26.4
Kent	23	50.0	3,760¼	53.2
Queen Anne's	10	25.6	1,364½	31.1
Gunpowder	5	13.9	730½	10.4
Monocacy	6	10.9	910¾	12.3
	88		12,871	

SOURCE: County Debt Books; Prerogative Court and County Court Probate Records, all at the Hall of Records, Annapolis, Maryland; Claim of Henry Harford, Public Record Office, Audit Office 12/79, ff. 129–43, London (microfilm copy available at the Hall of Records, Annapolis, Maryland).

table 2–10 shows, the percentage of land in the possession of nonresidents was about the same as their percentage of the total tenant population on every manor except Chaptico, where they held considerably less than their share of land. Therefore, the average nonresident tenant had about the same amount of land as resident tenants, indicating that outside investors and speculators had little interest in proprietary manor tracts.

To summarize, nearly all the productive land on the eight manors selected for consideration had been leased by the mid-1760s, when the proprietor decided to sell them. Most leaseholders were permanent rather than transient residents, with nearly four-fifths of the tenants in 1767 and 1768 being either the original leaseholders of their tracts or the direct descendants of original leaseholders. Although the stability of the manor populations was exceptionally high, about one-third of the original leaseholders had either died without heirs or had been forced by indebtedness to sell their tenements. As a result, land on the manors had become concentrated in the hands of a smaller number of individuals representing even fewer family groups. Some new entrants purchased the right to manor tracts from original leaseholders, although most never lived on their tenements. A few resident tenants were eventually able to acquire freehold land off the manor, but on every manor at least half of the tenant population resided on manor tracts, and except on Kent Manor, most tenants never owned freehold land. Thus, by the mid-1760s, the typical proprietary tenant had lived on his manor lot for many years, even decades; he had friends and family living on neighboring tenements; and both the past and future of the members of the remarkably stable rural community of which he was a part were inextricably bound to the proprietary manor.

Data gathered in the mid-1760s prior to the proprietor's attempt to sell the manors provide an indication of the stability of tenant populations, but determining the amount of economic opportunity manor tenants had requires closer examination. By concentrating on those tenants who actually resided on the manors and who did not own freeholds, some indication of the variations in life experiences of nonlandowners in different sections of the province can be discerned. As a result, the following discussion considers the sample manors regionally, concentrating on differences in natural resources and tenant wealth at death that might be attributable to the geographical location of the manors.

The four sample manors in St. Mary's and Charles counties were situated in the earliest settled section of the province, with some tenements having been leased for more than a half-century when the manors were surveyed in the 1760s in preparation for the proprietary sales. The surveyor's task was to describe the manors so that the commissioners appointed by the proprietor to conduct the sales could set a fair value on each tenement. Since the manors in St. Mary's and Charles counties were used primarily as agricultural land, the surveyor was careful to note the quality of the natural resources on each tenement. The most desirable agricultural tracts had fertile soil, an ample supply of timber for firewood, fences, and other needs, and an adequate source of water for man and beast.

Tenants on the lower Western Shore manors had always relied on tobacco as their staple cash crop and maize as their main crop for home consumption. Both tobacco and corn depleted soil nutrients and neither provided much ground cover, so erosion was a persistent problem.[12] The surveyor's descriptions of the tenements on the four sample manors on the lower Western Shore suggest that much of the land on the manors had never been particularly fertile and that years of cultivation had further impaired its quality.[13]

According to the surveyor, less than half the tenements on Beaverdam Manor in St. Mary's County had soil that could be termed intermediate ("middling") in quality or better, and only two lots had really fertile soil. In addition, six tenements, encompassing a total of 995 3/4 acres, were described as partly or entirely worn out from cultivation. The majority of Beaverdam leaseholds had an insufficient amount of wood, and six lots had an inadequate supply of water (*see* table 2–11).

TABLE 2-11
Natural Resources on Selected Proprietary Manors, 1767–1768

Manor	Soil Quality				Wood Supply			Water Supply		
	Good	Intermediate	Poor	All or Partially Worn Out	Sufficient	Insufficient	None	Good	Poor	None
Beaverdam	2	19	22	6	21	25	4	43	5	1
Chaptico	12	5	25	11	37	10	4	43	4	3
Zachiah	7	9	29	10	14	30	3	31	5	12
Calverton	—	20	5	6	9	21	—	29	1	1
Kent	13	25	7	7	18	30	—	—	—	—
Gunpowder	12	18	36	—	52	4	4	58	—	1
Monocacy	50	11	8	—	62	1	1	43	8	11

SOURCE: Gaius Marcus Brumbaugh, *Maryland Records, Colonial, Revolutionary, County and Church*, 2 vols. (1915–28; reprinted, Baltimore, 1967), 2:4–14; Claim of Henry Harford, Public Record Office, Audit Office 12/79, ff. 131–43, London (microfilm copy available at the Hall of Records, Annapolis, Maryland).

The other St. Mary's County manor, Chaptico, contained more good land than any other sample manor on the lower Western Shore. Twelve lots were described as having superior soil, although the land on nearly as many lots was exhausted from cultivation and twenty-five other tracts had poor quality or broken soil.[14] Most Chaptico tenements were adequately supplied with timber and water, with only fourteen of fifty-one lots being deficient in wood and seven lacking a satisfactory water supply. Thus, in every category the natural resources on Chaptico Manor were superior to those on Beaverdam.

Neither Charles County manor could equal the natural resources found on Chaptico. Seven Zachiah Manor tenements had good soil, but twenty-nine others were described as having poor soil, and the soil of ten others was completely or partially worn out from cultivation. Most good land on the manor was located between three large patented tracts, indicating that proprietary favorites had preempted the best land available. Zachiah tenements were poorly timbered, with only fourteen of forty-six tracts having an adequate supply of wood. Furthermore, although the manor bordered on Zachiah Swamp, seventeen tracts on the manor had either no fresh water or an inadequate supply to support the tenement.

The soil of Calverton Manor tenements was described as being light and sandy. No tract had good land, but twenty tracts had moderately good soil, and only five tracts had poor soil. The manor included some swampy land, however, and six tracts, encompassing nearly one-third of the manor, were described as being exhausted from cultivation. Like those on Zachiah Manor, most Calverton leaseholds were deficient in wood, with only nine tracts having a sufficient amount to support the tenements. Water was much more plentiful on Calverton Manor than on Zachiah Manor, however, with only two lots having either none or an inadequate supply.

One clear relationship indicated by the description of natural resources on the four manors in St. Mary's and Charles counties is that soil quality was higher on those tenements that were well timbered. Tracts covered with wood had either never been cleared or they had been allowed to grow back to woods years before the 1767 and 1768 surveys of the manors were conducted. Although timbered tracts often had moderate to good soil, the quality deteriorated rapidly once the land was cleared for cultivation. Therefore, to ensure a sufficient quantity of fertile land for his tobacco and maize crops, a tenant on the lower Western Shore manors had to leave a substantial portion of his leasehold in woods. But the poorest tenants were less able to rent large tenements than the more affluent nonresident tenants who used their manor land as extensions to nearby freeholds. Tenants who could afford 100 acres or less found it difficult to keep an adequate portion of their tenement in woodland, and some required so much of their land to accommodate exhausting crops that needed frequent rotation that their lots became entirely deforested. Three of the four leaselots on Beaverdam Manor that had no wood at all, for example, contained less than 100 acres each, and the fourth tract, which contained 195 1/2 acres in 1767, had originally been divided into two leaseholds. The relationship between the size of leaselots, quantity of woodland, and quality of the soil undoubtedly contributed to the relatively high rate of tenant emigration from the manors in Charles and St. Mary's counties (*see* table 2–5). Small leaseholders were forced to cut down most of the wood on their tenements in order to rotate their arable fields, but deforestation resulted in the depletion of the soil from leaching and erosion. The quality of the small tenants' crops was affected by their inability to allow fields to recuperate under a cover of forest growth, and eventually reduced profits could force them to relinquish their tenement to satisfy creditors.[15]

The poor quality of natural resources on the lower Western Shore manors and the low incidence of resident tenants owning freeholds suggest that most proprietary leaseholders on the sample manors in St. Mary's and Charles counties were probably very poor. Probate records provide information on the economic status of many people who lived in colonial Maryland, but the poor are underrepresented in them.[16] If most tenants were at the lower end of the economic spectrum as their non-landowning status and the poor quality of the natural resources on their tenements would imply, then few would have left the estate papers necessary for a detailed analysis of the personal property they owned at the time of their death. At best, the absence of tenants' names in the probate records can be interpreted as negative confirmation of poverty. The few tenant estates that are found must be interpreted with extreme caution, always bearing in mind that they are probably indicative of the property owned by the more affluent, and thus atypical, tenants on the manors.

The usefulness of probate records is especially limited for tenants on the lower Western Shore, because few St. Mary's County estate papers have survived for the period when many of the tenants died.[17] The meager evidence available suggests that most resident tenants on the manors in St. Mary's County who did not own freehold land had very few assets. The few resident tenants who did own freeholds were more prosperous; they frequently held larger tracts of manor land than the average resident tenant and they often owned slaves. Nonresident tenants who owned freeholds were generally considerably more wealthy than resident tenants, and a few were among the most affluent men in the county. Members of the Fenwick family, for example, were descended from one of the first settlers in Maryland; they owned large freehold tracts in southern Maryland and they were among the richest families in St. Mary's County. The Fenwicks owned Fenwick Manor, a large private estate that adjoined Beaverdam Manor, and different members of the family also leased manor tracts on Beaverdam as extensions to their freehold plantations. George Plater was another nonresident tenant on Beaverdam Manor. In 1767, Plater owned nearly 6,500 acres of freehold land in St. Mary's County, including 4,000 acres of the private estate called Resurrection Manor,[18] in addition to his 198-acre leasehold on Beaverdam Manor.

Probate records have survived for Charles County, but the names of few proprietary tenants are found in them. Calverton Manor is represented by only four estates of resident tenants, a number too small to afford a basis for comment. The names of twenty-five Zachiah Manor tenants appear in the probate records, but only fourteen of them resided on the manor (*see* table 2–12).[19] Of the fourteen, three had estates that were settled with negative balances, five others had estates valued at less than £50, one was worth between £50 and £99, and two were valued at between £100 and £199.[20] Thus, over one-half the resident tenants who appear in the probate records died with personal property valued under £50, and over three-fourths of the estates were worth less than £200. Furthermore, nothing in the probate records suggests that the vast majority of the tenants whose names cannot be found there were even as well off as those whose names do appear.

The inventories of eight of the fourteen resident tenants on Zachiah Manor contain no slaves or servants, a condition that must also have characterized most tenants whose names are not found in the probate records (*see* table 2–13). As a result, even though Charles County was a tobacco staple area where slaves provided much of the labor, most Zachiah tenants were dependent upon their own families for labor. Sons and daughters were undoubtedly put to work at an early age, but tenants with large families to support nevertheless had to devote much of their available land and labor to the cultivation of crops for home consumption.

Because of the small number of inventories that has survived for Zachiah tenants, none may accurately reflect the personal property of the average resident on the manor. The estate of Richard Vincent, however, indicates the kinds of personal property of one small leaseholder on the manor. Vincent had lived on the manor most of his life, although he did not acquire a leasehold in his own name until 1763. When he died six years later, the only land in Vincent's possession was his forty-three-acre leasehold, and he left very little personal property to support his widow and six children.

TABLE 2-12
Size of Estates at Death of Proprietary Leaseholders and Tenants

Value of Estate (£ current money)	Zachiah		Calverton		Gunpowde	
	Number	Percentage	Number	Percentage	Number	Perce
1–99	10	40.0	1	14.3	8	3
100–199	5	20.0	1	14.3	4	1
200–299	1	4.0	—	—	1	
300–399	3	12.0	2	28.6	1	
400–499	1	4.0	—	—	2	
500–749	—	—	—	—	2	
750–999	3	12.0	2	28.6	1	
1,000–1,499	—	—	—	—	2	
1,500–1,999	1	4.0	—	—	—	-
2,000 and above	1	4.0	1	14.3	1	
	25	100.0	7	100.1	22	10

SOURCE: Charles County Inventories and Accounts; Baltimore County Inventories and Accounts; Frederick County Inventories and Accounts; Queen Anne's County Inventories

The value of Vincent's personal property amounted to only £62.14.3 1/2. Livestock and fowl accounted for nearly one-third of the total, with three beds in the house adding another £12.0.0 to the valuation. Carpenter's tools, cooper's tools, and shoe-making tools were worth £2.2.6. Farming tools, the implements of Vincent's primary occupation, were valued at only £0.18.0, indicating both the simplicity of and the relatively small number of tools needed for small-scale plantation agriculture.[21]

The first accounting of Vincent's estate lists the crops harvested on his

TABLE 2-13
Slaves Held at Death of Proprietary Leaseholders and Tenants

Number of Slaves	Zachiah		Calverton		Gunpowder	
	Number	Percentage	Number	Percentage	Number	Percentage
0	15	60.0	—	—	13	59.1
1–2	3	12.0	1	14.3	1	4.6
3–4	1	4.0	—	—	2	9.1
5–9	4	16.0	3	42.9	3	13.6
10–14	1	4.0	1	14.3	—	—
15–19	—	—	1	14.3	3	13.6
20 or more	1	4.0	1	14.3	—	—
	25	100.0	7	100.1	22	100.0

SOURCE: Charles County Inventories and Accounts; Baltimore County Inventories and Accounts; Frederick County Inventories and Accounts; Queen Anne's County Inventories

Monocacy		Kent		Queen Anne's	
Number	Percentage	Number	Percentage	Number	Percentage
10	33.3	1	3.7	7	31.8
6	20.0	3	11.1	3	13.6
7	23.3	—	—	5	22.7
—	—	3	11.1	—	—
2	6.7	2	7.4	—	—
2	6.7	4	14.8	2	9.1
—	—	6	22.2	—	—
1	3.3	6	22.2	1	4.6
—	—	—	—	3	13.7
2	6.7	2	7.4	1	4.6
30	100.0	27	99.9	22	100.1

and Accounts; Kent County Inventories and Accounts; Prerogative Court Probate Records, all at the Hall of Records, Annapolis, Maryland.

tenement the year he died. Vincent's family had produced 1,476 pounds of tobacco, 15 1/2 barrels of maize, 24 bushels of wheat, 8 1/2 bushels of rye, 8 bushels of oats, and 1 1/2 bushels of beans.[22] To harvest this quantity of produce from the tenement, Vincent's family would have had about four acres planted in tobacco, four acres in wheat, five acres in Indian corn, and an additional two acres in rye, oats, and beans, for a total of about fifteen acres.[23] Only the eight acres of tobacco and wheat would have been sold, since the rye, oats, and maize would have been consumed by Vincent's family and livestock. Even if Vincent's manor plantation had been larger, his family probably could not have produced additional crops for sale. Vincent owned no slaves or servants, and he

Monocacy		Kent		Queen Anne's	
Number	Percentage	Number	Percentage	Number	Percentage
27	90.0	4	14.8	14	63.6
—	—	2	7.4	1	4.6
3	10.0	3	11.1	1	4.6
—	—	8	29.6	3	13.6
—	—	3	11.1	—	—
—	—	4	14.8	—	—
—	—	3	11.1	3	13.6
30	100.0	27	99.9	22	100.0

and Accounts; Kent County Inventories and Accounts; Prerogative Court Probate Records, all at the Hall of Records, Annapolis, Maryland.

and his family undoubtedly planted as many acres as they could manage by themselves. Therefore, Vincent's poverty was not the result of a lack of land, even though he leased very few acres, but of a shortage of labor to devote to the production of cash crops, coupled with a large family whose support necessitated that almost half the acreage cultivated be planted in consumables.

The majority of resident tenants on the lower Western Shore manors were probably faced with the same problem as Vincent. With little personal property, few assets, and a large family to support, a tenant had to be as self-sufficient as possible. But only by producing large cash crops could he hope to improve his economic condition. If a tenant grew tobacco at the expense of food, however, he could only fall more deeply in debt to the local planter or storekeeper who extended him credit for necessities. Even when a tenant attempted to be self-sufficient, he still had to purchase a few store goods each year and pay his rent, and expenses often consumed all the profit the tenant and his family could make from the tobacco and other cash crops they grew. Vincent's case is again illustrative. Although his personal property was valued at over sixty pounds, the legacy Vincent left to his widow and six children was limited to a lifetime of poverty and hard work, because the modicum of property he had accumulated was burdened by debts that exceeded his total assets by over fifteen pounds.[24]

The number of estate inventories for tenants on the proprietary manors in Charles and St. Mary's counties is too small to establish with certainty that Vincent was typical of other manor residents, but the poor natural resources on the tenements and the fact that most tenants left no probate records strongly suggest that poverty was endemic on the manors in the region. In an area dominated by freeholders and slaveowners, tenants who lived on the manors were not only unable to accumulate capital to buy land or slaves, but by leasing land and relying on their own families' labor they were just barely able to eke out a subsistence. The few wealthy freeholders who leased land on the manors may have been able to reap profits by working their tenements with slaves, but for tenants who were totally dependent on their leasehold for support, the manors on the lower Western Shore provided a small return for the labor invested in cultivating the soil. As a result, few resident tenants achieved any measure of economic mobility, and most lived in extreme poverty.

Of the two sample manors on the Eastern Shore, records showing the quality of natural resources on Queen Anne's Manor have not been found. Settlement on the manor began at about the same time as on the manors of the lower Western Shore, however, so many leaselots had been cultivated for decades by 1767 and 1768. In addition, tobacco and maize were grown extensively on the manor in the early years of settlement. Thus, deforestation and soil depletion similar to that on the lower Western Shore manors had probably occurred on many tenements by the mid-1760s.

Kent Manor was located a short distance upriver from Queen Anne's, so the quality of soil may have been similar on both manors. A larger amount of land on Kent Manor was described as being intermediate or good in quality than on any of the manors of the lower Western Shore, with only fourteen of the fifty-two tracts having poor or depleted soil (*see* table 2–11). The seven lots that were worn out from cultivation encompassed 14 percent of the manor, however, and deforestation may have contributed to the impairment of the soil's fertility. Every tenement had at least some woodland, but thirty of the forty-eight tracts that were described had an insufficient quantity to support the tenements. Although water was an essential resource, the Kent Manor surveyor failed to note whether lots on the manor were provided with an adequate supply.

The meager information available suggests that the Eastern Shore manors may originally have had very fertile soil, but decades of cultivation had taken their toll. Despite intensive cultivation and deforestation, however, the soil on most tenements was still fairly good in the mid-1760s. As a result, leaseholders on the Eastern Shore manors should have been able to produce more profitable crops than tenants on the manors in Charles and St. Mary's counties.

The average size leaselot on Queen Anne's Manor was the smallest of any on the eight sample manors, averaging just 112.7 acres per tenement (*see* table 2–3). In addition, of the twenty-nine tenants residing on the manor in 1767, only four owned freehold land off the manor. Both the small tenement size and the low proportion of tenants who owned freeholds suggest that Queen Anne's Manor was primarily populated by poor tenants.

Probate records were found for twenty-two of the twenty-nine tenants who were in possession of land on Queen Anne's Manor in 1767 (*see* table 2–12). Although the number of tenants who left estate records is far larger than for the lower Western Shore manors, the sample is still small and only tentative conclusions can be reached from it. More than any other manor, a dichotomy between the rich and poor appears to have existed on Queen Anne's Manor. Of the twenty-two tenant estates, seven were valued at less than £100 and eight others were worth less than £299. Five estates were valued at over £1,000 and only two were worth between £300 and £1,000. Just two of the largest estates belonged to tenants who resided on the manor, however, and the estates of all other resident tenants were valued at the lower end of the spectrum. Thus, the twenty-two tenant inventories indicate that the people who held leases on Queen Anne's Manor can be divided into two groups. The preponderance of tenants resided on their leaseholds, did not own land off the manor, and died with small estates. A much smaller number of leaseholders lived on freehold land, used their manor tenements as a quarter or extension to their freehold farms, and died with large personal estates. The dichotomy is also apparent in the number of slaves owned by tenants who left probate records. Fourteen of the tenants owned no slaves or servants and thus were entirely dependent on their own families for labor (see table 2–13). Five others owned between one and nine slaves, while the three richest tenants owned more than twenty slaves each. The Sparkes family, one of several large family groups on the manor, typified most residents on Queen Anne's Manor. Eight members of the family leased small tenements on the manor; all those who left probate records had small estates; and none owned slaves or servants when he died.

Even though Kent Manor was located only a short distance upriver from Queen Anne's, the pattern of landholding and the size of tenant estates differed markedly between the two. The proportion of tenants who owned freeholds and the number of nonresidents was higher on Kent Manor than on any of the other sample manors, suggesting that people who leased land on the manor were far wealthier than tenants on the other manors. Probate records have survived for twenty-seven Kent Manor tenants. Only one was valued at under £99, twenty-three were worth more than £300, and eight were valued at more than £1,000. In addition, just four of the Kent Manor tenants who left probate records did not own slaves or servants, while ten of the twenty-seven held ten or more slaves at the time of their deaths. In short, whereas little real or personal property characterized tenants on Queen Anne's Manor and the manors on the lower Western Shore, most Kent Manor leaseholders were well-to-do.

Kent Manor leaseholders had not become wealthy by farming their tenements. Nearly all the tenants who left probate records lived off the manor, and those who did reside on their tenements frequently owned large freehold tracts. Furthermore, not all the wealthy tenants were dependent upon agriculture for their livelihood. Several of the men leased freehold land to private tenants, receiving income as landlords.[25] One tenant, John Gleaves, Jr., was a miller and baker, and the presence of a pair of "French Burr mill stones" valued at seventy pounds in his inventory indicates that his mill was a large one.[26] George Garnett leased land on the manor, but he was an attorney who resided in Chestertown. The largest item in Garnett's inventory was his library, which included 193 titles, nearly all of which were books on law or political theory.[27] Another tenant, Isaac Perkins, was a wealthy merchant. In addition to a well-stocked retail store, Perkins had a malt and brew house, and at the time of his death he was erecting a sawmill, a fulling mill, and a gristmill.[28]

Another indication of the wealth of Kent Manor tenants is the number of inventories that contain cash. The sums of cash left by deceased Kent Manor tenants frequently exceeded the entire net worth of tenants on Queen Anne's Manor and the manors on the lower Western Shore. Henry Brooke, for example, left Pennsylvania money worth £223.6.0 when he died; Robert Maxwell's inventory listed £42.5.11 1/2; and John Graham left £58.7.2.[29] The value of beds in the inventories of Kent Manor tenants provides another contrast with the poorer tenants on other manors. William Merrit owned five beds valued at over £59.0.0; William Maxwell had eight "complete beds" worth nearly £63.0.0; and Charles Grooms's eight beds "with furniture" were valued at £74.0.0.[30] The personal property of most of the tenants on the lower Western Shore did not total as much as the beds alone of these three nonresident Kent Manor leaseholders.

In short, Queen Anne's and Kent manors were in close geographical proximity and probably had similar quality natural resources, but the tenant populations on the two manors were strikingly dissimilar. Queen Anne's Manor was dominated by relatively poor farmers who owned no other land and who were dependent upon their families for labor. Most of Kent Manor was leased by wealthy freeholders who resided off the manor and who only used their tenements as extensions to their freeholds or for subleasing to poorer tenants. The poverty of Queen Anne's tenants can be ascribed to their inability to produce more than small cash surpluses by farming their manor lots; Kent Manor tenants were wealthy because they had other sources of income. The average Queen Anne's tenant may have been somewhat better off than his counterpart on one of the lower Western Shore manors, but he was still quite poor; most Kent Manor tenants lived as comfortably as any wealthy freeholder in the colony. The principal difference between tenants on the two Eastern Shore manors was that a leasehold was only an incidental source of income for the one, while it was the principal means of support for the other. A proprietary tenant on the Eastern Shore could subsist, but he had to have much more than a small manor leasehold to achieve affluence.

Northwestern Maryland was the last-settled section of the province, so the two sample manors in the region were tenanted later than the other six manors that have been discussed. Leases were issued on Gunpowder Manor more than two decades before the first tenant moved onto Monocacy Manor, but both were relatively recently populated manors compared to those on the lower Western Shore and the Eastern Shore. Thus, the effects of habitation should not have altered the natural landscape as markedly on the upper Western Shore manors as elsewhere in the province, and the natural resources should have been less depleted when the manors were surveyed in the mid-1760s.

Gunpowder Manor was located in an area of Baltimore County that had been wilderness throughout the seventeenth century. Leases for land on the manor were issued as early as 1720, but the manor was not heavily populated until the mid-eighteenth century.[31] As a result, when the manor was surveyed in 1767, not a single tract on it was described as being worn out (see table 2–11). The absence of exhausted land, however, was not due to high quality soil. With the exception of a band of good to very rich land that stretched through the center of the manor, most tenements were described as having poor soil, much of which was hilly and broken. Originally, Gunpowder Manor had been heavily wooded, and in 1767 many tenements were still completely covered with timber. Only eight of the sixty-six leaselots had no wood or an insufficient amount to support the tenement. Furthermore, most lots on the manor were well watered, either by the Gunpowder River, by springs, or, in one case, by a well. Thus, although the soil on the majority of Gunpowder tenements was not exceptionally fertile, soil depletion was not yet evident by the 1760s and the ample supplies of wood and water were valuable assets to leaseholders on the manor.

Monocacy Manor, situated in Frederick County on the Monocacy River, was the last settled of the eight sample manors. The manor was endowed with excellent soil, and, except for a narrow band of poor, gravelly land that ran through one section of it, most tenements on the manor were described as having good or very good land in the mid-1760s. No land on the manor was exhausted, and the soil on only eight of the sixty-nine tenements was called poor. In addition, the manor was heavily wooded, with just two tenements having either no timber or an insufficient supply. Water was deficient on a portion of the manor, although less than one-third of the tenements had an inadequate supply. Thus, of the eight sample manors Monocacy had by far the best natural resources.

Despite the large number of tenements on Gunpowder Manor, probate records were found for only twenty-two of its leaseholders (see table 2–12). Eight of these estates were valued at less than £100 and another four were worth between £100 and £199, so over half the tenants whose names were found in the probate records had little personal property when they died. The other ten estates, however, were distributed fairly equally along the economic spectrum, with seven being worth between £200 and £999, and three worth more than £1,000. Thirteen of the tenants who left probate records owned no slaves, but three had fifteen or more and another three owned white servants (*see* table 2–13). Therefore, although the majority of the leaseholders who left probate records were quite poor, a larger number of Gunpowder tenants could be ranked as middle or upper class than on any other manor except Kent. In addition, two Gunpowder tenants whose names were not located in the probate records are known to have been affluent. Thomas Gittings, Sr. and Charles Baker both had extensive landholdings, both on and off the manor, as well as a number of slaves. The personal estates of both men must have exceeded £1,000, and Thomas Gittings's estate was probably worth at least twice that sum.[32] If probate records had survived for these two men the indication that the majority of tenants on the manor died with small estates would not be altered, but their omission tends to obscure the concentration of wealth in the hands of a few tenants on the manor. Gittings was certainly the dominant tenant on the manor, and his daughter's marriage to John Chamberlain united the two wealthiest families on the manor.[33]

When Monocacy Manor was surveyed for the proprietor, it was located on the extreme northwestern frontier of the province, and the first leases for land on the manor were not issued until 1741. Three of the four leases granted in that year were to persons of English extraction, but Germans moving down the Monocacy Trail from Pennsylvania soon came to dominate the manor population.[34] Monocacy Manor offered much in terms of natural resources to those persons willing to settle on the frontier, but clearing a homesite and fields out of the heavily timbered land must have been an arduous task. But the Germans and other settlers persevered, and by the mid-1760s most of the better land on the manor had been developed into improved homesteads.

Probate records were located for thirty of the tenants who lived on Monocacy Manor. One-third of the estates was valued at less than £100, and the personal property of thirteen others was worth less than £300, so the preponderance of the leaseholders whose names appear in the probate records had only modest estates at the time of their deaths. In addition, only three tenants owned slaves and they were by far the most wealthy men on the manor. The three held a total of only ten slaves, however. Not only was slave labor negligible on the manor,[35] but only one tenant owned an indentured servant. In short, the vast majority of the Monocacy tenants were dependent upon their own families for labor.

Although the number of small estates on Monocacy Manor was about the same as on Zachiah on the lower Western Shore, a qualitative difference in the types of goods owned by tenants on the two manors is discernible. As soon as a Zachiah tenant was able, he purchased a slave.

Slaves may have been a wise investment in a tobacco-growing area like Charles County, but the purchase of one did little, at least immediately, to improve the living conditions of the tenant and his family. Monocacy tenants preferred to invest in livestock, household goods, and buildings for their tenements, the kind of expenditures that improved the quality of life and made the land more productive. Furthermore, even though most Monocacy tenants had small personal estates, a larger number had assets that placed them above the very poorest class of free whites in the colony. Only one-fifth of the inventories of Zachiah tenants found in the probate records included personal property valued between £100 and £299, whereas one-third of the Monocacy estates fell within that range. Thus, most tenants on both manors were far from being well-to-do, but Monocacy leaseholders were somewhat better off and had a better chance of leaving at least something to be divided among their children when they died than Zachiah tenants.

Not only were their estates slightly larger than those of Zachiah tenants, but Monocacy tenants appear to have had more chance to invest in freehold land, even though they continued to reside on the manor.[36] Land was not included in estate inventories, so it is impossible to determine exactly how many small tenants owned freeholds. The estate of John Biggs, however, illustrates that tenants with very little personal property could still have a substantial amount of capital invested in land off the manor. Biggs died in 1761, a resident tenant on lot 2 on Monocacy Manor. His leasehold encompassed 175 1/2 acres, an ample amount of land to satisfy his crop requirements since he owned no slaves or servants. In addition to his leasehold, however, Biggs owned a 100-acre freehold in Frederick County and two lots in Frederick Town. Biggs's inventory in no way reflected his investments in land, since his personal property was valued at only £67.6.5.[37]

The fact that more Monocacy tenants seem to have been able to accumulate more surplus capital to invest in land than tenants on the lower Western Shore manors should not obscure the presence of genuinely poor tenants on the manor. Martin Adams, for example, was a shoemaker who leased lot 29. His 138 1/4-acre tract was the only land he possessed, and except for his log house, a log barn with a thatched roof, and a few head of livestock he had no other assets. When he died, Adams's inventory totaled only £33.14.1.[38] Another Monocacy tenant, Nathaniel Wickham, leased an 88-acre tract on the manor. Wickham's inventory totaled only £4.3.0, and his debts exceeded his assets by over £18.0.0.[39]

Perhaps Adams and Wickham were more typical of the average Monocacy tenant than the majority who left probate records. Three tenants are known to have moved off the manor, presumably in search of greater opportunity, and most tenants held small leaseholds.[40] But a large proportion of Monocacy tenants were the original leaseholders of their tracts, and the manor supported nearly as many tenants in 1767 as there had been original lessees (see tables 2–5 and 2–6). Both of these facts suggest that most tenants were able to support themselves on their leaseholds and that they could perceive no better opportunity for improving their condition by moving elsewhere. Therefore, both the stability of the manor population and the probate records that exist for tenants suggest that the standard of living of Monocacy tenants was superior to that of the average tenant on the lower Western Shore manors and that it was surpassed by only a few resident tenants on other manors in the province.

Stable communities of landless husbandmen populated the proprietary manors by the mid-1760s. Many tenants had lived on their leaseholds for decades and others had inherited their tracts from relatives who had lived and died on the manors. The incidence of tenants with a common surname leasing land on the same manor indicates that sons frequently settled on tenements near those of their fathers, and the marriage of daughters, although impossible to trace completely, must have further linked families on the same manor. Some land on every manor was leased by wealthy freeholders, but most resident tenants had only their leasehold for their families' support. A small number of resident tenants eventually accumulated sufficient capital to invest in freehold land or to purchase a slave, but the majority of tenants whose names can be found in the probate records left only modest personal estates to be divided among their heirs. Most resident tenants were dependent upon their own families for labor, and the soil of many tenements, originally quite poor, had been depleted by decades of cultivation and deforestation. A shortage of labor and poor natural resources dictated that most manor tenants who were dependent on their leaseholds for support could achieve only minimal economic mobility for themselves. More important, it meant that they could do little to accumulate sufficient capital to provide their children with greater opportunity.

CHAPTER THREE

Dwellings and Other Improvements

Students of the Chesapeake Bay region have described in detail the growth of architectural sophistication that culminated in magnificent eighteenth-century Georgian mansions and townhouses, many of which still survive as evidence of a style of gracious living and conspicuous consumption that has greatly influenced our impression of what life was like in colonial Maryland and Virginia.[1] Historians have become increasingly aware, however, that the lifestyle represented by the mansions was not enjoyed by the majority of the region's inhabitants. The dwellings of small planters and farmers were undoubtedly commensurate with the low economic status of their inhabitants in the same way that mansions reflected the great planters' affluence, but specific information concerning the dwellings and other improvements built by poor colonists is extremely meager.

One reason for the dearth of evidence regarding the houses and outbuildings owned by small planters and farmers is that they were cheaply constructed and rarely worth repairing when they began to decay. According to Thomas Jefferson, it would have been "impossible to devise things more ugly, uncomfortable, and happily more perishable" than the houses occupied by most laborers and small farmers at the time of the Revolution.[2] Many surviving eighteenth-century houses were built of brick, which made them more resistant to weather and fire than wooden structures. Most extant wooden houses dating from the colonial period were built by wealthy planters. The size of these dwellings, their architectural features, and their well-executed interiors made them worth repairing by the families who built them and worth restoring by modern owners. Therefore, existing examples of eighteenth-century domestic architecture cannot be considered typical of the buildings inhabited by poor people, and the architectural and structural features that account for their survival were undoubtedly lacking in the dwellings they built.

Compounding the problem of a low survival rate is the paucity of literary evidence concerning the buildings on small farms and plantations. Travelers who toured the Chesapeake colonies in the eighteenth

century frequently commented about improvements on large plantations, especially on the visual effect produced by the complex of outbuildings customarily built in close proximity to the dwelling house,
which, in Benjamin Latrobe's words, "seem to follow the dwelling house
as a litter of pigs their mother."[3] But contemporary descriptions of buildings on small plantations and farms are primarily confined to the
dwellings inhabited by people who lived on the frontier, and the small
log cabin of the backwoodsman may have borne little resemblance to the
houses of poor whites who lived in the older settled sections of the
region.

When Gov. Horatio Sharpe requested a survey of each manor prior to
the proprietary sales in the 1760s, he also asked that the surveyors return a list of improvements on each tenement to assist him in determining the value of the manor tracts. A detailed description of improvements does not exist for Queen Anne's Manor, but information concerning the dwellings, outbuildings, and orchards on the other seven sample
manors is available. The data are especially valuable because with the
names of such a small number of proprietary tenants appearing in the
probate records, the description of manor improvements provides a
more comprehensive source of information regarding the lifestyle of
tenants on the proprietary manors.

The small number of proprietary tenants whose names appear in the
probate records suggests that poverty was endemic among the populations on the sample lower Western Shore manors. Deforestation and soil
depletion, especially on smaller leaseholds, further indicate that manor
tenants in the region should have had little surplus capital to expend on
dwellings and other improvements for their tenements. Yet, according
to the terms of the developmental leases issued by the proprietor after
1733, each tenant was obligated to build a dwelling twenty feet wide by
thirty feet long with a brick chimney (see page 11). As table 3-1 indicates, however, tenants on the four lower Western Shore manors
(Beaverdam, Chaptico, Zachiah, and Calverton) often failed to build
anything on their leaseholds, and the dwellings they did construct were
generally smaller than the size prescribed by the proprietor.

If not in terms of quality, then at least in terms of quantity Beaverdam
Manor was the most heavily developed of the sample manors on the
lower Western Shore, with over three-fourths of the lots having
dwellings built on them. Furthermore, some lots had more than one
house, so that there was a total of seventy-nine different dwellings on the
fifty-two manor tenements. Some of the houses on lots that had two or
more dwellings may have been abandoned, but others were used by the

TABLE 3-1

Dwelling Houses on Sample Proprietary Manors, 1767-1768

Manor	Total Lots	Lots with Houses	Percentage	Total Dwellings	Number with Dimensions	Average Size (square feet)	Range (square feet)
Beaverdam	68	52	76.5	79	58	424.7	144–720
Chaptico	51	29	56.9	35	28	490.4	256–1,260
Zachiah	48	17	35.4	28	20	278.2	144–512
Calverton	30	21	70.0	23	20	394.9	192–884
Kent	53	40	75.5	42	40	484.0	192–760
Gunpowder	64	43	67.2	49	49	473.6	160–1,400
Monocacy	69	57	82.6	64	64	558.2	224–1,056

SOURCE: Claim of Henry Harford, Public Record Office, Audit Office 12/79, ff. 129–42, London (microfilm copy available at the Hall of Records, Annapolis, Maryland).
NOTE: Comparable information for improvements on Queen Anne's Manor is not extant.

families of sons and other relations of the leaseholder. The number of multiple dwelling tracts on Beaverdam Manor is consistent with the large number of family groups that resided on the manor and the high stability of the manor's tenant population (*see* tables 2–5 and 2–6). The houses on Beaverdam were quite small. Dimensions were given for fifty-eight dwellings, with individual structures ranging from 144.0 to 720.0 square feet. The average dwelling contained 424.7 square feet and measured 16.6 feet wide by 25.0 feet long.[4]

The other St. Mary's County manor, Chaptico, had only thirty-five houses on twenty-nine lots. Perhaps because the soil on this manor was better than on the other manors on the lower Western Shore, the tenants were able to construct slightly larger dwellings. The twenty-eight houses for which dimensions were given ranged in size from 256.0 square feet to one dwelling that contained 1,260.0 square feet of floor space. The average house on the manor contained only 490.4 square feet, however, and measured 19.6 feet wide by 24.5 feet long.

Zachiah Manor in Charles County had twenty-eight houses on seventeen lots when it was surveyed in 1767 prior to the proprietary sales. The number of multiple dwelling tracts was due in part to two or more members of the same family building on the same leasehold, made necessary because so many lots on the manor did not have a source of water to support a separate dwelling (*see* page 43). The dwellings on Zachiah Manor were the smallest of any of the manors on the lower Western Shore, with the average containing only 278.2 square feet of floor space. Individual structures ranged from 144.0 square feet—just 12.0 feet square—to 512.0 square feet, with the average measuring 14.6 feet wide and 19.0 feet long. The other Charles County manor, Calverton, had twenty-four houses on twenty-one lots. Dimensions were given for twenty of the houses, with the average dwelling containing 394.9 square feet and measuring 17.0 feet wide by 22.2 feet long.

The surveyor who examined the lower Western Shore manors prior to the proprietary sales provided little information concerning the dwellings on the manors beyond their dimensions. The surveyor's job was to record what added to or detracted from the value of a tenement. He noted the presence of a house, since that enhanced the value of the tract, but since the commissioners for the sale of the manors were aware of what ordinary tenant housing on the lower Western Shore was like, the surveyor only had to elaborate when there was something unusual about the structure. Therefore, the surveyor rarely mentioned the type of construction of dwellings on the manors, how chimneys were built, the number of rooms the houses contained, or how many stories high they were. The surveyor did note when a house was new, when it was constructed with superior materials, and other features that distinguished it from ordinary tenant dwellings. Thus, information concerning the physical appearance of tenant houses on the lower Western Shore manors must be largely extrapolated from what the surveyor indicated about the unusual dwellings on the manors.

One detailed description of tenant houses on a private estate on the lower Western Shore survives that provides detailed information concerning the construction of ordinary tenant dwellings. The list, itemizing the improvements on thirteen tenements owned by Col. George Plater, a wealthy St. Mary's County landowner, was compiled in 1802 as part of the valuation of his estate.[5] Each of the thirteen tenements had a dwelling house, with individual structures ranging in size from 16.0 feet square (256.0 square feet) to 36.0 by 16.0 feet (576.0 square feet). The average house on Plater's land contained 437.9 square feet and measured 27.7 by 15.7 feet. Thus, Plater's average tenant dwelling was slightly smaller than the average tenant's house on Chaptico Manor, but larger than those on Beaverdam, Zachiah, and Calverton manors. The type of construction is described for twelve of Plater's tenant houses. Eleven of the dwellings were framed structures covered with clapboards, and one was built of logs. Chimney construction is given for nine of the dwellings. Three of the houses had brick chimneys, three had single wooden chimneys, and the other three had two wooden chimneys each. Most of the dwellings on Plater's tenements apparently had no flooring, or at least not solid plank flooring. Two houses are described as having plank flooring covering half the house, and the floor of another was entirely covered with plank. Because flooring is specifically mentioned for only three of the houses, the others probably had nothing but packed dirt floors. No indication of room partitions is given for any of Plater's tenant houses, but most were large enough to have been divided into two rooms.

The description of Plater's tenements dates nearly forty years after the proprietor's surveyor examined the leaseholds on the lower Western Shore manors. J. F. D. Smyth saw similar structures in Virginia in the early 1780s, however, suggesting that the methods of construction and the types of materials used by poor people in building their dwellings changed little in the last half of the eighteenth century.[6] Thus, the information concerning Plater's tenements can serve as a guide for interpreting the remarks the surveyor made when he described the dwellings on the sample proprietary manors.

The type of construction is rarely mentioned in the surveyor's report concerning houses on the manors in Charles and St. Mary's counties. Not a single dwelling on Calverton Manor is described, and of the 142 houses on Beaverdam, Chaptico, and Zachiah manors, the type of construction is specified for just 30. Of those, 11 were frame buildings covered with clapboards, 8 had plank sidewalls, 9 were built of logs, and 2 were constructed of brick (*see* table 3–2).

TABLE 3-2

Types of Construction of Dwelling Houses on Sample Proprietary Manors, 1767–1768

Manor	Total Houses	Unspecified	Clapboard Covered	Plank Covered	Posted	Brick	Log and Frame	Log	Frame
Beaverdam	79	73	2					4	
Chaptico	35	15	9	8		2		1	
Zachiah	28	24						4	
Calverton	23	23							
Kent	42	16			1	1	3	9	12
Gunpowder	49	5			4		2	24	14
Monocacy	64	4						60	

SOURCE: Claim of Henry Harford, Public Record Office, Audit Office 12/79, ff. 129-42, London (microfilm copy available at the Hall of Records, Annapolis, Maryland).

Although the specific type of construction is not mentioned for the majority of the houses on the lower Western Shore manors, most were probably simple frame structures. Frame had been the basic type of house construction in England, and it was transplanted by English immigrants to the New World. A frame house consisted of a framework of sills, posts, girders, joists, plates, rafters, and braces constructed out of sawed timber. The interstices between the posts and studs in the walls were filled with one of several kinds of insulating material called "nogging." In England the nogging was often left exposed, resulting in what is called a "half-timbered house," but in the Chesapeake Bay region the nogging was generally covered with clapboards. Clapboards were boards split thinner on one edge than the other, which allowed them to be overlapped and nailed horizontally to the wallposts. Although most of the houses in southern Maryland were probably covered with clapboards, a few dwellings on the manors had plank sidewalls made from sawed boards two to six inches thick and nine or more inches wide. Planks were not overlapped like clapboards, but set on top of each other and nailed to the studs. Because of their greater thickness and width, planks were a more substantial, although more expensive, covering for frame houses. Bricks were an even better material for sidewalls, because they were more durable and fireproof than either plank or clapboards. But bricks were costly and required skill to lay. The small number of brick dwellings on the proprietary manors is indicative of the fact that most tenants could neither afford expensive building materials nor could they hire skilled laborers to assist them in constructing their homes.[7]

Most dwellings on the lower Western Shore were undoubtedly frame structures covered with clapboards, but the construction of fireplaces and chimneys in more problematical. Chimney construction is mentioned for only twenty-four of the houses on the manors in St. Mary's and Charles counties, and all these chimneys were made of brick (*see* table 3–3). Since the surveyor generally noted only those features of a house that were unusual, the fact that brick chimneys were mentioned on a few dwellings suggests that most houses had chimneys that were built with inferior materials. The majority of Plater's dwellings had wooden chimneys, and most proprietary tenants must also have constructed that type of chimney for their houses.

Wooden chimneys could be built in several ways, but most often the firebox was lined with brick, clay, stone, or some other heat-resistant material, while the chimney itself was made by packing clay around a framework of sticks. Wooden chimneys were extremely hazardous, because the clay in the chimney deteriorated over time, leaving the wooden framework exposed to sparks from the fireplace.[8] Brick chimneys were

TABLE 3-3
Materials Used in Chimney Construction on Dwelling Houses
on Sample Proprietary Manors, 1767–1768

		Type of Chimney Construction			
Manor	Total Dwellings	Unspecified	Brick	Stone	Brick and Stone
Beaverdam	79	69	10		
Chaptico	35	24	11		
Zachiah	28	28			
Calverton	23	20	3		
Kent	42	18	24		
Gunpowder	49	41	8		
Monocacy	64	28	9	26	1

SOURCE: Claim of Henry Harford, Public Record Office, Audit Office 12/79, ff. 129–42, London (microfilm copy available at the Hall of Records, Annapolis, Maryland).

considerably safer, but bricks cost money whereas a wooden chimney could be constructed with materials readily available for nothing. The small size of the average house on the lower Western Shore manors indicates that tenants were only able to provide their families with the minimum requirements for shelter. The poverty that forced them to live in cramped dwellings must also have induced many tenants to build wooden chimneys.

Flooring and room partitions are rarely mentioned in the description of houses on the lower Western Shore manors. Many tenants' houses probably had no flooring at all or were only partly covered with planks, as were two of the houses on Plater's land. The number of rooms is specified for just two houses on the proprietary manors. One was the dwelling of George Maxwell, a wealthy freeholder who resided on Calverton Manor. Maxwell's house was twenty-six feet wide and thirty-four feet long—one of the largest houses on the lower Western Shore manors—and it was divided into four rooms. Not only was Maxwell's dwelling far larger than most houses on the manors, but the building was unusual in another respect—it had a "hipp'd roof," an architecturally advanced roof design. Most tenant houses undoubtedly were simple gable-ended structures.[9] The other house the surveyor noted as having more than a single room was also on Calverton Manor. Described as being old, the house, whose dimensions were not given, was divided into two rooms.[10] Although the surveyor failed to mention the number of rooms in other dwellings on the lower Western Shore manors, very few were large enough to have been divided into as many as four rooms. The smallest tenant houses were undoubtedly single room structures, in which the

"Kitchen, living room, bed room and hall are all in one room into which one enters when the house door opens."[11] The average dwelling on all the lower Western Shore manors was sufficiently large to have been divided into two rooms, and those containing a larger than average amount of floor space may have had a hall and two small chambers on the ground floor. No dwelling on the lower Western Shore manors was described as being two stories high, so houses with a single story and loft must have predominated.[12]

In short, the average proprietary tenant on the lower Western Shore lived in a very small frame house covered with clapboards. His dwelling measured about sixteen or seventeen feet wide and twenty-four or twenty-five feet long. The fireplace that dominated one end of the house had a chimney constructed of wood and clay, and only if he was one of the more fortunate tenants was he able to provide a safer brick chimney for his dwelling. The ground floor of the house was divided into two, or at most three, small rooms, although some of his neighbors lived in one-room houses and only the wealthiest tenants, most of whom owned freehold land off the manor, had as many as four rooms in their dwellings. Part of the ground floor of the typical tenant's house might have been covered with planks, but the remainder of the floor was probably nothing but packed earth, especially at the end of the house where sparks from the fireplace caused a greater fire hazard. The living space on the ground floor of the tenant's house was supplemented by a loft that served as storage space and sleeping quarters. In physical appearance, the average tenant's house lacked any suggestion of architectural refinement; it was cheaply and unskillfully constructed, and it was ugly. Little wonder that travelers so rarely described the dwellings of the poor people in Tidewater Maryland—they were an uninviting blemish on the landscape.

A dwelling was the only improvement necessary to make a tenement habitable, but many leaseholders constructed additional buildings on their lots. One type of dependency commonly found on plantations in southern Maryland was a detached kitchen, a building a short distance from the dwelling where, among other things, the family's meals were cooked.[13] A separate kitchen reduced the danger of fire in the dwelling and kept the house cooler during the hot summer months. Despite the advantages of a separate kitchen, few proprietary tenants built them. Most tenants cooked in the open or over a fire in their dwellings, not by choice but because they could not afford to erect a special building for that purpose.

Only fourteen of the seventy-nine houses on Beaverdam Manor had detached kitchens, and the number on the other three manors on the lower Western Shore ranged from less than one-third on Zachiah Manor to a little more than one-half the total dwellings on Chaptico Manor (*see* table 3–4). Dimensions were given for thirty-three of the detached kitchens, and nearly all were quite small. The largest kitchens were on Beaverdam Manor, with the average measuring 14.0 feet wide and 19.1 feet long, while the smallest were on Calverton Manor, where the average was 13.0 feet wide and 18.0 feet long.

The manor surveyor provided even less information about the construction of kitchens than he did about dwellings. One kitchen on Zachiah Manor was constructed of logs, but most were probably built of the same type materials as the dwelling with which they were associated. Thus, clapboard-covered frame structures undoubtedly were most common, but since kitchens were used primarily for cooking and were probably erected by the more well-to-do tenants, a larger percentage of kitchens than dwellings may have had brick chimneys rather than the more hazardous wooden chimneys.

Because the principal cash crop grown on the lower Western Shore was tobacco, the most common type of crop storage building found on manor tenements in the region was the tobacco house. One argument against the tobacco staple was that curing the crop required large buildings that were used only a few weeks of the year.[14] The description of tobacco houses on the lower Western Shore manors gives credence to this charge, because even though most resident tenants were poor to-bacco houses were the largest improvement on most tenements, nearly always exceeding the size of the dwellings.

There were fifty-one tobacco houses on Beaverdam Manor, ranging in size from 256.0 square feet to 640.0 square feet. The average tobacco house on the manor contained 517.6 square feet and measured 18.7 feet

TABLE 3-4
Detached Kitchens on Sample Proprietary Manors, 1767–1768

Manor	Total Dwellings	Total Kitchens	Percentage of Dwellings with Detached Kitchens	Number of Kitchens with Dimensions	Average Size (square feet)
Beaverdam	79	14	17.7	14	273.2
Chaptico	35	19	54.3	12	257.3
Zachiah	28	8	28.6	1	240.0
Calverton	23	8	34.8	6	233.3
Kent	42	15	35.7	0	—
Gunpowder	49	2	4.1	0	—
Monocacy	64	3	4.7	3	285.3

SOURCE: Claim of Henry Harford, Public Record Office, Audit Office 12/79, ff. 129–42, London (microfilm copy available at the Hall of Records, Annapolis, Maryland).

TABLE 3-5

Crop Storage Facilities on Sample Proprietary Manors, 1767-1768: Tobacco Houses and Corncribs

Manor	Total Lots	Tobacco Houses				Corncribs		
		Total Number	Number with Dimensions	Average Size (square feet)	Range (square feet)	Total Number	Number with Dimensions	Average Size (square feet)
Beaverdam	68	51	35	517.6	256–640	16	5	105.6
Chaptico	51	33	18	679.6	400–960	7	2	248.0
Zachiah	48	25	12	636.0	400–792	6	0	—
Calverton	30	23	19	665.3	240–768	3	1	260.0
Kent	53	2	0	—	—	0	—	—
Gunpowder	64	32	32	887.2	400–1,500	0	—	—
Monocacy	69	1	1	600.0	—	0	—	—

SOURCE: Claim of Henry Harford, Public Record Office, Audit Office 12/79, ff. 129–42, London (microfilm copy available at the Hall of Records, Annapolis, Maryland).

wide by 27.5 feet long. Tobacco houses on Chaptico Manor were even larger, although there were fewer of them. Dimensions were given for eighteen of the thirty-three tobacco houses, with the average containing 679.6 square feet and measuring 20.8 feet wide by 32.6 feet long. Tobacco houses on Zachiah Manor were smaller than those on any other sample manor on the lower Western Shore. Of the twelve that were measured, the average contained 636.0 square feet and was 21.3 feet wide by 29.7 feet long. Nineteen of the twenty-three tobacco houses on Calverton Manor were measured. The average structure contained 655.3 square feet and was 21.4 feet wide and 31.1 feet long.

The principal food crop grown by tobacco planters in southern Maryland was maize, and although most tenants must have relied heavily on it for the support of their families and livestock, the surveyor noted few corncribs on the sample manors. Only sixteen Beaverdam Manor tenements had corncribs, and the number was even smaller on the other three sample manors on the lower Western Shore (*see* table 3–5). Dimensions were given for only eight corncribs. Of the five on Beaverdam Manor that were measured, the average contained 105.6 square feet of floor space and was 8.0 feet wide and 13.2 feet long. The two corncribs on Chaptico averaged 12.0 feet wide by 20.0 feet long, and contained 248.0 square feet. The single corncrib on Calverton for which dimensions were given measured 13.0 feet wide by 20.0 feet long. Because of the small number of corncribs on the lower Western Shore manors, most tenants must have stored their annual crop of maize in other buildings. Tobacco houses could be used for storing corn, and once the ears were packed in barrels the crop could be kept in any building or shed that was relatively dry and protected from vermin.[15] Many tenants undoubtedly kept corn in the lofts of their dwellings or in the sheds that some houses had attached to them. The main reason for the small number of corncribs on the manors was that unlike tobacco, corn did not have to be cured in specially constructed buildings. Since most tenants grew little surplus maize in addition to what was necessary to feed their families and livestock and to provide seed for the next season, the size of the annual crop was insufficient to require construction of a separate storage facility.

Although every tenant who resided on the lower Western Shore manors owned livestock, few provided shelter for their animals. Cattle and horses were allowed to range in pastures or on grassland during the winter months. Hogs foraged in the woods throughout the year, while poultry ran unconfined in the house yard and adjacent fields. The absence of adequate shelter was a major reason for the low quality and high winter mortality of farm animals in the Chesapeake colonies, but even large planters usually ignored the problem. If their wealthy neighbors

TABLE 3-6

Barns on Sample Proprietary Manors, 1767–1768

Manor	Total Lots	Number of Barns	Percentage of Lots with Barns	Barns with Dimensions	Average Size of Barns (square feet)	Range (square feet)
Beaverdam	68	0	—	—	—	—
Chaptico	51	2	3.9	0	—	—
Zachiah	48	0	—	—	—	—
Calverton	30	1	3.3	1	600.0	—
Kent	53	8	15.1	5	764.0	400–936
Gunpowder	64	11	17.2	11	676.0	360–1,250
Monocacy	69	49	71.0	46	1,022.1	340–2,700

Source: Claim of Henry Harford, Public Record Office, Audit Office 12/79, ff. 129–42, England (micro-film copy available at the Hall of Records, Annapolis, Maryland).

failed to provide barns and stables for their animals, it is not surprising that few tenants constructed shelters for their livestock.[16]

Only three tenements on the lower Western Shore manors had barns (*see* table 3–6). Two of the barns were located on Chaptico Manor, and the third was on Calverton Manor. Dimensions were only given for the Calverton Manor barn, which measured twenty feet wide by thirty feet long. Stables were the other type of structure that could be built to house animals. Just one was recorded on the four sample manors on the lower Western Shore, however, that being a building of unspecified size on Beaverdam Manor.

In addition to the large structures already mentioned, tenants frequently constructed smaller buildings on their leaseholds that served a variety of purposes. The surveyor usually failed to note the size or use of these outbuildings and in many cases they were probably nothing but multipurpose sheds. Among the outbuildings on Beaverdam Manor that were specifically noted by the surveyor were nine dairies, with two of the three that were measured being eight feet square and the other eight feet wide by twelve feet long (*see* table 3–7). There were also three small slave quarters on Beaverdam Manor, as well as a meat house, a cock house, and a "mill house on a good stream [with] 2 p[ai]r [of] stones." One Chaptico Manor tenement also had a mill, described as "a sorry grist mill on Budds Creek."[17] Other Chaptico outbuildings included five slave quarters, one of which was sixteen feet square and built of brick; two storehouses; a schoolhouse; and Pile's warehouse, one of the county's tobacco inspection warehouses.

Only a fourth of the tenements on Zachiah Manor had outbuildings on them. Small gristmills were located on three lots, but the only other buildings specifically named were three dairies and a single slave quarter. Just two outbuildings on Calverton Manor were specified as to use, one being a slave quarter and the other a dairy. Over one-half the tenements on Calverton Manor had outbuildings on them, however, but the surveyor failed to note their use.

A final improvement found on many tenements on the lower Western Shore manors was an orchard of fruit trees. According to the terms of their leases, tenants were required to plant and maintain an orchard of 100 or more trees. Not every tenant abided by the lease provision, but most did plant at least a few trees and some had very large orchards. As table 3–8 shows, at least one-half of the leaselots on each of the lower Western Shore manors had an orchard. The number of trees ranged from as few as 10 to as many as 500, with the average orchard on every manor containing over 100 trees. The apple was the type of fruit tree most frequently planted by tenants. Zachiah Manor orchards, for example, contained over 3,000 apple trees, slightly more than 1,200 peach

TABLE 3-7
Outbuildings and Other Improvements on Sample Proprietary Manors, 1767–1768

Manor	Total Lots	Lots with Outbuildings or Other Improvements	Percentage of Lots with Improvements	Slave Quarters	Stables	Dairies	Meat House
Beaverdam	68	22	32.4	3	1	9	1
Chaptico	51	28	54.9	5			
Zachiah	48	12	25.0	1		3	
Calverton	30	18	60.0	1		1	
Kent	53	7	13.2				1
Gunpowder	64	36	56.3		1		
Monocacy	69	42	60.9		18		

SOURCE: Claim of Henry Harford, Public Record Office, Audit Office 12/79, London

trees, and one orchard contained 6 cherry trees. The fruit from the orchards, either fresh or preserved, must have been an important supplement to the tenants' diet, but most of the crop was undoubtedly processed into cider or brandy.

From an examination of the improvements on the lower Western Shore manors, supplemented by other information gathered in 1767 and 1768 prior to the proprietary sales, the following picture of tenancy in that region emerges. The majority of the proprietary tenants had lived on their leaseholds for decades. The manor was their permanent family home, and most tenants undoubtedly built the best improvements they could afford. But building and maintaining well-constructed dwellings and dependencies required money, something that tenants

TABLE 3-8
Orchards on Sample Proprietary Manors, 1767–1768

Manor	Total Lots	Number of Orchards	Percentage of Lots with Orchards	Orchards with Number of Trees Specified	Average Number of Trees	Range
Beaverdam	68	44	64.7	43	124.0	30–500
Chaptico	51	27	52.9	27	101.5	15–300
Zachiah	48	24	50.0	24	190.7	30–500
Calverton	30	21	70.0	19	120.0	10–500
Kent	53	23	43.4	23	99.6	30–200
Gunpowder	64	35	54.7	35	141.6	20–400
Monocacy	69	42	60.9	42	97.4	8–360

SOURCE: Claim of Henry Harford, Public Record Office, Audit Office 12/79, ff. 129–42, London (microfilm copy available at the Hall of Records, Annapolis, Maryland).

			Types of Specified Outbuildings					
Weavers' Shops	Smiths' Shops	Tan-yards	Store-houses	Ware-houses	Cock-houses	Schools	Churches	Mills
					1			1
			2	1		1		1
								3
							1	
	1	1						1
2	3						1	

(microfilm copy available at the Hall of Records, Annapolis, Maryland).

who lived in a tobacco-producing area, where the economic advantage lay with the large landowner and slave owner, rarely had. The inferior quality of the natural resources on the lower Western Shore manors, as well as the fragmentary evidence from probate records, suggest that most resident tenants in St. Mary's and Charles counties were very poor. The tiny clapboard-covered dwellings and the small number of outbuildings in addition to tobacco houses that dotted the landscape of the manors in the region certainly reinforce this impression.

The two sample proprietary manors on the Eastern Shore had been settled almost as long as the manors on the lower Western Shore, and as on the latter deforestation and decades of cultivation had impaired the fertility of the soil. Nevertheless, the quality of the soil was somewhat better on Kent and Queen Anne's manors than on the lower Western Shore manors, and probate records suggest that resident tenants made slightly better profits from growing wheat as their principal cash crop than did the tenants on the lower Western Shore who relied on tobacco.

Because such a high proportion of the leaseholders on Queen Anne's Manor were resident tenants, it is unfortunate that no list of improvements for that manor is known to exist. The improvements on nearby Kent Manor, however, do not reflect the affluence of the nonresident leaseholders who dominated the manor, but rather the poverty of the people to whom they sublet their tracts. Thus, the improvements on Kent Manor reflect the kinds of improvements poor people on the Eastern Shore usually built, not the types of buildings and dependencies that the actual leaseholders of most Kent Manor lots could afford.

Nearly every Kent Manor tenement had a dwelling house, indicating that most of the manor was cultivated even though the majority of the manor tracts were held by nonresident freeholders. Dimensions were given for forty of the forty-two dwellings on the manor (*see* table 3–1). The smallest house contained only 192.0 square feet, and the largest 760.0 square feet of floor space. The average dwelling on the manor contained 484.0 square feet and measured 18.4 feet wide by 25.6 feet long. Although the average house on the manor could have been divided into two or three small rooms, it was still a very small structure, and living conditions must have been extremely cramped for even a moderate sized family.

The type of construction is specified for twenty-six Kent Manor dwellings. Twelve were frame buildings; one was described as "posted," another type of frame construction;[18] one house was built of brick; and twelve others were either built of log or a combination of frame and log construction (*see* table 3–2). Log houses were somewhat more common on Kent Manor than on the lower Western Shore manors. Constructing buildings of horizontally stacked logs was a practice introduced into America by non-English immigrants, especially the Scandinavians and Germans. The Swedes and Finns who settled in the Delaware Valley in the seventeenth century built log houses, and the idea probably spread from there to the Eastern Shore of Maryland. But tenants on Kent Manor also had close commercial ties with Pennsylvania, where both German and Scotch-Irish immigrants built houses and outbuildings of logs.[19] Although Kent Manor residents were familiar with log construction, most built frame dwelling houses covered with clapboard, a reflection of the cultural preferences of Marylanders of English ancestry for that type of building.

Dimensions are given for twenty-five of the Kent Manor houses for which the type of construction is known. As table 3–9 shows, there was a direct relationship between the size of the dwelling and the type of material used in its construction. Houses built of unspecified log construction—presumably round logs with saddle notched corners— were smallest, averaging only 364 square feet. Dwellings built of hewed logs with dovetailed joints, a superior type of log construction, averaged 465 square feet. Frame houses were larger than either type of log structure, averaging 479 square feet. The three dwellings that were part hewed log and part frame construction were the result of either the log or frame section being added to a preexisting dwelling. These composite houses were large, averaging 660 square feet. The single brick dwelling on the manor measured 25 feet wide and 30 feet long, or 750 square feet. The largest dwelling on the manor was a posted structure, which contained 760 square feet. Not surprisingly, those residents who could afford better quality building materials were also able to build larger

TABLE 3-9
Size of Dwellings on Kent Manor Described
According to Type of Construction, 1767

Type of Construction	Number of Dwellings	Average Size (square feet)	Range (square feet)
Log	5	346	320–450
Hewed log and dovetailed log	3	456	360–684
Frame	12	479	288–750
Hewed log and frame	3	660	648–684
Brick	1	750	—
Posted	1	760	—
	25		

SOURCE: Claim of Henry Harford, Public Record Office, Audit Office 12/79, f. 130, London (microfilm copy available at the Hall of Records, Annapolis, Maryland).

houses. The poorest residents on the manor who could only afford to build houses out of unhewn logs also lived in the smallest dwellings.

In at least one respect houses on Kent Manor were noticeably superior to those on the lower Western Shore manors. Twenty-four of the forty-two houses on the manor had brick chimneys. Thus, although the average house on Kent Manor was quite small, the majority of the tenants were able to build chimneys for their houses that were considerably safer than the wooden ones that seem to have dominated on houses in Charles and St. Mary's counties (see table 3-3).

In addition to a dwelling fifteen Kent Manor tenements had separate kitchen facilities (see table 3-4). Neither size nor method of construction is specified for any of the kitchens. The fact that nearly two-thirds of the residents on Kent Manor had to cook in their houses confirms that the wealth revealed in the probate records of leaseholders inaccurately indicates the economic condition of the people who actually resided on the manor.

Although the Eastern Shore had originally been a tobacco-growing region, wheat had become the dominant staple throughout much of the area before the middle of the eighteenth century. That tenants on Kent Manor had almost entirely abandoned tobacco in favor of grain is reflected in the presence of only two tobacco houses on the manor (see table 3–5). Dimensions are not given for either structure, nor is the method of construction described. No Kent Manor tenement had a corncrib, but eight had barns. Dimensions are given for five of the barns, which ranged from 400.0 square feet to 936.0 square feet in size, with the average containing 764.0 square feet and measuring 21.8 feet wide by 34.8 feet long (*see* table 3–6).

Not only were there few crop storage buildings and barns on Kent Manor, but the number of other outbuildings was also very small. Only 13.2 percent of the tenements on the manor had outbuildings, a number so low that it suggests the surveyor simply omitted mentioning small structures that he considered of little value (*see* table 3–7). Just two of the outbuildings the surveyor did note are specified as to use. One was a meat house and the other was a church. Less than one-half of the tenements on the manor had orchards. The twenty-three orchards on the manor contained from 30.0 to 200.0 trees, with the average having 99.6 trees (*see* table 3–8).

In short, although the probate records of Kent Manor leaseholders indicate that many of the people who held leases on the manor were wealthy, improvements on the manor tenements reflect the lifestyle of the people who actually resided there. Although a few leaseholders may have cultivated their tracts with slaves and an overseer, the absence of slave quarters on the manor suggests that most sublet their lots to people who were too poor to purchase land of their own. These subtenants were able to build houses that were slightly larger and better constructed than those of tenants on the lower Western Shore, but their buildings were still very small and they were able to provide few additional amenities for themselves, their families, and their livestock. The grain farmers who resided on Kent Manor may have had slightly larger disposable incomes than their counterparts who grew tobacco in St. Mary's and Charles counties, but the difference was hardly discernible in the kinds of improvements they could afford to construct on their manor tenements.

More recently settled and characterized by moderately good to excellent soil and bountiful woodlands, Gunpowder and Monocacy manors offered their tenants a distinct advantage over the other proprietary leaseholders in terms of natural resources. But carving homesteads and arable fields out of the forest required arduous labor, and the probate records suggest that the profits from farming and animal husbandry were so small that the majority of the manor residents remained near the bottom of the economic spectrum. The residents of both upper Western Shore manors quickly learned to exploit the ample supplies of timber on their tracts for constructing improvements, however, and in the case of German-dominated Monocacy Manor, the residents enjoyed a noticeably better standard of living than other tenants—at least in terms of improvements on their leaseholds.

Slightly more than two-thirds of the Gunpowder tenements had dwellings on them, and dimensions were given for each of the forty-nine houses on the manor (*see* table 3–1). The house on lot 10 had the distinction of being the largest dwelling on any of the sample manors. Owned by James Gittings—son of Thomas Gittings, who had first leased land on the manor in 1737 and was the wealthiest tenant on the manor—the frame dwelling with brick chimneys measured thirty-five feet wide and forty feet long. In addition to his dwelling, Gittings had a detached kitchen, five tobacco houses, a stable complex, a barn, a smith's shop, six other outhouses, and an orchard of 150 fruit trees. Gittings either leased or coleased six other tenements on the manor, and he also owned freehold land off the manor.[20]

Gittings's dwelling was exceptionally large, but the majority of Gunpowder tenants lived in houses that were about the same size as those on other proprietary manors. The average dwelling on the manor contained 473.6 square feet of floor space and measured 17.8 feet wide by 25.6 feet long. The type of construction is indicated for all but five of the forty-nine dwellings on the manor. Fourteen were frame, four were posted, two were a combination of log and frame, and twenty-four were built of logs (*see* table 3–2). The German and Scotch-Irish immigrants who settled in large numbers in northern Maryland in the middle of the eighteenth century popularized log construction in the area, and since much of Gunpowder Manor was heavily timbered, logs were a logical building material. As on Kent Manor, however, log houses were generally smaller than dwellings built with other materials. Log houses on Gunpowder Manor averaged only 382.5 square feet, whereas posted dwellings averaged 481.0 square feet, frame structures contained 617.6 square feet, and the two houses that were both log and frame averaged 725.0 square feet (*see* table 3–10). As these last dwellings were undoubt-

TABLE 3-10
Size of Dwellings on Gunpowder Manor Described
According to Type of Construction, 1767

Type of Construction	Number of Dwellings	Average Size (square feet)	Range (square feet)
Log	24	382.5	160–784
Posted	4	481.0	384–560
Frame	14	617.6	384–1,400
Log and frame	2	725.0	640–810
	44		

SOURCE: Claim of Henry Harford, Public Record Office, Audit Office 12/79, f. 131, London (microfilm copy available at the Hall of Records, Annapolis, Maryland).

edly houses that had been enlarged, frame construction was the type of building preferred by those who could afford large houses. Frame dwellings were not necessarily easier to build or more comfortable to live in than well-constructed log houses, but most Gunpowder tenants had English ancestors, and like the tenants on Kent Manor they built frame dwellings when they had sufficient wealth to choose which materials to use in constructing their houses.

The type of chimney construction on Gunpowder Manor houses is specified in only eight cases, and in each case the chimney was made of brick (*see* table 3–3). Six of the eight houses with brick chimneys were frame dwellings, and the other two were a combination of log and frame construction. The average size of the houses with brick chimneys was 764.3 square feet. Thus, not only did the wealthier tenants construct frame dwellings, but they were also able to build safer and more permanent brick chimneys for their houses. The majority of the houses on the manor, however, probably had wooden chimneys.

Only two homes of tenants on Gunpowder Manor had detached kitchens. One was on the dwelling plantation of James Gittings, the manor's richest tenant, and the other was located on an adjacent tract that Gittings held in partnership with John Chamberlain. Because the climate of the area in which Gunpowder Manor was located is cooler than southern Maryland or the lower Eastern Shore, even those tenants who could afford a separate kitchen may have decided not to build one.

Tobacco was an important staple crop on Gunpowder Manor, although by the 1760s most tenants had diversified their crop base and were relying increasingly on wheat as their major cash crop. Tobacco houses were still the most common type of crop storage structure found on the manor, however, and dimensions were given for each of the thirty-two (*see* table 3–5). The tobacco houses ranged in size from 400.0 square feet to 1,500.0 square feet. The average tobacco house on the manor contained 887.2 square feet and measured 21.2 feet wide by 41.6 feet long, considerably larger than similar structures on the tobacco-growing manors on the lower Western Shore.

Eleven Gunpowder tenements had barns built on them. Six of the barns were constructed of logs, two were posted, two were frame, and one was of an unspecified type of construction (*see* table 3–11). The barns ranged in size from 360.0 square feet to 1,250.0 square feet, with the average containing 676.0 square feet and measuring 19.4 feet wide by 36.2 feet long. One of the log barns on the manor had a thatched roof, but the type of roofing on the others was not specified. Only one tenement on the manor had a stable, that being on James Gittings's dwelling lot.

TABLE 3-11

Types of Construction Used for Barns on Gunpowder and Monocacy Manors, 1767–1768

Manor	Total Barns	Number with Type of Construction Indicated	Type of Construction					
			Unspecified Log	Round Logs	Squared Logs	Round Logs with Clapboards	Posted	Frame
Gunpowder	11	10	6	—	—	—	2	2
Monocacy	49	41	17	18	4	1	—	1

SOURCE: Claim of Henry Harford, Public Record Office, Audit Office 12/79, ff. 131, 142, London (microfilm copy available at the Hall of Records, Annapolis, Maryland).

Over one-half of the Gunpowder leaselots had one or more outbuild-ings in addition to the major structures that have been mentioned (*see* table 3–7). James Gittings had built a number of outbuildings on his home lot, and he owned a gristmill on another tenement on the manor. A tanyard with a large tanning house built of logs was located on lot 24, which Gittings coleased with George Hunter. Although the surveyor failed to specify the use of other buildings on the manor, the total number of outbuildings on Gunpowder tenements was much larger than on any of the other sample manors previously discussed. Finally, the majority of Gunpowder tenements had orchards planted on them. The thirty-five orchards ranged in size from 20.0 to 400.0 trees, with the average having 141.6 trees (*see* table 3–8).

To summarize, improvements on Gunpowder Manor tenements were more numerous and larger than those on Kent Manor or the manors on the lower Western Shore. If James Gittings had not built his dwelling, tobacco houses, stables, barns, tanyard, and mill, however, the improve-ments on the manor would not have been much better than those on the other sample manors. Gittings was very wealthy, and he had invested heavily in developing his manor tracts, but the majority of Gunpowder tenants lived in houses that were as small as those inhabited by proprie-tary tenants on the lower Western Shore. Most of the smaller houses on Gunpowder Manor were built of logs, but otherwise only minimal dif-ferences are discernible between the improvements made by the poorer Gunpowder tenants and those made by resident tenants on the other sample manors.

Monocacy Manor was the last settled of the sample proprietary man-ors, but its tenants had built larger, better, and more numerous im-provements on their leaseholds than residents on any other sample manor. Most Monocacy tenants were Germans who had moved into the region in the 1740s and 1750s, and the fragmentary evidence from the probate records indicates that the majority left small estates when they died. But the description of improvements on the manor indicates that the average Monocacy tenant had invested a considerable amount of labor and capital in improving his tenement, the value of which would not have been reflected in his estate inventory.

All but twelve Monocacy leaselots had houses built on them when the manor was examined in 1767 prior to the proprietary sales. Dimensions were given for all the sixty-four dwellings on the manor, which ranged in size from 224.0 square feet to 1,056.0 square feet. The average dwelling contained 558.2 square feet and measured 19.4 feet wide by 28.2 feet long. Even though the average house on the manor was less than the 20.0- by 30.0-foot structures specified in the proprietary leases, houses on Monocacy Manor were still larger than those on the other sample manors, and they were more than double the size of the average house on Zachiah Manor.

Not only were Monocacy dwellings larger than the houses owned by other proprietary tenants, but they were also constructed of different materials. The type of construction is given for sixty dwellings on the manor, and all were built of logs. The specific type of log construction is mentioned for forty-nine of the houses. Thirty-six of the dwellings were built of round logs, twelve were built of squared logs, and one was built of a combination of round and squared logs. Round-log construction was the easiest method of building with logs, since the structure consisted of stacked logs, often unbarked, which were joined at the corners with a simple saddle joint. Round-log houses could be completed in from one to three days and no tools except an axe were required. Squared-log construction was more complicated and required more tools, but the end product was an excellent house.[21] Since squared-log construction was superior to round-log construction, not surprisingly houses that were built of squared logs or a combination of squared and round logs were larger than the average house on the manor. The thirteen houses constructed of squared logs or both squared and round logs averaged 657.7 square feet of floor space, nearly 100.0 square feet more than the average house on the manor. The largest house on the manor, however, was a twenty-two- by forty-eight-foot dwelling that was built entirely of round logs. Thus, although squared logs were generally preferred by those who could afford to build large dwellings, round logs were not confined to the smaller houses on the manor.

The type of chimney construction is mentioned for thirty-six houses on Monocacy Manor (see table 3–3). Nine of the dwellings had brick chimneys, one had a brick and stone chimney, and twenty-six had stone chimneys. Although the other twenty-eight dwellings on the manor probably had wooden chimneys, a larger proportion of houses on Monocacy Manor had relatively permanent and fireproof chimneys than on any other sample manor.

The surveyor who examined the tenements on Monocacy Manor added one detail concerning the construction of dwellings and outbuildings that was rarely mentioned by those who examined the other proprietary manors. He specified the type of roof covering for fifty-seven of the dwellings on the manor, as well as for a smaller number of the other buildings on the individual tenements (see table 3–12). Nearly all dwellings were covered with shingles, although four had what was described as a "cabbin roof." Many buildings on Conegocheague Manor, a proprietary manor located on the extreme frontier in Frederick County, had cabin roofs. Anticipating that the commissioners appointed to sell

TABLE 3-12
Materials Used for Roofing on Buildings on Monocacy Manor, 1768

Type of Building	Total Number	Number with Roof Construction Specified	Type of Material			
			Shingles	Cabin Roof	Thatch	Tile
Dwellings	64	57	53	4	—	—
Barns	49	39	19	—	20	—
Stables	18	10	3	1	6	—
Outbuildings	58	18	12	3	2	1

SOURCE: Claim of Henry Harford, Public Record Office, Audit Office 12/79, f. 142, London (microfilm copy available at the Hall of Records, Annapolis, Maryland).

the proprietary manors might not be familiar with this type of roof, the surveyor of that manor added an explanatory note to his report. A cabin roof, he wrote, was made by "splitting Trees into thin pieces which they lay one upon another for a [roof] cover, it saves the expence of Nails & is said to be as tight as Clapboards."[22]

A cabin roof was usually found on only the simplest and smallest log structures on Monocacy Manor. Thin staves of wood secured by heavy poles created a functional roof, but the absence of nails rendered it precarious protection from wind and rain. As a result, cabin roofs on Monocacy dwellings were replaced with shingles as soon as the occupant could afford to do so. The four Monocacy houses that had cabin roofs were among the smallest on the manor, averaging only 278 square feet each. Three of the four were of round-log construction, and the other was of unspecified log construction. All four houses were built on tenements that had been leased in the early 1760s, so they were undoubtedly only temporary shelters for families that had just recently moved onto the manor.

Only three tenements on Monocacy Manor had separate kitchens, and all three were leased by men with English surnames (see table 3–4). The three kitchens were larger than those on the other sample manors, averaging 285.3 square feet and measuring 15.3 feet wide and 18.7 feet long. The small number of separate kitchens on the manor was due to the cooler climate of Frederick County, as well as to the Germans' preference for cooking in their dwellings.

Monocacy Manor residents had never relied on tobacco as a major cash crop, and as a result there was only one tobacco barn on the manor. Furthermore, the surveyor did not note a single corncrib on the manor, but most tenants were nonetheless well supplied with storage space for their crops because the majority had barns. Barns were found on over 70 percent of the Monocacy tenements, and dimensions were given for forty-six of them (see table 3–6). The barns ranged from 340.0 square feet to a mammoth structure that contained 2,700.0 square feet, and many undoubtedly had more than one story. The average barn had 1,022.1 square feet of floor space and measured 23.9 feet wide by 41.7 feet long. The type of construction was noted for forty-one barns. One was frame, another was a combination of round logs and clapboard, four were built of squared logs, and the remainder were of round-log or unspecified log construction (*see* table 3–11). Although the frame barn was large, containing 1,920.0 square feet, the largest barn on the manor was built of logs. The type of roof covering was specified for thirty-nine of the barns. Nineteen were shingled, but twenty were thatched. With the exception of the single barn on Gunpowder Manor, no other example of thatching was noted on the other sample manors, and its use on Monocacy barns was undoubtedly due to the large number of Germans on the manor. A thatched roof was less permanent than a shingled roof and it was more of a fire hazard, so Monocacy tenants preferred shingles, or even a cabin roof, for their dwellings. Thatching provided an adequate and economical roof for outbuildings, however, and the tenants used it extensively, even on the largest barns on the manor.

Not only did Monocacy tenants have more barns than tenants on the other sample manors, but they also frequently provided stables for their livestock. There were eighteen stables on the manor, and whenever the type of construction is mentioned it was round-log construction. The type of roof covering is specified for ten of the stables. One had a cabin roof, three were shingled, and the remainder were thatched.

Over 60 percent of the Monocacy tenements had some type of outbuilding in addition to the major structures that have been discussed (*see* table 3–7). In most cases, the surveyor only noted that there were one or more outbuildings on a lot, but he specifically mentioned two weaver's shops, three smith's shops, and a "Dutch Church" as being on the manor. Of the fifty-eight different outbuildings on the manor, twelve were shingled, three had cabin roofs, two were thatched, and one had a tile roof. Monocacy orchards were among the smallest on the sample manors, but over 60 percent of the tracts had at least a few trees. Individual orchards ranged in size from 8.0 to 360.0 trees, with the average orchard containing 97.4 trees (*see* table 3–8).

Examination of the improvements on the various proprietary manors reveals that by the mid-1760s tenants on the two upper Western Shore manors had invested considerably more labor and capital in improving their leaseholds than had residents on the other sample manors. One particularly wealthy tenant on Gunpowder Manor, James Gittings, accounted for a large proportion of the development on that manor, but other tenants had also invested in very large tobacco houses and slightly larger dwellings than had the other tenants that have been examined. In part, Gunpowder Manor tenants were able to construct larger and more numerous improvements because of the abundance of timber on the manor, but most residents still preferred frame construction, reserving logs for barns, stables, and other outbuildings.

The Germans on Monocacy Manor had no hesitancy about utilizing log construction, and they exploited the timber resources on their leaseholds to the fullest, constructing sturdy, well-built dwellings that were, compared to the dwellings on the other sample manors, almost commodious. Log construction may have been introduced onto Monocacy Manor by Germans, but everyone soon recognized the superiority of logs, both in terms of durability and economy. All the tenants on Monocacy Manor lived in log houses, regardless of their ethnic background, and logs were customarily used in the large number of outbuildings that were found on the manor. Some dwellings were very small, and not every tenant had been able to construct a barn or stable by the mid-1760s, but compared to tenants on the other sample manors, Monocacy residents were both able and willing to provide adequate shelter for man and beast.

Although the kinds of improvements on the sample manors ranged from tanyards to churches, most proprietary tenants built very little on their leaseholds. Improvements on the lower Western Shore manors were smallest in number and poorest in quality. Most tenants in that region lived in diminutive frame dwellings with little else on their leaselots except a tobacco house, one or two small outbuildings, and an orchard. Houses on Kent Manor on the Eastern Shore were not much larger than those on the manors on the lower Western Shore, although they were somewhat better constructed and a larger number did at least have brick chimneys. Improvements on Gunpowder Manor were superior to those on the manors on the Eastern and the lower Western shores, but the best dwelling and outbuildings were owned by a single tenant. The average Gunpowder tenant seems to have been just slightly better able to provide himself with a decent house and outbuildings than were leaseholders on the other sample manors. The improvements on Monocacy Manor were markedly superior to those on the other manors, especially considering the late date of settlement in the area. Houses were relatively large and the tenants had built barns and a variety of other outbuildings on their leaseholds. Most structures on Monocacy Manor were built of logs and stone rather than the clapboard and clay or brick that was preferred by proprietary tenants in other areas of the province. Nevertheless, most Monocacy leaseholders had certainly been able to invest more labor, and in all probability more capital, in improving their tenements than had the proprietary tenants on the other sample manors.

The most striking observation that can be made on the basis of the improvements on the sample proprietary manors, including Monocacy, concerns the small size of the tenants' houses. Probate records indicate family size for a few tenant households on every manor. Although the number of families that can be reconstructed is small, the data suggest that tenants often had six or more children (*see* table 3–13). Even if the eldest child had established a separate household by the time a tenant's last child was born, the large families indicated by the probate records would have been exceedingly crowded given the size of the average house on the proprietary manors.

The most important factor concerning housing on the eight proprietary manors—what it was like to live in such an environment—is not revealed in the description of the manor tenements. Many, perhaps most, of the dwellings must have been little better than hovels. Their small size coupled with large families must have taxed tempers, as well as sanitary conditions, to the limit. Privacy within the house, if desired, would have been difficult to achieve. Furthermore, the physical appearance of the tenant's house was both a result of his poverty and a constant reminder of his economic condition. How this environment affected tenants and their children can only be imagined. Literary sources provide little information concerning the life of poor whites in the Chesapeake Bay region. Chastellux observed "miserable huts inhabited

TABLE 3-13
Size of Families at Time of Father's Death: Leaseholders and Tenants
on Selected Proprietary Manors

| | | Siblings | | | | | |
| | Number of Families | Male | Female | Sex Unknown | Total | Average Siblings per Family | Average Family Size[a] |
Manor							
Beaverdam	9	32	30	0	62	6.9	8.9
Chaptico	5	18	13	0	31	6.2	8.2
Zachiah	11	28	40	17	85	7.7	9.7
Calverton	9	22	25	9	56	6.2	8.2
Kent	10	30	30	0	60	6.0	8.0
Queen Anne's	11	27	30	9	66	6.0	8.0
Gunpowder	15	38	48	2	88	5.9	7.9
Monocacy	18	47	43	36	126	7.0	9.0

SOURCE: Wills, Accounts, and Distribution Books for Charles, Baltimore, Frederick, Kent, and Queen Anne's counties, all located at the Hall of Records, Annapolis, Maryland.

[a]Assumes leaseholders were survived by a spouse.

by whites, whose wane looks and ragged garments bespeak poverty" in his travels through Virginia, and Ebenezer Hazard divided Virginians into two classes, rich and poor, characterizing the latter as "ignorant & abject."[23] Both descriptions could probably have been applied to many proprietary tenants in Maryland. John Beale Bordley, accusing lower class farmers in Maryland of idleness and dissipation, wrote that they "fly from their own happiness in the moment when they mount their horses and hurry to the tavern, the race, nine-pins, billiards, excess upon excess of toddy, and the most nonsensical and idle chat, accompanied with exclamations and roaring, brutal and foreign to common sense and manners as the mind of wisdom can conceive of depraved man."[24]

Bordley was repelled by the life led by poor whites in the Chesapeake Bay region. He was the product of a different culture, one in which the sons of the gentry had all the advantages of education and social status in addition to comfortable houses, imported clothing, and adequate diets that were denied by birthright to the children of nonlandowners. A great many tenants may have been shiftless carousing drunks, but understanding the physical environment in which they lived renders the pejorative statements of upper class critics seem less like aristocratic snobbery and more like a commentary on the mental and motivational impairment that could result from abject poverty. The tenants on Lord Baltimore's manors were fortunate to have secure tenures and low annual rents, which raised them at least marginally above the very poorest class of free whites in Maryland in the late colonial period. But their life was still exceedingly difficult, and even those who resisted the succor of toddy could do little to improve their situation or to ensure something better for their children.

CHAPTER FOUR

"Gloomy and Barbarous Practices": Tenant Agriculture

The general outlines of the agricultural development of the Chesapeake Bay region during the colonial period are well known. Tobacco early became the staple crop in Virginia and Maryland, and during the first half-century of settlement fortunes could be made growing the plant. After the 1680s, however, rising costs of production and lower prices for tobacco made the staple a precarious source of profit. The search for a more lucrative staple occasionally erupted in enthusiasm for a specific crop that led planters to divert a large portion of their labor force away from tobacco. Indigo, hemp, and flax each in turn seemed to promise relief from declining tobacco profits, but none proved to be a satisfactory substitute for Chesapeake planters. Only wheat, and to a lesser extent corn, were successful in making inroads into tobacco's hegemony as the primary cash crop in the region. By the end of the colonial period, much of lower Tidewater Virginia, the Northern Neck, the Eastern Shore of Maryland and Virginia, and northern Maryland had shifted from tobacco to a diversified crop base with wheat as the dominant cash staple.[1]

Although the movement away from tobacco occurred gradually, agriculture in the Chesapeake Bay region was markedly different at the end of the colonial period from what it had been at the beginning of the eighteenth century. The following discussion concerns what effect the kinds of crops grown in a particular area had on the tenants who resided on the proprietary manors in Maryland.

Tenants are a particularly useful group to study for several reasons. First, although tenants could benefit from an advantageous shift in the crop base, they could not effect such a change themselves. Few tenants had the labor or risk capital necessary to experiment with new crops, and the annual production of a tenant and his family was insufficient to ensure that a new crop could be easily and economically conveyed to market. Many large planters, on the other hand, had both the labor and surplus capital necessary to try new crops, and furthermore, they had better access to trade networks that would allow them to test a new crop on the market. The inability of tenants to alter the crop base was particularly important when the dominant planters' decision either to change to a new crop or to refuse to do so was detrimental to the economic interests of the small-scale producer. Because of the differences between large and small planters in terms of land, labor, and capital, the economic interests of the two groups were frequently at variance.

Second, the tenant farmer's annual income was almost entirely derived from agriculture. Unlike that of the large planters, who could preserve or increase family fortunes through professional, governmental, or mercantile activities, the preponderance of a tenant's income was derived from the soil, augmented to some extent by day-labor wages and home manufactures.[2] As a result, the effects of a change in the agricultural base of an area should be especially evident among tenants, because they had few sources of income besides what they received from their crops.

Third, because of their dependence upon agriculture, the ability of tenants to acquire freehold land was directly related to their success in producing cash surpluses from their crops. Tenancy could only be a temporary stage in the rise toward freehold status if leaseholders were able to accumulate capital from their crops. If small producers could not make a profit from cultivation of the soil, tenants would have little hope of improving their economic condition, and tenancy as a form of land tenure would flourish, providing that people who could not acquire land of their own rejected or did not have alternate forms of employment and remained—whether by choice or necessity—geographically immobile.

Finally, nonlandowners comprised approximately one-half of the householders in the older settled counties of Maryland by the War for Independence (see appendix A). Although the exact proportion of the wheat, tobacco, corn, and other crops produced by tenants cannot be established, members of the group contributed substantially to the economy of the region. Furthermore, in addition to the crops tenants marketed themselves, many paid their rents in tobacco or wheat, which augmented their landlords' annual crop shipments.[3] Given the importance of tenant agriculture in the Chesapeake Bay colonies, any alteration or improvement in the crop base or in planting methods not only affected the tenants themselves, but the economy of the entire region as well.

Planters in some sections of Maryland had diversified their agricultural base by the late colonial period, but this was not the case on most of the lower Western Shore. Tenants, as well as large planters there, continued to rely on tobacco as their staple cash crop until after the War for Independence. Because of the dearth of probate records for St. Mary's County residents and the underrepresentation of the poor in the probate records of Charles County, few inventories listing crops have survived for proprietary tenants on the manors in those counties. Only fifteen crop inventories were found and all were for residents on Calverton and Zachiah manors. The fifteen inventories do indicate, however, that tobacco was still the principal cash crop grown by proprietary tenants on the lower Western Shore during the last half of the eighteenth century, and this conclusion is supported by the large number of tobacco houses on the manors prior to the proprietary sales in the mid-1760s. The production of tobacco per laborer—defined as slaves, servants, or freemen in the household sixteen years of age or older—indicated in the crop inventories seems to have diminished during the period represented, but because the sample is so small the trend is only suggestive (see table 4–1). Other sections of the province were decreasing their dependence on tobacco, however, and a gradual diversification of crops grown on the lower Western Shore did occur by the end of the eighteenth century. Data are too sparse to establish what alternative cash crops were adopted by tenants on the manors in Charles and St. Mary's counties, although wheat would have been a logical choice. But even if tenants did begin planting a greater variety of crops, tobacco remained the primary cash staple grown in the region throughout the colonial period.

Tenants on Kent and Queen Anne's manors on the Eastern Shore relied on tobacco during the early years of settlement, but grain became increasingly important in the second and third decades of the eighteenth century. Production figures for the Eastern Shore manors are either not available or do not shed light on the exact time when the proprietary tenants began turning away from tobacco or where the change first occurred. John Beale Bordley, a Queen Anne's County planter and agricultural innovator, maintained that the cultivation of wheat as a major cash crop originated in Pennsylvania, and that the "culture of wheat . . . travelled southward, from county to county through Maryland," and, as a result, "the tobacco culture declined."[4] As Philadelphia increased in size and began operating as an export center for grain and as the West Indian market for food expanded, the demand for wheat increased, causing grain merchants to draw from an ever-increasing orbit of surrounding territory.[5] Grain was easily transported by water or over land, thereby enabling the people on the Eastern Shore to market wheat in Philadelphia. Later, additional grain centers arose, including Baltimore, Wilmington and New Castle in Delaware, and smaller towns along the

TABLE 4-1
Production of Tobacco on Zachiah and Calverton Manors, 1750–1798

Date of Crop Inventory	Manor	Total Laborers	Tobacco per Laborer (in pounds)	Date of Crop Inventory	Manor	Total Laborers	Tobacco per Laborer (in pounds)
1750	Zachiah	2	1,055.4	1778	Calverton	11	262.5
1751	Zachiah	1	1,975.0	1779	Calverton	13	871.7
1767	Zachiah	1	2,543.0	1783	Calverton	2	352.5
1769	Zachiah	1	1,476.0	1784	Zachiah	5	525.6
1769	Zachiah	2	249.0	1792	Calverton	5	350.0
1775	Zachiah	1	862.0	1795	Zachiah	8	264.1
1775	Zachiah	1	154.0	1798	Calverton	9	242.7
1776	Calverton	1	638.0				

SOURCE: Prerogative Court Inventories; Charles County Inventories, Hall of Records, Annapolis, Maryland.

TABLE 4-2
Major Cash Crops Grown on Kent Manor, 1751–1793

Date of Crop Inventory	Number of Laborers	Wheat (bushels)	Tobacco (pounds)	Production Per Laborer	
				Wheat (bushels)	Tobacco (pounds)
1751	4	392.00	—	98.0	—
1756	7	644.75	3,518	92.1	502.6
1762	6	278.00	2,100	46.3	350.0
1768	7	123.00	—	17.6	—
1768	11	644.00	156	58.6	14.2
1770	1	50.00	—	50.0	—
1770	1	97.00	—	97.0	—
1772	6	846.00	—	141.0	—
1774	5	398.00	—	79.6	—
1779	2	353.00	—	176.5	—
1784	7	335.00	—	47.9	—
1793	7	256.00 (est.)	—	36.6	—

SOURCE: Prerogative Court Inventories; Kent County Inventories and Accounts, Hall of Records, Annapolis, Maryland.

Eastern Shore.[6] By the Revolution, the Eastern Shore was the breadbasket of the province, producing large surpluses of grain for consumption within the colonies and for export.[7]

Crop inventories for the tenants on Kent and Queen Anne's manors (*see* tables 4–2 and 4–3) and the small number of tobacco houses on Kent Manor (improvements on Queen Anne's are not recorded) suggest that

TABLE 4-3
Major Cash Crops Grown on Queen Anne's Manor, 1767–1791

Date of Crop Inventory	Number of Laborers	Wheat (bushels)	Tobacco (pounds)	Production Per Laborer	
				Wheat (bushels)	Tobacco (pounds)
1767	1	48.0	—	48.0	—
1768	1	29.0	—	29.0	—
1775	1	210.0	900.0	210.0	900.0
1775	1	156.5	—	156.5	—
1787	1	102.0 (est.)	340.0	102.0	340.0
1787	1	181.0	—	181.0	—
1787	1	250.0	—	250.0	—
1788	9	804.0 (est.)	—	89.3	—
1788	1	219.0 (est.)	2,108.0	219.0	2,108.0
1790	1	76.0	—	76.0	—
1791	6	275.0	2,500.0	45.8	416.7

SOURCE: Prerogative Court Inventories; Queen Anne's County Inventories and Accounts, Hall of Records, Annapolis, Maryland.

by the late colonial period wheat was the tenants' principal cash crop. Three of the twelve inventories for Kent Manor tenants include tobaccco, as did four of the eleven inventories for Queen Anne's Manor tenants, but in every case the principal cash crop listed was wheat.

As indicated by the numerous tobacco barns on the tenements, large quantities of tobacco were cultivated on Gunpowder Manor on the upper Western Shore (*see* table 3–5). The tenants' reliance on tobacco as a cash crop appears to have decreased in the 1760s, however, although most tenants probably continued to grow some tobacco as part of a more diversified agricultural base. The evidence for the movement away from the tobacco staple on Gunpowder Manor is partly based on nine crop inventories, dating between 1750 and 1786, that exist for tenants on the manor (*see* table 4–4). Tobacco is the only cash crop listed in the inventories for 1750, 1751, and 1758; both tobacco and wheat are present in the inventories for 1767 and 1769; and all subsequent inventories list only wheat as a cash crop. Nine inventories are inadequate to establish positively an alteration in the type of cash crop grown on the manor, but the suggestion receives confirmation from a statement made by William Strickland, an Englishman, who was dispatched by the Board of Trade in 1794 to survey American agriculture. Strickland wrote that the "Incumbent of St. John's Parish, on [the] Gunpowder, till 1760, received his Pol[l] Tax *mostly* in *Tobacco* according to law, from all who made Tobacco.... By the year 1770 very little of Tobacco was specifically paid him; because little was made—and now there is scarcely any made there. Wheat has turned away Tobacco; and the erection of Grist Mills and the growing of Wheat go Hand in Hand, increasing yearly, every where."[8]

TABLE 4-4
Cash Crops Grown on Gunpowder Manor, 1750–1786

Date of Crop Inventory	Number of Laborers	Wheat (bushels)	Tobacco (pounds)	Production Per Laborer	
				Wheat (bushels)	Tobacco (pounds)
1750	1	—	1,056.0	—	1,056.0
1751	3	—	974.0	—	324.7
1758	2	—	4,225.0	—	2,112.5
1767	1	79.0	1,598.0	79.0	1,598.0
1769	8	285.0	7,951.0	35.6	993.9
1770	4	150.0	—	37.5	—
1775	9	305.0	—	33.9	—
1780	1	69.0	—	69.0	—
1786	1	47.0	—	47.0	—

SOURCE: Prerogative Court Inventories, and Baltimore County Inventories and Accounts, Hall of Records, Annapolis, Maryland.

TABLE 4-5
Cash Crops Grown on Monocacy Manor, 1753–1792

Date of Crop Inventory	Number of Laborers	Wheat (bushels)	Rye (bushels)
1753	1	72	—
1777	1	132	54
1783	1	120	—
1788	1	120	—
1792	1	84	—

SOURCE: Prerogative Court Inventories; Frederick County Inventories, Hall of Records, Annapolis, Maryland.

NOTE: Production figures for both wheat and rye are estimates, because all inventories for tenants list crops in the ground rather than actual production statistics. Estimated yields for planted crops are based on six bushels per acre for both rye and wheat, a realistic figure for most land in Maryland during the eighteenth century, but probably much too low for the rich land of the Monocacy River Valley.

Thus, a fairly rapid change to diversified agriculture appears to have occurred on Gunpowder Manor in the decade before the Revolution. Tenants may have continued to grow some tobacco, but wheat increasingly became the dominant cash crop on the manor.

On the other upper Western Shore manor, Monocacy, tenants relied on grain as their principal agricultural commodity. Wheat, and to a lesser extent rye, were the main cash crops grown from the earliest settlement on the manor, due perhaps to the large number of Germans who settled in the Monocacy Valley, but also to the great distance a bulky tobacco crop would have to have been transported to reach a market. The only evidence that tobacco had ever been grown in quantity on the manor was the presence of a single tobacco house on one tenement when the manor was examined prior to the proprietary sales in the mid-1760s.[9] None of the crop lists in inventories for Monocacy Manor tenants includes tobacco among the cash crops (*see* table 4–5).

While tenants in other parts of the province were decreasing their dependence on the tobacco staple, most residents on the lower Western Shore manors continued to rely on the crop throughout the colonial period. Tobacco offered tenants several advantages as a cash staple. First, unlike wheat or other grains that required large tracts of land for cultivation, tobacco could be grown on a small amount of arable land, although the need to rest tobacco fields every few years partly offset this advantage.[10] Large families necessitated that the average tenant plant much of his cultivated acreage in maize and vegetables, and even though older children could work in the fields, the amount of labor that could be devoted to cash crops was greatly restricted. Of the fifteen Zachiah and Calverton Manor tenants whose estate inventories contain crop lists, eleven produced under 1,000 pounds of tobacco and only one harvested more than 2,000 pounds in the half-century from 1750 to 1798 (see table 4–6). Even on low-quality soil that had been cultivated for a number of years, no more than three acres of land would have been required to produce a 1,000-pound tobacco crop.[11] The small acreage required for their tobacco crops meant that tenants did not have to clear much land when a reduction in yields signaled the need to lay out new tobacco plots. Furthermore, small tobacco fields could be worked without plows and draft animals, an important consideration for poor tenants.

Another beneficial feature of tobacco was that by the mid-eighteenth century the methods of cultivating the crop were well understood and the marketing system was highly developed. Tobacco had been grown since the first years of settlement in the colony, and by the eighteenth century people born in those areas where tobacco was the staple acquired the skills necessary for producing the crop as a natural by-product of growing up. Scottish and English factors and native-born merchants handled the marketing of the crop, thereby greatly simplifying this part of the crop cycle for tenant planters.[12] In addition, large slave owners in the area found the labor-intensive nature of the crop

TABLE 4-6
Estimated Acreage Planted in Tobacco on
Calverton and Zachiah Manor Tenements, 1750–1798

Number of Acres Planted	Number of Crop Inventories	Percentage of Total Estates
less than 1	4	26.7
1–2	4	26.7
2–3	3	20.0
3–4	1	6.7
4–5	1	6.7
5–6	1	6.7
6–7	—	—
7–8	1	6.7
	15	

SOURCE: Prerogative Court Inventories and Accounts; Charles County Inventories and Accounts, Hall of Records, Annapolis, Maryland.

helpful in keeping their slaves fully employed, thus limiting the marketing options for tenant farmers who might have benefited from a staple crop that required less effort to produce.[13] In sum, planters on the lower Western Shore remained strongly attached to the tobacco staple because it could be grown on less land than alternative crops; it required little capital investment in tools; its production utilized universally understood skills; and it was easy to market through well-established commercial channels.

But tobacco had several important disadvantages as a cash crop, some of which bore especially heavy on the small producer. First, the crop was so labor intensive that it required almost year-round attention. The tobacco planter was busy from late winter when he laid out the seed beds, through the transplanting in the spring, the constant weeding, suckering, topping, and deworming, concluding with the cutting of the crop in the fall, after which it had to be hung, dried, sorted, and packed into hogsheads. What little time remained between crops was employed making hogsheads, repairing tobacco barns and fences, and clearing new tobacco fields.[14]

Tobacco was also easily damaged during the growing and curing periods. John Beale Bordley noted that crop failure could result from "frost, drought, or fly; want of seasonable weather for planting; destruction by the groundworm, webworm, hornworm; buttening low, for want of rain; curling or frenching, from too much rain; house-burning or funking whilst curing; frost before housed; heating in bulk or in the hogshead; inspection culling, &c."[15]

Furthermore, tobacco was a luxury crop, which meant that it had to be marketed in Europe, rather than being a food crop that could be sold locally. The need to ship tobacco abroad reduced the planter's profits because of expenses for transportation, insurance, and profits to middlemen. Furthermore, the small producer grew too little tobacco to enable him to ship his crop directly to England, so the tenant usually had to sell it locally to storekeepers, factors, or large planters, all of whom took a share of the profits for their trouble. In addition, the price of tobacco could be dramatically affected by world events, and foreign wars could even prevent the planter from disposing of his crops.[16]

The debilitating effect of tobacco on the soil is a well-known, albeit exaggerated, problem. Tobacco did deplete the soil, but probably no more than wheat or maize, and if a planter manured any of his crops the tobacco fields received preferential treatment. Bordley maintained that most Maryland planters manured their tobacco fields, but he noted that the amount of animal fertilizer produced on most farms and plantations was inadequate for the much larger corn and wheat fields. Even though tobacco had been grown on the lower Western Shore manors for decades, the small amount of land described as worn out indicates that the crop had not resulted in general soil depletion (*see* table 2–11).[17]

Although tobacco was the major cash crop grown by tenants on the lower Western Shore, maize was their principal food crop. The diet of most tenants was confined to what they could raise or gather on their leaseholds, and as William Eddis commented, "Indian corn, beaten in a mortar and afterwards baked or boiled, forms a dish which is the principal subsistence of the indigent planter. . . ."[18] Hardy and dependable, maize was not nearly so difficult to cultivate as tobacco, but it was extremely debilitating to the soil. Planted in widely spaced rows (generally six feet apart), individual corn hills were usually planted five or six feet apart in the row, resulting in about 1,200 to 1,500 hills per acre. Cornfields had to be kept free of weeds, so the unprotected soil between the widely spaced hills was subject to erosion during much of the growing season. Furthermore, unlike potatoes, beans, peas, and other leafy plants that add nitrogen, or at least humus, to the soil, virtually every part of the maize plant, from the stalk to the tassel, was consumed by man or beast.[19]

Crop inventories and contemporary accounts provide some indication of what the typical proprietary tenant who lived on the tobacco-staple manors grew and how he organized his fields. Because most resident tenants did not own slaves or servants, the labor supply that could be devoted to the production of crops was confined to family members. Free hired laborers were rarely employed on the tobacco-staple manors, because the labor required for tending both tobacco and maize was distributed fairly evenly throughout the growing season. William Tatham remarked that "he who would have a good crop of tobacco, or of maize, must not be sparing of his labour, but must keep the ground constantly stirring during the whole growth of the crop."[20] Given the labor requirements of both tobacco and corn, little advantage could be achieved by hiring free laborers or slaves at harvest or for any other limited period of time, and tenants were rarely able to afford full-time help. Therefore, the tenant planted enough maize to support his family and cultivated only as much additional acreage in tobacco as could be tended by the members of his own family. Evidence from tenant inventories, supplemented by an additional sampling of Charles County estates, indicates that the production of tobacco per household without slaves or servants averaged less than 1,000 pounds yearly after passage of the Tobacco Inspection Act of 1748.[21] Because of the small amount of land required for tobacco production, the fields could be prepared with care, and if any manure was available it was applied to the small tobacco fields. The tenant could continue growing tobacco on the same field for three or four years until a decrease in the crop's quality or productivity forced him to lay out a new one- to three-acre tract.

Indian corn, or maize, required a much larger plot of land on the average tenant's leasehold than did tobacco. The number of acres planted in corn depended on the size of the tenant's family, with those having a large number of children to support necessarily devoting a great deal of land to the crop. Johann David Schoepf reported that the produce from two bushels of seed would support a "large household." Two bushels of Indian corn planted in hills five feet apart in rows six feet wide with four kernels in each hill required between seventeen and nineteen acres of land.[22] The few crop inventories for tenants on Zachiah and Calverton manors indicate that most planted about fifteen acres of corn. Thus, the average tenant on the lower Western Shore had at least five times as much land in corn as he did in cash-producing tobacco. Most of the corn harvested from the fifteen or so acres the tenant had in that crop was generally consumed by the tenant's family and livestock. Overplanting to guard against a partial crop failure, however, meant that tenants usually had a few barrels of surplus corn to sell after most harvests.[23] The tenant's cornfield could also be the source of profit in another way. Shortly before the maize was harvested in the fall, tenants frequently planted a grain crop between the widely spaced corn rows. Winter wheat was the usual grain sown in cornfields, although rye or some other grain was occasionally substituted.[24] Yields from grain planted in cornfields were very low, so the profit from such crops was quite small. In light of the small amount of land the average tenant could plant in tobacco, however, any supplemental income from surplus maize or cornfield grain crops must have been welcome.

Planting patterns undoubtedly varied to some extent from one tenement to another, but the typical plantation of resident proprietary tenants in southern Maryland was centered around two fields and two principal crops. The tobacco field was small, almost always less than three acres, and it received special attention, both in terms of the amount of animal fertilizer placed on it and in the care given the growing crop. The maize field was much larger, and it was often interplanted with a winter grain crop in the fall. Some of the tenants may have used a three-field system, which added a fallow field that was kept free of weeds by periodic plowings and harrowings. In alternate years maize was grown on the fallow field and the maize field was allowed to lie fallow. Only the most progressive tenant farmers employed a four-field system, which added a pasture to the tobacco, corn, and fallow fields. The pasture in the four-field system was generally an old cornfield that was covered with whatever native grasses and weeds happened to appear when the field was not plowed.[25] The separate fields, whether two, three, or four, were normally enclosed with fencing.

The number of acres cultivated by tenants varied with the amount of labor available to them and the type of field system employed. Tenants

without extrafamilial laborers who practiced two-field agriculture usually had less than twenty acres in cultivation, allowing three acres for
tobacco, about fifteen acres for maize, and two or three acres for a
vegetable garden and orchard. A three-field system required an
additional fifteen acres for the fallow field, increasing the total arable
land to about thirty-five acres. The pasture in the four-field system
added another fifteen acres, increasing the size of the four-field plantation to approximately fifty acres of arable land. By the late 1760s, the
average tenement on Zachiah Manor contained 135.5 acres, and since
the average leasehold on the other manors in the region was even larger,
most proprietary tenants on the lower Western Shore manors had ample
land for two-, three-, or four-field husbandry.[26]

The fact that many planters on the Eastern Shore turned from tobacco
to wheat as their principal cash crop early in the eighteenth century, and
that large quantities of wheat were grown on the upper Western Shore by
the middle of the century, indicates that increasing numbers of
Marylanders had found wheat to be superior to tobacco as a cash crop.
Some planters experimented with flax, hemp, and other alternative cash
crops, but most discovered that wheat was the most viable substitute for
the tobacco staple.

Farmers did not begin planting wheat as their major cash staple in
order to conserve land. Estimating how many acres the average tenant
farmer could plant in wheat is problematical, but crop inventories
suggest that most tenants produced at least 100 bushels of wheat per
year. Wheat yields averaged from 6 to 8 bushels per acre in most parts of
Maryland, so from thirteen to sixteen acres of land was required to
produce 100 bushels of wheat, or about five times the amount of land a
planter without slaves or servants needed for a tobacco field.[27]

Nor did planters turn to wheat in order to preserve their soil, because
wheat, like tobacco, was a debilitating crop. Wheat may even have been
more damaging to the land than tobacco when planted over a number of
years, because the larger size of wheat fields made it far less feasible to
manure them than the much smaller tobacco fields. Livestock was usually not penned by residents of the Chesapeake Bay colonies, which
restricted the quantity of manure available. Manure salvaged from feeding areas was sometimes adequate to fertilize small tobacco fields, but it
was not sufficient for the much larger wheat fields.[28]

Although conservation of land and soil depletion were not factors that
influenced people to turn to wheat cultivation, the crop did offer several
important advantages over tobacco. First, wheat required relatively little
labor compared to tobacco. The land had to be prepared before seeding

by plowing and harrowing, but when wheat was sown in maize fields between the rows of corn the soil was already sufficiently loose because of the hoeing that had been given the corn. If a new or additional field was used for wheat, it usually had been in fallow, in which case the field was relatively free from weeds, and it could be readied for planting with little additional effort. Sown broadcast in the fall, the growing crop could not be cultivated, so no labor at all was required until the crop was harvested the following summer.[29]

Harvest was the only time during the entire growing season when large amounts of labor had to be expended on a wheat crop. More than any other factor, the harvesting phase of wheat culture encouraged the use of free hired labor in preference to slaves. A farmer could plant and tend many more acres than he could harvest, as long as he could secure additional laborers during the two or three weeks of harvest.[30]

In addition to requiring less labor to grow than tobacco, wheat was also easy to process for market after it had been cut in the field. Unlike wheat farmers in England and in the northern colonies who extracted the kernels by flailing, most Marylanders trod out their wheat with horses or cattle. John Beale Bordley commented that the thought of "treading out small corns [i.e., grains] with *horses* may entertain persons who are unacquainted with the practice" and admitted that he had not been enthusiastic about the idea himself when he first began grain farming. Bordley feared that the wheat would be contaminated by the horses, but later concluded that horse treading was superior to flailing, as long as the farmer was careful about "taking off the horse-dung directly as it is dropped, and let not the horses stop to stale, until each journey ends and they are led off."[31]

Although horse treading was "an universal practice within the penninsula of [the] Chesapeak[e],"[32] the scale of operation varied with the size of the grain farm. Some of the larger farmers had a permanent plank treading floor several hundred feet in diameter, but tenants and other small farmers generally had much smaller dirt floors that were enclosed by a fence. The sheaves of wheat were laid on the ground and a number of horses were then led into the enclosure. Humane farmers led or rode the horses around the floor in harness, but more commonly the horses were confined as closely as possible and then excited by shouts and gesticulations. According to Bordley, the result of each horse "pressing to be foremost to get fresh air, jostling, biting, and kicking the others with bitterness" was that the wheat sheaves were pulverized, separating the grains of wheat from the heads. Treading was hard on horses, but it remained the customary practice among grain farmers in Maryland into the nineteenth century. The principal advantage of treading over flailing was that by the latter method one man could beat out only about 1 bushel of wheat per day, whereas up to 500 bushels per day could be extracted by treading.[33]

Wheat was superior to tobacco as a cash crop in several respects, most notably because of the ease with which it could be grown and processed. In addition, most farmers probably made more money growing wheat than if they had planted tobacco. Although this hypothetical advantage was undoubtedly the most important reason for the change from to-bacco in much of the province, proving the proposition is difficult and gauging its effect on tenants who rarely had extrafamilial laborers is even more problematical.

One thousand pounds of tobacco can safely be considered the maximum amount grown by most tenants who did not own slaves or servants. Estimating the amount of wheat produced by the average ten-ant is complicated by the element of hired labor and by the ability of a man to plant and tend more acres than he could harvest with members of his family alone. An average laborer in mid-eighteenth-century Mary-land, including men, women, girls, and boys, could harvest about three-fourths of an acre of wheat per day.[34] Harvest had to be completed in two or three six-day weeks, so a grain farmer could plant between 9 and 13 1/2 acres of wheat per laborer available for harvest. At 6 bushels per acre, this number of acres would have produced between 54 and 81 bushels of wheat per laborer. But most tenant grain farmers who did not own slaves or servants produced at least 100 bushels of wheat per year, which would have required about 16 2/3 acres of land and the labor of from one and one-half to two persons during harvest. Many tenant farmers had more than two laborers in their own families, and others could hire additional laborers or trade their labor with neighbors during harvest. Therefore, 100 bushels of wheat can be considered the minimum annual production of proprietary tenants who relied on wheat as their primary cash crop.[35]

Based on an estimate of 1,000 pounds of inspected tobacco and 100 bushels of marketable wheat per tenant household, the value of the two cash crops can be compared. Table 4–7 shows the price of wheat and tobacco as valued in tenant inventories recorded between 1750 and 1790. In every year for which there are inventories in which both wheat and tobacco are valued, wheat produced a larger return for an average crop than tobacco. In all but three years, 100 bushels of wheat was worth at least twice as much as 1,000 pounds of tobacco, and in three years wheat was at least three times as valuable as tobacco. In addition, the price of wheat was less erratic than tobacco, with a general trend toward increasing prices. Tobacco, on the other hand, showed no trend either to

TABLE 4-7
Price in Maryland Currency of Wheat and Tobacco Cash Crops
from Inventories of Proprietary Tenants, 1750–1790

Year	Wheat (100 bushels)	Tobacco (1,000 pounds)	Year	Wheat (100 bushels)	Tobacco (1,000 pounds)
1750		£12.10.0	1771		
1751	£17.10.0	10. 0.0	1772	28.15.0	
1752			1773		
1753			1774	25. 0.0	
1754			1775	24.11.8	13.15.0
1755			1776	20. 0.0	15. 0.0
1756	18.15.0	8. 6.9	1777		
1757			1778		
1758		10. 0.0	1779		
1759			1780		
1760			1781		
1761			1782		
1762	22.10.0	6. 5.0	1783		
1763			1784	37.10.0	17.15.10
1764			1785		17.10.0
1765			1786	27.10.0	
1766			1787	30. 0.0	10. 0.0
1767	23.15.0	10. 0.0	1788		7.10.0
1768	23. 7.0	8. 0.0	1789		
1769	19.11.8		1790	40. 8.4	10. 0.0
1770					

SOURCE: Prerogative Court Inventories and Accounts; Inventories and Accounts for Charles, Queen Anne's, Kent, Baltimore, and Frederick counties, all at the Hall of Records, Annapolis, Maryland.

higher or lower prices, with wide variations in value from one entry to another. The prices of wheat and tobacco may not precisely reflect the value of the two crops when grown and marketed by large planters, but given his labor supply and marketing alternatives, wheat appears to have been a more profitable crop for the small producer after the mid-eighteenth century.[36]

Not only did tenants who grew tobacco make less, but they had to market their crop through local merchants, planters, or the factors of English or Scottish tobacco houses, all of whom expected to profit from the transaction. Because most of them were chronically short of cash, tenants were usually forced to market their tobacco through storekeepers who would extend them credit for needed store goods during the year. The storekeeper's dual role as crop purchaser and merchant created a strong tie between him and the small planter. One study of a Prince George's County storekeeper indicates that most planters, including slave owners who were above the ranks of the very poor, were indebted to the store and that the amount of indebtedness generally increased over time.[37] Perhaps the most important implication of such a debt structure was that it could impede tenants from adopting alternative cash crops that promised larger cash incomes. The storekeeper profited both on goods that he sold and on the tobacco he exported. If tenants accepted store credit against future tobacco crops, the storekeeper could insist that he either settle the account in cash or continue growing tobacco to make payments on his debt. If the return from an average tobacco crop was insufficient to allow a tenant to live at or above the subsistence level, and if he achieved subsistence by buying on credit from the store, even though it meant increasing his indebtedness annually, the storekeeper gained almost complete economic control over the tenant. The storekeeper ensured himself of an annual supply of tobacco by subsidizing people who might otherwise have been forced to seek a more profitable cash crop, and the subsidy in the form of store credit may have been an important reason that the culture of tobacco was perpetuated for so long on small farms in southern Maryland.[38]

One important benefit of wheat was that it enabled grain farmers to achieve independence of the storekeeper. Bordley noted that "as the culture of *wheat*, and the manufacturing it into *flour* travelled southward, the people became more happy, and independent of the British storekeepers who had kept them in debts and dependent."[39] Grain farmers might be tempted by merchandise offered in a factor's store, but they were at liberty to take their business elsewhere if they chose.

After mid-century, wheat appears to have been a more profitable cash crop than tobacco, at least for tenants who did not own slaves or servants. Wheat had replaced tobacco as the principal cash crop on much of the Eastern Shore in the early eighteenth century, and before the War of Independence it had begun to replace tobacco as a cash staple throughout much of the upper Western Shore. Tenants on the lower Western Shore continued to grow tobacco, however, and their apparent inability to break away from the tobacco staple raises the question of how Eastern Shore tenants had been able to accomplish the transition early in the eighteenth century and how tenants on Gunpowder Manor had been able to diversify their crop base in the 1760s. A complete answer to the question must await a detailed economic study of the debt and credit structure of the various regions in the province, but several possible explanations can be advanced.

The geographical progression of the transition from tobacco to wheat appears to have been an important factor in determining when tenants could begin growing grain as their major cash crop. The spread of wheat culture southward down the Eastern Shore from the locus of the trade in

Philadelphia, and the emergence of secondary market centers in Delaware and along the Chesapeake Bay, suggest that trade networks were crucial for enabling planters to adopt wheat as a cash crop. Grain merchants were probably willing to advance cash to planters so that they could settle store debts and become grain farmers. The grain buyer benefited by collecting interest on the loan as well as by assuring himself of additional bushels of wheat, and the planter was enabled to free himself from the storekeeper and adopt a more lucrative cash crop. Furthermore, as the grain-trade network moved closer to a particular tobacco-growing area, the planter was able to sow more of his land in wheat because it was easier and more economical for him to transport whatever he could raise to market. Over a period of several years, he could gradually convert his land to wheat, still producing some tobacco for the storekeeper, but eventually accumulating enough surplus capital from wheat to pay his store debts and completely convert to the more profitable cash crop.[40]

Another factor that facilitated diversification on the Eastern and upper Western shores was that planters in the regions were not deeply committed to slave labor when the transition to wheat occurred. The Eastern Shore had a large slave population by 1783, but in the early decades of the century when the planters began to diversify their crop base the number of slaves in the area was much smaller.[41] As late as 1783, the proportion of slaves in the total population of Baltimore County in which Gunpowder Manor was located was only about one-half as large as in the counties on the lower Western Shore, and the majority of the tenants on the manors had no slaves when they began to adopt wheat as their primary cash staple.[42]

Large slave populations posed a serious impediment to diversification, because wheat and other grains were far less labor intensive than tobacco. Small planters with few slaves or servants could shift to wheat as soon as the trade network enabled them to market grain crops economically, but planters with large numbers of slaves were faced with the problem of employing their labor force productively if they abandoned the cultivation of tobacco. Furthermore, many slave owners found that they had insufficient arable land to convert their entire plantation into wheat farms. A planter with ten slave laborers, for example, could plant, tend, and harvest no more than 30 acres of tobacco. The same ten laborers could plant and harvest between 86 and 130 acres of wheat, and to take advantage of the wheat grower's ability to plant and tend more acres than he could harvest, the slave owner would have had to plant at least 166 acres of wheat. On a well-managed farm, one-half the acreage was always left in woods,[43] and if the remaining land was cultivated according to a four-field system (wheat, maize, fallow, and pasture), only one-eighth of the plantation could be devoted to wheat.[44] Therefore, to fully employ ten slave laborers, a four-field grain farm would have had to contain over 1,333 acres. Plantations in excess of 1,000 acres were unusual in southern Maryland, but many landowners had more than ten slave laborers. In short, some tobacco planters resisted switching away from tobacco because wheat culture would have required that they either purchase more land, sell some of their slaves, or devise alternative forms of employment for their laborers.

A final factor impeding the transition away from the tobacco staple on the lower Western Shore was the planter's traditional, technological, and psychological attachment to the crop. The lower Western Shore had been producing tobacco longer than any other region in the colony. The tobacco trade provided a direct link between the southern counties and England, a connection that was highly valued by the large planters. Furthermore, the population of the southern counties was less heterogeneous than that of other sections of Maryland, where non-English immigrants helped to break traditional customs and to introduce new agricultural practices. Finally, the tobacco counties were dominated by a relatively small number of men who had large holdings of land and slaves. The planting elite could have fostered the adoption of wheat as the staple cash crop, either by changing to the crop themselves or by requiring that tenants on their land pay rents in grain. Perhaps large landowners in southern Maryland were as securely tied to British creditors as were tenants to the local stores. Or perhaps for reasons cited above, they did not believe it would be in their economic interest to change their crop base. In any case, tenants as well as large landlords on the lower Western Shore continued to rely on tobacco throughout the colonial period despite the economic advantage that might have been achieved, at least by tenants, from the adoption of an alternative cash crop.

Agriculture was an important, and perhaps the decisive, factor accounting for the economic condition of tenants on the Maryland proprietary manors. The fact that most resident manor tenants were very poor can be directly attributed to the low returns from small-scale agriculture. A shortage of land was not a problem for tenants, because a 100- to 150-acre tenement was ample for the two- to four-field system of cultivation followed by small planters. Neither was soil exhaustion an important factor, since most tenements were large enough to permit regular crop rotation. The principal impediments to tenant economic mobility and capital accumulation were a shortage of labor and for some an inability to adopt new cash crops. The large number of children in the average family meant that tenants had to devote much of their arable land to the production of maize and other crops for home consumption. Older sons and daughters undoubtedly worked in the fields until they married or moved away from home, but the ratio of dependents to laborers in most tenant households nevertheless remained high. The acreage that could be planted in cash crops was insufficient to produce much surplus after the tenant paid his rent and made essential purchases and expenditures. Those tenants who relied on tobacco were in an even worse economic condition, and many had to rely on local storekeepers for subsistence. Even where tenants were able to alter their crop base to the more profitable wheat culture, however, few were ever able to achieve economic mobility. Most tenants never accumulated enough capital to purchase a freehold; the majority could not even afford to make substantial improvements on their tenements; and the average tenant died with a very small estate. Although wheat provided better cash returns than tobacco and helped free tenants from local storekeepers, no one in late colonial Maryland, unless he owned high-quality land and many slaves, could accumulate large capital surpluses if his income was derived exclusively from agriculture.

CHAPTER FIVE

The Sale of the Proprietary Manors

Small estates at death, no slaves or servants, and poor improvements on tenements all reflected the poverty that characterized the majority of tenants who resided on the proprietary manors. Most tenants had little or no surplus capital, and given the poor returns from small-scale agriculture, the possibility that they could ever acquire freehold land of their own was slim. Nevertheless, twice within little more than a decade the proprietary leaseholders were given the opportunity to purchase their tenements. Lord Baltimore put his manors up for sale in the 1760s, and the land that was not purchased was confiscated and sold by the state during the War for Independence. Both sales offered tenants the chance to become freeholders, but both also placed those tenants who were unable to buy their land in jeopardy of losing their homes. Because most resident tenants were poor, they must have awaited the day appointed for auctioning off their tenements with apprehension. If the tenant was fortunate, a lack of competitive bidding would enable him to acquire his tenement at a low price. But especially if he had worked hard making improvements that had enhanced the value of his tract, he could find himself bidding against wealthy outsiders who were willing to pay more than he could possibly offer for land that he and his family had lived on for years. The following discussion examines the response of tenants to the two sales of the manors and explores the amount of dislocation the tenant population experienced as a result of them.

Although Gov. Horatio Sharpe protested the proprietor's order to sell the manors, Lord Baltimore remained adamant. The proprietor's second sale order, addressed to Sharpe in February 1766, left no doubt about Baltimore's intention: he wanted all his manors and reserved lands in the colony sold as expeditiously as possible. The sales were to be conducted by a commission composed of Governor Sharpe, Daniel Dulany, deputy secretary of the province, and John Morton Jordan, a merchant and friend of the proprietor who had personally carried the second sale order from England.[1]

In his first set of instructions, written in January 1765, Baltimore had directed that the manors be sold for not less than fifty pounds sterling per 100 acres, or ten times the amount usually charged as caution money for uncultivated land.[2] The terms of sale were altered in the second sale order, but the proprietor still requested that the commissioners charge at least twenty shillings sterling per acre for cultivated land and six shillings sterling per acre for uncultivated tracts.[3]

Governor Sharpe immediately began gathering information about the manor tenements in order to place a value on each leasehold. Despite the proprietor's wishes, Sharpe concluded that land in the Baltimore Reserves was worth an average of only £0.1.6 sterling per acre, and on the other manors he rated only the best land that was highly improved as high as £0.20.0 sterling per acre.[4] After the necessary information concerning improvements and encumbrances on each leasehold had been compiled, the sales commenced. Anne Arundel Manor was the first tract scheduled for sale. In late May 1766, the commissioners inserted a notice in the *Maryland Gazette* informing the public that the tenements on Anne Arundel Manor would be auctioned off "at a House near the Mannour on the 14th of July."[5]

The sale of Anne Arundel Manor had to be postponed temporarily because of a dispute over Lord Baltimore's title to the land,[6] but between September 1766 and April 1768 the commissioners traveled to all parts of the province to sell the other proprietary manors. Table 5–1 sum-

TABLE 5-1
Proprietary Manors and Escheated Tracts Sold Prior to April 1768

Manor or Escheat Tract	Acres Offered for Sale	Acres Sold	Total Price Paid (sterling)
Anne Arundel	10,680⅞	9,101¼	£10,883.17.1½
White Plains[a]	812	812	620.0.0
Abbington[a]	109	109	168.19.0
Queen Anne's	6,000	936¾	855.8.3
Collington	1,297¼	1,297¼	1,459.0.7½
Gunpowder	7,265¼	1,080¼	1,046.9.6
Conegocheague	11,586	897¾	861.6.6
Chaptico	8,671¾	2,120	2,029.16.0
Calverton	6,020	661	416.17.6
Kent	6,721¾	—	—

SOURCE: Executive Papers, portfolio 3, folder 19, Hall of Records, Annapolis, Maryland; *Archives of Maryland,* ed. William Hand Browne et al., 72 vols. to date (Baltimore, 1883–), 14:335–36, 411, 420, 422, 424, 436, 463–64, 477–78, 485.
[a] Escheated tracts.

TABLE 5-2
Proprietary Manors and Escheated Tracts Sold, 1766–1771

Manor	Total Acres Offered for Sale	Acres Sold		Total Acres Sold	Total Paid (sterling)	Average price per Acre (sterling)
		Prior to April 1768	April 1768 through 1771			
Anne Arundel	10,680⅞	9,101¼	889¾	9,991	£12,045.0.0	£ 1.4.1
White Plains[a]	812	812	—	812	620.0.0	0.15.3
Abbington[a]	109	109	—	109	168.19.0	1.11.0
Queen Anne's	6,000	936¾	743¼	1,680	1,694.0.0	1.0.2
Collington	1,297¼	1,297¼	—	1,297¼	1,459.0.7½	1.2.6
Gunpowder	7,265¼	1,080¼	581¾	1,662	1,789.0.0	1.1.6
Conegocheague	11,586	897¾	—	897¾	861.6.6	0.19.2
Chaptico	8,671¾	2,120	441	2,561	2,414.0.0	0.19.10
Calverton	6,020	661	1,035	1,696	1,037.0.0	0.12.3
Mill	2,607	—	254	254	157.0.0	0.12.4
Nanticoke	5,249	—	673	673	501.10.0	0.14.11
Kent	6,721¾	—	2,725	2,725	3,771.14.0	1.7.8
Snowhill	926	—	208	208	133.0.0	0.12.9
Zachiah	5,407	—	102	102	58.0.0	0.11.14
Pangaiah	1,451	—	360	360	259.0.0	0.14.5
Baltimore Reserves	45,000	—	24,984	24,984	5,262.0.0	0.4.3
	119,304	17,015¼	32,996¾	50,012	32,230.10.1½	

SOURCE: Executive Papers, portfolio 3, folder 19, Hall of Records, Annapolis, Maryland; Claim of Henry Harford, Public Record Office, Audit Office 12/79, f.127, London (microfilm copy available at the Hall of Records, Annapolis, Maryland).
[a]Escheated tracts.

marizes the amount of land sold by the commissioners prior to April 1768. In several cases, more than one visit was made to a manor, but despite their efforts, the commissioners were able to sell only a small portion of the total acreage put up for auction.[7]

In April 1768, John Morton Jordan returned to England. He took a summary of the manor sales with him, as well as a description of unsold manor lots so that Lord Baltimore could sell land to emigrants embarking for the province.[8] After Jordan's departure, the two remaining commissioners discontinued traveling to the manors for auctions. The sales continued, however, although people desiring to purchase manor land had to contact the commissioners at the Revenue Office in Annapolis. Table 5–2 summarizes the sales of manor land through the year 1771. Virtually no evidence of later sales has been found, and the commissioners undoubtedly ceased actively seeking purchasers after word of the proprietor's death in September 1771 reached the colony.[9]

In March 1768, Governor Sharpe wrote to Lord Baltimore that he was "sorry it was not in our power to sell more of the Lands than we have for I am afraid our Remittances will fall vastly short of what your Lordship expected to receive from the Mannours. . . ."[10] The account that Sharpe sent to Baltimore in April 1768 showed that only £6,510.5.6 1/2 sterling had been forwarded to the proprietor on sales amounting to £18,341.14.5 sterling. The manors were sold on three-years' credit, with the first quarter due at the time of purchase and another quarter due each year thereafter.[11] Some purchasers should have made their second payment by April 1768, but many were slow in remitting money to Sharpe.[12] The governor attempted to schedule the auctions in the fall to coincide with the time when planters received cash or bills of exchange for the year's tobacco crop, but despite this precaution many purchasers were unable to make their payments on time.[13]

Not only were purchasers slow in paying for land purchased from the proprietary commissioners, but on the whole the sales were disappointing. By April 1768, the commissioners had sold only 17,015 1/4 acres, and when the sales ended in 1771, just 50,012 acres of a total of 119,807 7/8 acres offered for sale had been purchased. Furthermore, nearly 25,000 acres of the land that had been sold were located in the Baltimore Reserves, extremely poor land that brought an average of only £0.4.3 sterling per acre.[14] The record of the sales, however, was not entirely bleak. The commissioners had entirely disposed of Collington Manor in Prince George's County, as well as the escheat tracts known as White Plains and Abbington in St. Mary's County, and they had been able to sell nearly all the land on Anne Arundel Manor once the legal objections to the auction had been resolved. The same factors of superior location and soil quality that had permitted the proprietor to extract high rents on short-term leases for Anne Arundel tracts had enabled the commissioners to sell tenements on the manor at the very high average price of £0.24.1 sterling per acre.[15] With the exception of these four manors and escheat tracts, however, the majority of the land on the manors remained in the possession of tenants at the conclusion of the proprietary sales.

The eight sample manors were typical of most proprietary tracts in the province in that the commissioners were able to sell only a few tenements and the sales resulted in minimal disruptions to the resident manor populations. No land was sold on Beaverdam and Monocacy manors, and only a single vacant lot was disposed of on Zachiah Manor. On four other manors—Chaptico, Gunpowder, Kent, and Queen Anne's—between about one-fifth and one-third of the leasehold land was sold, although even here the number of new entrants—people who had not previously held land on the manor—and the amount of displacement of resident tenants was small (see table 5-3).[16]

Except on Chaptico, the proprietary commissioners had little success in disposing of land on the lower Western Shore manors. Four men purchased a total of more than 2,500 acres at the Chaptico Manor sale. Three of the four purchased tracts they already held by lease, but the fourth man did buy lots leased to other individuals. All the leaseholders displaced by the sale resided off the manor, however, so it did not result in any resident tenant being forced from his land.

The proprietary sales were most successful on the Eastern Shore

TABLE 5-3

Land Sold on Sample Proprietary Manors and Resultant Tenant Dislocations, 1766–1771

Manor	Acres Sold	Percentage of Total Land Offered for Sale	Number of Purchasers	Number of New Entrants	Tenants Dispossessed
Beaverdam	0.0	—	—	—	—
Chaptico	2,561.0	29.5	4	1	9
Zachiah	102.5	1.1	1	1	0
Kent	2,725.5	35.6	10	3	10
Queen Anne's	1,677.3	28.0	8	1	2
Gunpowder	1,662.0	22.9	4	1	1
Monocacy	0.0	—	—	—	—

SOURCE: Claim of Henry Harford, Public Record Office, Audit Office 12/79, f. 129, London (microfilm copy available at the Hall of Records, Annapolis, Maryland); County Patented Certificates of Survey; Manor Plats; Maryland State Papers (Series F—Confiscated Property), Hall of Records, Annapolis, Maryland.

manors. Eight persons bought a total of 1,677 1/4 acres at the auction of Queen Anne's Manor, or slightly more than one-quarter of the land offered for sale. Only one new entrant resulted from the sales, however, and he was probably related by marriage to a manor tenant. Although most of the purchasers at the Queen Anne's sale confined themselves to land they already held by lease, two tenants did lose possession of their leaseholds because of the sale.

The commissioners sold 2,725 1/2 acres of Kent Manor, or slightly over 35 percent of the land on the manor. A major reason for the success of the sale was that three new entrants purchased land at the auction. All three were wealthy freeholders who owned land adjoining the manor or who were related by marriage or tied by commerce to manor tenants. William Frisby purchased John Gleaves's leasehold, but Gleaves's son William was Frisby's son-in-law, and when Frisby died in 1779 he devised the land back to his son-in-law. Isaac Briscoe owned freehold land adjoining the manor, and he seems to have purchased the seventy-two-acre manor tract in order to expand the size of his freehold farm. The third new entrant, James Black, purchased three leaseholds totaling 253 1/2 acres at the Kent Manor sale. Black was a wealthy miller in New Castle, Delaware, who invested in Maryland wheat land to ensure a supply of grain for his mills. By the time of his death in 1794, Black owned several hundred acres of land in Kent County in addition to his manor land. Although Black did not cultivate any of his Maryland farms himself, he undoubtedly required tenants leasing his land to market their grain through him.[17]

The commissioners sold 1,662 acres of Gunpowder Manor on the upper Western Shore, with four men accounting for the sales. Three of the four—Benkid Willson, Michael Jenkins, and James Gittings—were among the wealthiest tenants on the manor. The three confined their purchases to lots they already held by lease, however, so no tenant was displaced by the sales. The fourth purchaser, Henry Brown, bought a 279-acre tract that was leased to another man, thus terminating the original leaseholder's right to his tenement.

The most striking facts about the proprietary sales of the eight sample manors is that most tenants were unable or unwilling to purchase their tenements and that other people failed to bid on their lots. The proprietary sales were least successful on the lower Western Shore, confirming Governor Sharpe's apprehension that tenants in the region would be "in general very poor & unable to bid" at the proprietary auctions.[18] The largest number of acres sold were on the grain-growing manors, which tends to corroborate the greater profitability of grain cultivation for tenant farmers. Not only did a larger number of wheat-growing tenants have the capital necessary to bid on their lots, but their farms were sufficiently valuable to attract some outside bidders to the proprietary auctions. Nevertheless, the number of tenants on the manors of the Eastern and upper Western shores who could afford to buy their tenements was only a small proportion of the total leaseholders. Furthermore, most purchasers at the proprietary sales were nonresident leaseholders who were much wealthier than tenants who actually lived on the manors. Thus, even on the grain-growing manors, tenants who resided on their leaselots and derived their major source of income from crops grown on their tenements were rarely able to purchase land at the proprietary sales.[19]

Although tenants who raised wheat were better able to purchase their tenements than those who cultivated tobacco, the proprietor failed through the sales to divest himself of his manor land in Maryland. Several factors prevented the commissioners from disposing of all the lots on the proprietor's manors. First, the price the proprietor expected was more than most tenants could afford; but since the proprietor was anticipating large receipts, his commissioners refused to auction a tenement unless there was a good chance for active bidding.[20] Second, most tenements were encumbered by lives or years remaining on the lease. When a tenant held a valid lease, he had the right to remain on his tenement until it expired, so all the commissioners could sell was the reversion to the lease. The proprietor expected that most tenants would purchase their own lots, in which case lease encumbrances would not have affected sales. Even when a tenant refused to buy his leasehold, the proprietor believed that others would be willing to buy the tract despite an encumbrance, because the purchaser could collect rent from the tenant in addition to owning the tract as a freehold at the expiration of the lease.[21] The sales proved that the proprietor's expectations were unfounded, however, and very few leaseholds that were encumbered were purchased by either tenants or outsiders.

A third reason for the failure of the proprietary sales was the "Scarcety of Money in the Province" that limited the number of individuals who could command the ready cash demanded by the proprietor for the initial payment on manor lots.[22] Sharpe occasionally allowed purchasers an extra month for the first payment, but even this concession was insufficient to induce many people to become purchasers.[23] Finally, the minority of proprietary tenants who were well-to-do generally refused to bid on their neighbors' tenements, because, as Sharpe noted, they thought "it would be ungenerous to purchase over their heads."[24] Thus, although those few tenants who were wealthy frequently took the opportunity to buy their leaseholds at the proprietary sales, the poorer tenants generally retained possession of their tenements under the terms of their old leases with the customary right to renew them when they expired.

Proprietary sales were discontinued in 1771, but a new threat to the stability of the tenant populations on the manors soon arose. With the outbreak of war with England, the problem of financing the military campaigns and the desire of many Marylanders to penalize Loyalists induced the General Assembly to approve a series of confiscation acts. The largest block of property seized by the state belonged to the proprietor, and a major component of the sequestered proprietary assets consisted of unsold manor lands. With state confiscation, the tenants on the manors were again confronted with the possibility of losing their leaseholds if they were unable or unwilling to purchase the right of reversion to their land.

The state did not immediately embrace a policy of confiscation. Confiscation was universally recognized, although not necessarily condemned, as a drastic measure, and some leading men in the province objected to the policy and fought every attempt to pass such legislation. Charles Carroll of Carrollton, for example, was a strident opponent of confiscation, objecting to the "danger of the precedent" of seizing property owned by any widely defined group and contending that only the property of known enemies of proven guilt should be seized. Carroll's position was supported by influential and wealthy men in the province who feared that similar legislation might be directed at their own property if the lower classes were ever able to divest the upper class of its privileged position in the state's government.[25]

As early as November 1777, the Continental Congress had recommended that the states confiscate and sell property belonging to Loyalists, but the Maryland Assembly did not pass a confiscation bill until December 1779. The unanimously approved House bill passed at that time was rejected by the Senate, however, thus postponing the issue until the following year. The crucial factor in eroding senatorial opposition to confiscation was the refusal of the Bank of England to redeem stock valued at £29,000 held by the state. The action of the Bank of England placed Maryland in an untenable economic position, alienating a sufficient number of senators to allow a confiscation bill to pass both houses of the General Assembly in 1780. Additional legislation amplifying and extending the conditions for confiscating property belonging to British subjects and American Loyalists was passed during legislative sessions in 1781 and 1782.[26]

Although some members of the Maryland Assembly doubtless supported confiscation from a vindictive desire to penalize persons whom they deemed to be traitors, the most compelling consideration was the financial distress of the province.[27] Parcels of confiscated property were designated to finance specific activities essential for the prosecution of the war, including completing a warship under construction by Stephen Steward at West River, raising money to pay soldiers, paying state debts, backing bills of credit issued by the state, and raising bounty money for enticing Maryland men to enlist in the Continental Line. Confiscation appeased those who desired to punish Loyalists, but even more important, it enabled the state to finance a host of war projects that could never have been contemplated without the security represented by the sequestered estates.[28]

Loyalist property confiscated by the State of Maryland can be divided into two broad categories: private estates and proprietary property. Private estates of all sizes were confiscated. Over one-fifth of the private estates were worth less than £100 Maryland currency, and more than half sold for under £500 (see table 5–4). Being poor clearly did not exempt a Tory from having his property seized by the state.[29]

The most lucrative private properties confiscated, however, were the estates of a few wealthy individuals and businesses. The property of Daniel Dulany of Daniel netted the state over £80,000.0.0, and the estate of Daniel Dulany of Walter sold for over £38,000.0.0 The Principio Iron Works brought in over £71,000.0.0 and the Nottingham Company Iron Works netted over £83,000.0.0. The most valuable mercantile firm confiscated was the property of Robert and James Christie, which sold for

TABLE 5-4
Net Return from Sale of Private Confiscated Estates

Amount Realized From Sale	Number of Estates Confiscated	Percentage of Estates Confiscated	Cumulative Percentage of Estates Confiscated
£1–99	22	22	22
100–499	31	31	53
500–999	13	13	66
1,000–1,999	10	10	76
2,000–2,999	5	5	81
3,000–3,999	5	5	86
4,000–4,999	1	1	87
5,000–9,999	7	7	94
10,000–49,000	3	3	97
50,000–100,000	3	3	100

SOURCE: Confiscated Property—Accounts, n.d., Scharf Collection, Maryland Historical Society, Baltimore, Maryland.

nearly £6,000.0.0, and the Jameson and Company property netted nearly £1,800.0.0. Among the smaller individual estates seized was that of Jonathan Boucher, noted tutor and Anglican minister, whose property sold for £6,233.13.3. The state confiscated a total of 100 private estates during the war, with sales of the property grossing more than £409,000.0.0.[30]

The second large category of land seized by the state was property belonging to the proprietor, Henry Harford, heir of Frederick, the last Lord Baltimore. In his claim for compensation after the war, Harford enumerated the assets he had lost because of state confiscation: (1) quit-rents on all freehold land; (2) manor rents; (3) the real value of manor and reserved lands; (4) the duty of twelve pence per hogshead on all tobacco exported and fourteen pence per ton on all shipping; (5) the value of alienation fines; (6) miscellaneous fines and forfeitures; (7) the value of 125,300 acres of unpatented land on the frontier west of Fort Cumberland; and (8) the value of the Revenue Office building in Annapolis. Furthermore, Harford had lost his "Royalties, Right of Patronage and Presentation, and all vacant Lands within his Domain," but because of the difficulty of ascertaining a monetary value for these assets, he waived his claim for loss of revenue on them. Harford estimated the value of his confiscated property at £477,000 sterling.[31]

The State of Maryland netted only £193,406.7.4 1/2 from the sale of Henry Harford's property, but the sum was nearly one-third the total receipts from the sale of all confiscated property.[32] A larger amount of property, both in terms of acres and of value, was confiscated from the proprietor than from any other individual. According to Harford's accounts, the state seized 244,904 5/8 acres of his land, approximately one-half of which was manor land (see table 5–5). Because so many acres of the proprietor's land were tenanted, the impact of the confiscation of Harford's property was quite different from the seizure of private estates in the province. The 100 private individuals and business firms whose property was sequestered suffered a varying amount of financial loss, and the families of some experienced real hardship. The proprietor's British citizenship provided the rationale for confiscating his estate in Maryland, but the citizens of the province who resided on his manors, not just Henry Harford, were directly affected by the state's action. By sequestering the proprietor's property in Maryland, the state in reality seized the farms and plantations of scores of his tenants without regard to their loyalty.

Although manor tenants were not immediately deprived of their land as long as they held valid leases, the state made no provision for renewing them. Thus, confiscation eliminated the security tenants had enjoyed under the proprietor and even if no one purchased their tenements at

TABLE 5-5
Manors and Reserves Confiscated from Henry Harford, 1781

Manor or Reserve	Total Acres	Acres Sold By Proprietor Prior to Confiscation	Acres Confiscated
Anne Arundel	10,680⅝	10,379⅝	301
Gunpowder	7,265¼	1,662	5,603¼
Kent	7,647½	2,725½	4,922
Queen Anne's	6,000	1,677¼	4,322¾
Nanticoke	5,449¼	673½	4,775¾
Calverton	5,209	1,616½	3,592½
Woolsey	3,131⅜	—	3,131⅜
Chaptico	8,671¾	2,561	6,110¾
Pangaiah	1,451	350	1,101
Mill	1,921¾	254¾	1,667
Snow Hill, St. Barbara's, and St. John's	982½	208	774½
West St. Mary's	1,370¼	—	1,370¼
Zachiah	5,407	102½	5,304½
Beaverdam	7,680	—	7,680
Monocacy and Monocacy Reserve	13,148	—	13,148
Elk River	6,000	—	6,000
North East	12,000	—	12,000
My Lady's	10,000	—	10,000
Susquehannah (New Connaught)	32,000	—	32,000
Land west of Fort Cumberland	121,000	—	121,000
	267,115¼	22,210⅝	244,904⅝

SOURCE: Claim of Henry Harford, Public Record Office, Audit Office 12/79, ff. 127, 155, London (microfilm copy available at the Hall of Records, Annapolis, Maryland).

the state sales, the tenants' tenure was certain to terminate as soon as their leases expired. The probability that tenants could remain on their leaseholds was further jeopardized by the promise that the state auctions would be more successful than the proprietary sales. The terms for purchasing land from the state varied from one manor to another, but they were universally more generous than those offered by the proprietor.[33] In addition, the atmosphere in which the state sales were conducted ensured a large number of bidders. The reluctance of outside investors and wealthy tenants to purchase land held by poor tenants was offset by the easy terms of purchase and by the fact that buyers would be viewed as performing a patriotic service in helping to finance the war. In short, by confiscating the proprietor's property in Maryland, the state government acquired a large amount of land crucial for supporting wartime spending. But confiscation also posed an unprecedented risk for tenants who desired to retain possession of their homes and improvements, especially since for many the value of these improvements constituted the bulk of their assets.

The administrative apparatus established by the state legislature to locate, manage, and sell property subject to confiscation was relatively simple. In conjunction with the first confiscation act, a bill was passed appointing three commissioners to supervise the identification, preservation, and sale of property owned by Loyalists and British subjects. William Paca, Uriah Forrest, and Clement Hollyday were named to the commission and were invested with the authority to take possession of all confiscated property and to "preserve and keep the same from waste and destruction."[34]

The commissioners held their first meeting on Friday, February 23, 1781, at the State House in Annapolis. William Paca did not attend, but Hollyday and Forrest proceeded to select Gabriel Duvall as their clerk and began drafting letters to the county sheriffs and tax assessors enlisting their aid in identifying property subject to forfeiture.[35] Speed was important, especially where personal property was involved, in order to prevent looting and the destruction of livestock, household goods, and crops. The commissioners frequently appointed a manager or agreed to lease out confiscated property until it could be sold. A large amount of property was undoubtedly lost or destroyed, but the commissioners attempted to inventory all estates to guarantee that as much as possible was preserved for the benefit of the state.[36]

The property that was most valuable, least perishable, and yet frequently most difficult to prepare for sale was land. Many privately owned tracts could be sold immediately, because the boundaries had been established by recent patents or surveys. Because of the confusion and misadministration of the proprietary manors, however, each tenement should have been completely resurveyed before the state sold the land, but pressing financial needs forced the General Assembly to pass appropriation bills that required the immediate sale of the proprietor's property. Therefore, most of the manors were auctioned off before they were resurveyed, with the commissioners basing their description of tenements on the best information available.[37]

Before any proprietary manor lots could be sold, however, the commissioners had to determine what encumbrances of lives or years remained on the tenants' leases. As with the proprietary sales, the state could only sell the reversion on leases. But by 1781 when the state sales began, far fewer lots were encumbered than in the 1760s when the

TABLE 5-6

Encumbrances on Lots Sold at State Sales of Selected Proprietary Manors, 1781–1782

Manor	21-Year Leases			3-Life Leases					Expired Leases	Status Unknown	Total Lots
	Number	Average Years Unexpired	Unspecified	Number	Lives Remaining						
					1	2	3	Unspecified			
Beaverdam	12	1.7		50	22	20	8		21		83
Zachiah	7	3.0		33	11	18	4		11		51
Calverton	3	4.0		20	11	7	2		6		29
Monocacy			24	37				37	?	61	61
Kent	6	2.8		18	10	7	1		3		27
Queen Anne's	4	4.8		11	8	1	2		15		30
	32		24	169	62	53	17	37	56	61	281

SOURCE: Manor lists in Maryland State Papers (Series F—Confiscated Property), Hall of Records, Annapolis, Maryland.

proprietor had attempted to sell the manors. The proprietor's refusal to grant three-life leases after the late 1750s meant that all subsequent leases were for twenty-one years, and by the early 1780s many of these had nearly expired. Furthermore, when the proprietor decided to sell his manors he prohibited Governor Sharpe from issuing any new manor leases. Although the proprietor's order was rescinded in the early 1770s, most leases that had lapsed in the interim were never renewed. Finally, after the outbreak of hostilities in 1775, the state refused to issue new leases or to renew those that expired.[38]

Table 5–6 summarizes the data on encumbrances remaining on leaseholds confiscated by the state. Information is not available for Chaptico and Gunpowder manors, but on the six other sample manors most twenty-one-year leases were near their expiration and only a single life remained on almost one-half the three-life leases. Some leases on every manor had lapsed, ranging from a low of one-ninth of the total number on Kent Manor to a high of one-half on Queen Anne's Manor. Thus, although tenants had the right to remain on their tenements as long as they held a valid lease, the majority could not anticipate long tenures on their leaseholds unless they were successful in acquiring possession of their tracts at the state sale.[39]

Between September 13, 1781, and November 26, 1782, the state commissioners disposed of £126,121.0.6 worth of proprietary manor land. Tenements were auctioned off at a public place on or near the manor being sold. At least one commissioner was present at each auction, although the actual sale was conducted by an auctioneer hired for that purpose.[40] The sales were generally well attended and bidding was frequently very competitive, especially for highly improved tracts.[41]

The terms for purchasing manor tenements at the state sales varied. The majority of the manors, including all those in St. Mary's, Kent, Charles, Queen Anne's, Dorchester, Somerset, and Worcester counties, were sold for specie (usually paid in an equivalent amount of one of several types of paper currency) or red money on three-years' credit. The 121,100 acres of manor land west of Fort Cumberland were set aside for the redemption of land certificates issued to soldiers. On three manors—Susquehannah, My Lady's, and Monocacy—purchasers were given the option of paying for land with soldier's pay certificates accepted at face value.[42]

A major factor accounting for the success of the state sales was that both paper money and army certificates were subject to depreciation. Merchants, army officers, and other persons in strategic positions in the economic structure who had acquired paper money and certificates for a fraction of their face value were anxious to convert them into real estate.[43] Furthermore, the state sales were widely advertised, and they attracted bidders from all parts of the state as well as from adjoining provinces.[44] The motives of state officials were clear and defensible— they wanted to encourage as much bidding as possible—but intense bidding was a distinct disadvantage for tenants who wished to purchase their leaseholds at a moderate price.

Most proprietary manor tenements had been sold by the end of 1783. The commissioners were unable to sell a few tracts, and other tenements reverted to the state because of forfeitures, so some sales were made as late as the early nineteenth century.[45] But the bulk of the business in the years after 1783 was devoted to formalizing the sales made at the state auctions by collecting the sums due from purchasers and by issuing patents on the tracts that had been sold. Since most manor tenements were sold prior to being resurveyed, finalizing the state sales was not always a simple matter. When the tracts were actually surveyed, some were found to lie in rivers, others were consumed by adjacent freeholds, and purchasers occasionally alleged that the commissioners had defrauded them by inaccurately describing the tenements that had been put up for sale.

An example of the kind of confusion that could result from the state selling manor tracts prior to resurvey can be seen in Richard Carnes's purchase of lots 34 and 42 at the Chaptico Manor sale. Carnes paid the high price of £2.2.6 per acre for lot 34 on the basis of the commissioners' assertion that it included two tenements that leased for 2,000 pounds of tobacco each per year. Carnes bid an exceptionally high £6.12.0 per acre for lot 42, because the lot was said to contain an operating water mill. But after Carnes and his security, John Cartwright, had posted bond for the purchases, William Compton, the owner of a patented tract adjacent to Carnes's lots, had the second line of his freehold resurveyed. In a deposition, Luke Huntington described the effect of the resurvey on lot 34. Compton's new line, Huntington stated, runs ". . . along and took these three houses and chief of the Tobacco Ground . . . and Chief of the fence rails so that the land laid off to Carnes and Cartwright was without any rails to fence it and that reduced this part of the land to little or no value as there is neither houses or fence rails on this part. . . ." Compton's resurvey also intersected the millseat lot. Philip Key deposed that "he was present at the sale of the land [lot 42] . . . and that at the time of the sale it was considered that the land was very valuable as there was a mill seat thereon and that he . . . bid for the said land upwards of six pounds per acre; believing there was a mill seat thereon was one of the inducements with him for going so high a price. He [was] also well convinced that no mill can now be erected on the run passing through the land . . .

without the permission of those who hold land adjoining. . . ." Carnes and Cartwright were granted their request to void the sale, but not until they had prosecuted an expensive and time-consuming chancery case.[46]

Even more vexing for the state than solving the problems that arose when tenements were resurveyed was collecting the money due for tracts that had been sold. The state was forced to levy high taxes on its citizens to prosecute the war and to pay the accumulated debts after hostilities ended. Money, never in ample supply in the province, was particularly scarce at the conclusion of the war, and much of the cash that was available was spent on imported goods once trade with England resumed. The adverse economic conditions affected all Marylanders, rich as well as poor. Samuel Chew expressed the concerns of wealthy landowners in a letter to Daniel of St. Thomas Jenifer, dated September 5, 1782: "I am heartily tired of the Times, & have Paid Enough for them, but I am affraid the worst is not come Tho' bad Enough at present for I [am] sure this Tax cant be collected for never was money so scarce now with us & Country Produce will not raise it. Every Gentleman who has a large Country Estate of Lands & Negroes must Sink, for they will not pay the assessment."[47] Writing two years later to former Gov. Horatio Sharpe, John Ridout commented on the economic distress in the months following the peace: "You will easily conceive how much distress't the People are in general & how unable to pay the heavy Taxes imposed on them in consequence of the late unhappy ruinous War. Money was never more scarce, much having been exported last Year by the foreign Adventurers who poured in Quantities of Goods from Europe on the Cessation of Hostilities & got for them most of the Specie that was then in Circulation."[48]

Because of the economic hardships described by Chew and Ridout, many purchasers of manor tracts were unable to make the required payments. Even men who were well-to-do were faced with the prospect of losing the manor lots they had purchased unless they were granted an extension by the state. Nine purchasers of Kent Manor lots, all wealthy freeholders, explained in a letter written to the intendant, Daniel of St. Thomas Jenifer, in August 1782: "We find ourselves under such Difficulties in regard to the first payment that we fear it will be utterly out of our power strictly to comply with the Terms, as we are so circumstanc'd that it is absolutely necessary for us to look forward to a future Crop. . . ." The petitioners' plea for "a little further time for the first payment" was rejected by the intendant, although he promised to take their case to the commissioners of confiscated property and to the General Assembly.[49]

Because the nine Kent Manor petitioners were freeholders, they would not have been divested of all their land if they had been forced to forfeit their manor tracts to the state. But other purchasers at the state sales were resident tenants who owned no other land; if unable to pay for their lots, they faced the prospect of losing their homes.

Even some of the poorest manor tenants successfully bid on their lots at the state sales, desperately hoping that they, in some way, could raise the money needed to pay for their land or that the state would not force them to forfeit their tenements. John Murphy, for example, had been a tenant on Susquehannah Manor for forty-six years when the state put his tenement up for auction. Murphy's leasehold was large, encompassing two tracts and 220 acres, but he assured the intendant that "it is a truth that may be made manifest that more than one third within the aforesaid bounds, is not worth 2 coppers an acre, the Scrub of timber that grows upon it excepted." Murphy's "little family" consisted of a "tender sickly wife, a Daughter of 13 years old, & my self that was born on the 11th of June in the year 1708." He asked that Jenifer "take it under consideration, that when I am unable to Raise my bread off the place, hard pinched to get money once a year to pay my taxes, it surely would be vanity with a wittness, for me to pretend to Raise money to pay for Land." Nevertheless, Murphy had offered the highest bid for his tenement at the state sale of the manor, and he was now faced with the problem of how to retain possession of at least a portion of it. In his petition to the indendant, Murphy offered a suggestion: ". . . all the way that I can think of, & that[']s in my power, to satisfie you Sir, is this, if you would be pleased to have the quantity of the Land Examined, Lay a moderate price upon it, Enable me to Share, what[']s Right would be for it when the money was paid, then, I will Endeavor to sell the Greatest part of it, with my Improvements, to Satisfie you Sir, & build me a Little house on Sum [sic] part [of] it to Spend the Residue of my Daies In."[50] Paying for manor land was difficult for many who purchased tracts at the state sales, but for tenants like Murphy, who were old, had few assets, and no place to turn, the prospect of being forced from their lifelong homes must have been agonizing.

Initially, the attitude of state officials was intransigent toward delinquent debtors, and some forfeitures of manor tracts occurred because purchasers were unable to make their payments.[51] With the cessation of hostilities, however, the state could afford to be more lenient and tenants who had paid at least part of the purchase price for their lots were generally indulged with additional time. In fact, final payment on some lots was not made until the second decade of the nineteenth century. The total number of forfeitures for nonpayment was small, but this does not necessarily imply that the persons who were successful in bidding for land were able to pay for it. Far more frequently than forfeiting, a purchaser simply assigned his right to the land to another person. An assignment required nothing more than a statement by the purchaser regarding his decision to transfer the tract, and in most cases no monetary sum was mentioned. Since a large number of assignments were executed within a few months of the state sales, most assignors probably received nothing but relief from the obligation of paying for the land. At any time prior to patenting, a tract purchased at one of the manor sales could change ownership by assignment. Some tenements were never transferred by the original purchaser, but others went through numerous assignments before finally being patented.[52]

Because of the ease with which manor tracts could change hands after they were sold at the state auctions, the ownership of each tenement must be traced until it reached a state of quiet possession, defined as that point in time when the purchase price of a tract had been paid and the land was in the possession of a person who intended to keep it for his own use rather than for speculative resale. Most tenements purchased at the state sales achieved a state of quiet possession when they were patented or shortly thereafter. Some manor tracts were never patented, with the purchasers apparently being satisfied that their right to the land was secured by completion of payment. In the discussion that follows, in those instances where no patent was issued, possession of tracts was traced to the year 1800, or in cases where the land was held by a speculator, as far into the nineteenth century as was necessary to establish when quiet possession was attained.

An examination of purchasers, intermediate possessors, and patentees of tracts on the eight sample manors demonstrates that the effects of confiscation varied widely from one manor to another, depending on the quality of the land and improvements and on the terms the state established for purchasing manor tenements. As table 5–7 shows, the size of the average tract sold at the state auctions was not particularly large, ranging from a low of 165.3 acres on Gunpowder Manor to a high of 430 7/10 acres on Queen Anne's Manor. On every manor, however, at least one sale of over 400 acres was recorded, led by a 2,374 5/8-acre purchase on Queen Anne's Manor.[53] The importance of following tracts to the point of quiet possession is evident from table 5–8, because the average holding per patentee was higher than the average holding per purchaser on all but two manors.[54] One general statement regarding the effect of confiscation on the manor populations can be made on the basis

TABLE 5-7

State Sales of Selected Proprietary Manors

Manor	Acres Sold	Number of Purchasers	Average Acres Purchased	Median Acres Purchased	Range	Family Names Represented	Average Acres Purchased Per Family
Beaverdam	7,192¾	41	175.4	130½	30¾–540	26	276.6
Chaptico	4,875⅛	24	203.1	148	36¾–744	20	243.8
Zachiah	4,486½	25	179.5	156	60–510	21	213.6
Calverton	3,431	17	201.8	206	33–417	14	245.1
Kent	2,846	16	177.9	168	16¾–453	14	203.3
Queen Anne's	4,807⅛	10	430.7	216	98–2,374⅝	9	478.8
Gunpowder	5,621½	34	165.3	145½	68–402	30	187.4
Monocacy	8,365	34	246.0	177	52½–791½	34	246.0

SOURCE: Sale Book, 1781–1785, Hall of Records, Annapolis, Maryland.

TABLE 5-8
Patentees or Persons in Quiet Possession to ca. 1800

Manor	Total Acres on Manor	Patentees	Families Represented	Average Acres Held per Patentee	Range	Average Acres Per Family
Beaverdam	7,337¾	39	26	188.0	30¾–1,104½	282.2
Chaptico	4,875⅛	20	16	243.8	36¾–665½	304.7
Zachiah	4,382	21	19	208.7	43–771½	230.6
Calverton	3,431	16	13	214.4	33–532	263.9
Kent	2,846	14	13	203.3	16¾–453	218.2
Queen Anne's	4,307⅛	12	10	358.9	98–1,218½	430.7
Gunpowder	5,621½	28	27	200.8	83–972	208.2
Monocacy	8,365	34	32	246.0	14–1,674	261.4

Source: Return Book for Reserved Lands; Patented and Unpatented Certificates of Survey, all at the Hall of Records, Annapolis, Maryland.

TABLE 5-9

Average Acreage Held by Leaseholders, Tenants in Possession in 1767–1768, Purchasers, and Patentees
on Sample Proprietary Manors

Manor	Average Acreage per Leaseholder	Average Acreage per Tenant, 1767–1768	Average Acreage per Purchaser	Average Acreage per Patentee
Beaverdam	143.6	157.3	175.4	188.2
Chaptico	146.2	182.9	203.1	243.8
Zachiah	115.6	135.5	179.5	208.7
Calverton	154.3	232.7	201.8	214.4
Kent	144.3	153.3	177.8	203.3
Queen Anne's	—	112.7	430.7	358.9
Gunpowder	155.6	194.5	165.3	200.0
Monocacy	125.7	134.8	246.0	246.0

SOURCE: Gaius Marcus Brumbaugh, *Maryland Records, Colonial, Revolutionary, County and Church*, 2 vols. (1915–28; reprinted, Baltimore, 1967), 2:4–73; Claim of Henry Harford, Public Record Office, A. O. 12/79, f. 129, London (microfilm copy available at Hall of Records, Annapolis, Maryland). Sale Book, 1781–1785; Return Book for Reserved Lands; Patented and Unpatented Certificates of Survey; documents at the Hall of Records, Annapolis, Maryland.

of data presented in table 5–9: the tendency toward larger size holdings observed between leaseholders and the tenants in possession in 1767 and 1768 was augmented by the state sales, with patentees on every manor owning more acreage than the average tenant had held. Although some concentration of landholdings occurred on every manor, each manor must be examined individually to fully appreciate the impact confiscation had on the resident tenant populations.

The first of the four sample manors on the lower Western Shore to be sold was Beaverdam Manor, with the auction being held at Leonardtown on September 13, 14, and 15, 1781.[55] Nearly everyone who leased land on the manor attended the auction, and the poorer tenants must have been relieved to see few strangers in the crowd. Several wealthy men were in attendance, particularly George Plater of "Sotterly" and Enoch Fenwick of "Squabbles Ridge," but most were nonresident leaseholders who probably had little interest in other tenants' land. Although the resident tenants had reason to hope that they would not be outbid when their lots were put up for auction, the first four tracts sold went to persons other than the tenants in possession. As the sale continued, however, most tenants were able to purchase at least some land on the manor, and by the time the auction had ended only three tenants had actually lost their right to land on the manor (*see* table 5–10). Five new entrants purchased land on Beaverdam Manor at the state sale. Two were wealthy men who owned both slaves and freeholds, and two others held their land only a short time before selling it, suggesting that they probably purchased the land as a speculative venture. Everyone else who bought land appears to have intended to keep it, however, so speculators must have found little to attract them to the sale.

Two of the new entrants and three persons who had previously been tenants on Beaverdam Manor were unable to pay for the land they bought at the state auction and lost possession of their tracts. Three of the five forfeited lots were purchased by additional new entrants, with the others being sold to persons who already held land on the manor. In short, most Beaverdam Manor tenants were able to buy their tenements at the state auction and to retain possession of them until they were patented. Just five lots changed ownership because of the sales, and the number of forfeitures was so small that only three new entrants purchased onto the manor after the initial sale.

One important factor accounting for the minimal dislocation of the tenant population on Beaverdam Manor was that most tenants resided on the manor and were related to other tenants. The forty-one purchasers at the state auction represented only twenty-six family names, a far larger concentration of family groups than was recorded at the sale

TABLE 5-10

Population Stability on Sample Proprietary Manors Sold as Confiscated British Property

Manor	Total Tenants, 1767–1768	Purchasers			Patentees			
		Tenants	New Entrants	Total	Purchasers	Former Tenants but not Purchasers	New Entrants	Total
Beaverdam	45	37	4	41	36	—	3	39
Chaptico	39	21	3	24	17	1	2	20
Zachiah	29	15	11	26	17	—	4	21
Calverton	18	14	3	17	15	—	1	16
Kent	46	13	3	16	11	—	3	14
Queen Anne's	39	4	6	10	9	1	2	12
Gunpowder	36	26	8	34	24	—	4	28
Monocacy	55	1	30	31	15	6	13	34
	307	131	68	199	144	8	32	184

SOURCE: Sale Book, 1781–1785; Return Book For Reserved Lands; Patented and Unpatented Certificates of Survey, all at the Hall of Records, Annapolis, Maryland.

of any other proprietary manor. Beaverdam leaseholders had a vested interest in retaining possession of their land because of family ties and the length of time many had lived on their manor tracts. A serious disruption of the manor population might nevertheless have occurred had speculators and outside investors been interested in the land. Most tenements had poor soil and unimpressive improvements, however, so Beaverdam tenants faced little competition from outside bidders. The majority of lots sold for less than £0.15.0 per acre, with one bringing only £0.4.7 per acre. Thus, even though the average Beaverdam tenant was quite poor, most people who lived on the manor were able to acquire their lots at a moderate price and, perhaps with the assistance of friends or neighbors, successfully complete paying for the land to become freehold owners of their tracts.

The sale of Chaptico Manor was held at the village of Chaptico on September 18 and 19, 1781. As with the sale of Beaverdam Manor, the tenants assembled for the auction must have been relieved to see few strangers in the crowd. A few wealthy men were in attendance, however, including Philip Key, who was a nonresident leaseholder on the manor, and Richard Carnes, who had come specifically to bid on two highly improved lots.

By the time the auction of Chaptico Manor had ended, eight tenants, five of whom were long-term residents on the manor, had lost possession of their tracts. Just three new entrants bought land at the sale, however, with nonresident freeholders accounting for most of the purchases in which tenants lost possession of their land. At least two of these wealthy nonresident tenants bought Chaptico lots as a speculative investment. Philip Key leased 316 3/4 acres, but he purchased 744 acres at the state auction. Key did not retain possession of all the land, however, later selling all but 275 acres that he had purchased at the auction. Hanson Briscoe bought 419 3/4 acres at the state sale, disposing of it all by assignment before the land was patented.

Subsequent to the sale of Chaptico Manor, seven purchasers lost possession of their tracts. One tenant, Samuel Higgs, leased 132 1/4 acres, but he was only able to purchase 60 acres at the state auction. Higgs bid a very high price of thirty-one shillings per acre for the land and soon discovered that he could not make the payments on the tract. Higgs ultimately fled from the state with the two men who had signed as securities for his purchase bond.[56] Another of the forfeited tenements was purchased by Edward Gardiner, the son of a tenant who had been unable to buy his land at the state sale. Two other forfeited lots were purchased by additional new entrants, while the remaining tracts were acquired by persons who already owned land on the manor.

Although Chaptico Manor had better natural resources than other proprietary manors in St. Mary's County, most tenants were still able to purchase their tenements without facing severe competition from outside bidders. A number of tenants lost possession of their land because of the state sales, but nonresident leaseholders who already had an interest in the manor, rather than speculators and outside investors, were the ones who most frequently bid against them.

Although the natural resources and improvements on most Chaptico lots were insufficient to attract much attention, one lot did generate a considerable amount of excitement. As was previously noted, lot 42 was considered very valuable because it was supposed to encompass a water mill. Philip Key was outbid for the lot by an outside investor, Richard Carnes. According to Carnes, the millseat was the "only object of the purchase."[57] Carnes's purchase of lot 42 illustrates one factor that could result in active bidding competition at the state sales. If the tenement included a valuable improvement, or if it had potential for the development of such an improvement (in this case, some bidders believed there was only a mill race on the lot), then outside investors like Carnes, as well as wealthy nonresident tenants such as Key, would bid very high prices for the land regardless of who held the lease. The fact that most manor land in St. Mary's County sold for low prices was a reflection of the poor natural resources on the tenements, the lack of potential for developing valuable improvements on them, and the consequent apathy of investors and speculators.

The natural resources and improvements on Zachiah Manor in Charles County were poorer than on any other manor on the lower Western Shore, so the tenants who resided there might have expected little bidding competition from speculators. The majority of the tenants on the manor were very poor, however, and judging from the small size of houses on their tenements and the lack of other improvements, most had fewer assets than residents on other manors in the region. As a result, when the manor leaseholders gathered at Sirlatt's Tavern near Bryan Town on October 11, 1781, they must have felt little satisfaction in seeing few wealthy outsiders in the crowd, because regardless of how cheaply the land sold most tenants must have known that paying for their leaseholds would be difficult or impossible.

Nearly all the Zachiah Manor tracts auctioned off at the state sale brought low prices, but despite this, only fifteen of the twenty-nine tenants on the manor were able to purchase land. Five of the fifteen bought more acreage than they held by lease, with the most impressive gain being made by Hezekial Reeves, who was a tenant on only 171 acres but purchased 510 acres. Furthermore, unlike purchasers of land on St. Mary's County manors, new entrants comprised an important segment of the people who bought land at the Zachiah Manor sale, accounting for eleven of the twenty-six purchasers. Henry Hardy, a resident of Prince George's County, made the largest purchase of any new entrant, buying five tracts containing a total of 473 acres.

By the time all the land on Zachiah Manor had reached a state of quiet possession, eleven of the twenty-one families that had leased land on the manor had lost possession of their tenements, and two other families that were able to pay for and patent their land sold it before 1800. The Robey family exemplifies the effect confiscation could have even on tenants who had long been established on the manor. Over the years, six members of the Robey family had leased lots on Zachiah Manor, with the family holding seven tracts totaling 692 1/4 acres by 1767. Although the Robeys had been able to pay their rents to the proprietor, they could not afford the relatively low price they bid at the state auction to retain possession of their land. One by one various members of the family were forced to relinquish their tracts. By 1797, only one Robey owned land on the manor, and his lot encompassed just 151 acres.[58]

Speculators and outside investors showed more interest in Zachiah Manor than they did in any of the manor auctions in St. Mary's County. Even though the natural resources and improvements on Zachiah tenements were poor, the fact that most tracts sold very cheaply, some for as little as £0.9.4 per acre, made the manor an attractive investment.[59] The most prominent new entrants were Alexander Hamilton and Randolph B. Latimer. Hamilton, the Piscataway factor for the Scottish firm of James Brown and Company, probably acquired his 243 acres on the manor in settlement for a debt, because the tract was assigned to him by the person who bought it at the state sale. Latimer, a wealthy Annapolis resident, engaged in extensive speculation in confiscated property, acquiring in addition to the tracts on Zachiah Manor, 1,742 acres of land west of Fort Cumberland.[60]

The other Charles County manor, Calverton, was auctioned off at Benedict Town on October 13, 1781. Few speculators attended the sale, and only three new entrants bought land at the auction. Two men, Robert Young who purchased 417 acres and Edward Anderson who bought 254 acres, disposed of their land by assignment within a year of the sale, but whether they made speculative profits cannot be determined. Only one additional new entrant purchased Calverton land between the state sale and the time when tracts on the manor had reached a state of quiet possession. As a result, the state sale of Calverton Manor caused only minimal dislocations to the resident tenant population. Just three leaseholders lost possession of their tenements, and two of them were women who may not have been dependent upon their manor land for support.[61]

The commissioners in charge of confiscated property traveled to the Eastern Shore in early 1782 to auction off land on the two sample proprietary manors in that section of the state, Kent and Queen Anne's. Kent Manor differed from the other sample manors in that the majority of the leaseholders were wealthy landowners who did not reside on the manor. Because of the number of affluent men already associated with the manor, few outside bidders purchased land at the state sale when it was held on February 18, 1782. Three new entrants bought land at the state auction, and three others later acquired tracts by assignment from the original purchasers, but none of the six appear to have been motivated by speculative interests. Three of the new entrants were well-to-do Kent County freeholders, while the others were small farmers who cultivated the land they purchased.

Despite the dearth of outside investors, fourteen tenants were dispossessed because of the sale of Kent Manor, with their tenements being purchased by wealthy men who already held land on the manor. The most notable purchaser at the state sale was James Black, the Delaware grain merchant who had first bought land on the manor at the proprietary sale in the 1760s. Black bought two additional Kent Manor tracts, containing a total of 221 acres, at the state auction, and in 1786 he acquired by assignment from John Wallace, Jr., another 158-acre lot in exchange for paying the remaining two-thirds of the purchase price and the accumulated interest on the debt. Except for Wallace, only one other purchaser at the Kent Manor sale is known to have lost possession of his land because of an inability to make payments. Aquilla Page bought a 277-acre tract that encompassed lots leased by his family for nearly forty years, but he was forced to forfeit it in 1787 because of bankruptcy.[62]

The effect of the state's confiscation and sale of Kent Manor was to dramatically increase the holdings of the wealthiest leaseholders, nearly all of whom were nonresidents who already controlled the preponderance of land on the manor. If speculators were present at the auction of the manor they must have found little to interest them. Most tenements sold for very high prices, generally over forty shillings per acre, and there was an ample number of nonresident tenants and neighboring freeholders who were willing and able to pay large sums for land on the manor.[63]

Speculation of a most unusual sort characterized the state sale of the other Eastern Shore manor. The auction of Queen Anne's Manor was held at Church Hill on January 14, 1782, with the sale being supervised by two of the commissioners of confiscated property, Clement Hollyday and Gabriel Duvall. During the course of the day, Duvall purchased eight manor lots for himself and two other men, William Hindman, a Talbot County lawyer-planter, and William Perry, a Talbot County planter. Acting on behalf of himself and the other two, Duvall executed a bond to the state for £7,186.13.3 in payment for the tracts, which encompassed 2,374 5/8 acres, over 55 percent of all the land sold at the auction. The purchase was a short-term speculative venture, with the three men signing agreements in October and December 1784 and August 1785 disposing of their holdings to three Queen Anne's County residents, two of whom had earlier been leaseholders on the manor. William Perry died intestate before one of the purchasers had completed paying for his part of the tract, however, and since the three had not relinquished title to the land, Perry's intestacy created legal problems with transferring title to the new owners. The case was eventually settled in chancery, but the last patent on the land purchased by Duvall, Perry, and Hindman was not issued until December 1811.[64]

Although Duvall might have argued that he was performing a public service by bidding more than private citizens were willing to pay for land on Queen Anne's Manor, his purchases were nonetheless a clear case of conflict of interest. Most tenants on Queen Anne's Manor were quite poor and might have been unable to pay for their tenements under any conditions. But outside bidding pressure, particularly from one of the commissioners supervising the sale, must have greatly exacerbated the problem for those tenants who hoped to retain possession of their land. Because of Duvall's purchases, compounded by the poverty of the tenants not affected by his acquisitions, the dispossession of tenants on Queen Anne's Manor was nearly complete, with only four being able to acquire land at the state auction.

Later in 1782, the commissioners journeyed to the upper Western Shore to dispose of tracts on the two sample manors in that region, Gunpowder and Monocacy. The state sale of Gunpowder Manor in Baltimore County, which was held in Baltimore on Friday, September 27, 1782, resulted in a considerable engrossment of land and the displacement of a number of resident tenants. The deleterious effects of confiscation were not due to purchases by outside speculators, however, but to acquisitions by a man who already owned land on the manor. James Gittings, the wealthiest tenant on the manor, had already purchased 907 acres of land at the proprietary sale of the manor. Gittings bought only one additional tract at the state sale, but in the decade that followed he obtained title to four other tracts by assignment from the original purchasers or in settlement for debts owed to him. By 1800, Gittings had amassed a total of 1,879 acres, or just over one-fourth of the entire manor.[65]

Eleven tenants lost possession of their land at the state auction of Gunpowder Manor, including seven who had been long-term residents on their tracts. In addition, six tenants who bid successfully on their tenements at the state sale lost possession before they could pay for and patent the land. Thus, confiscation resulted in a substantial dislocation of the tenant population on Gunpowder Manor. One resident tenant, however, rather than outside investors, was the principal beneficiary of the former tenants' inability to retain possession of their leaseholds.

The sale of Monocacy Manor differed from that of the other sample manors because land on Monocacy could be purchased with army pay certificates. The auction of the manor was held at Grost's Tavern in Frederick Town on September 10, 1782, and the tenants who assembled for the sale, many of whom were first generation German immigrants who had worked hard improving their leaseholds, must have been appalled at the number of high-ranking army officers and affluent storekeepers who had come to bid against them for their land. Monocacy tenants were among the most prosperous of any on the proprietary manors, and yet few could hope to compete with men who could pay for land with certificates that had been acquired for only a fraction of face value.[66]

The tenants' worst fears were confirmed as the auctioneer knocked down the first lot, a fifty-four-acre tract of very rich land leased by Simon Shover. The tract was purchased by Gen. Thomas Johnson, who bid £350 and paid for it in army certificates.[67] The pattern set by the sale of the first lot continued throughout the auction. Only one tenant, Joseph Wood, Jr., was able to purchase land from the state, and he was an army officer who was able to pay for his 320 acres with certificates. Wood incorporated one of the lots he purchased with adjacent freehold land into a resurveyed tract on which he founded the town of Woodsborough.[68] Most other purchasers of Monocacy Manor land, however, were not interested in developing their manor holdings. Speculators bought land on the manor because it offered them the opportunity to exchange their accumulated pay certificates at par for high-quality real estate. The rights to tracts on the manor, purchased for only a fraction of their real value, became negotiable commodities that could be traded and sold from one party to another. Speculators from all sections of Maryland, as well as residents of Virginia and Pennsylvania, engaged in the trading of Monocacy Manor tracts.[69] Many tenements on the manor were not finally patented until well into the nineteenth century, and then only after the sale certificate had passed through the hands of a half-dozen or more speculators. When a tract eventually did reach a state of quiet possession, the owner was usually a resident of Frederick County, rather than one of the speculators. Although the lots frequently ended up in the possession of Frederick County inhabitants, the owner was in most cases not the original tenant, but rather one of the more affluent residents of the county.[70] Thus, the confiscation and sale of Monocacy Manor resulted in an almost complete and permanent displacement of the resident tenant population.

One example will illustrate the complex speculative transfers in which some Monocacy Manor tracts were involved. Lot 12, containing 248 acres, was purchased and paid for in army certificates by Michael Montgomery. In 1783, Montgomery deeded the tract to Christian Orendorff and George Adams. Later the same year, Orendorff conveyed his interest in the lot to Adams. Adams mortgaged the lot to the Rev. Frederick Henop in September 1783. When Henop died, the executor of his estate deeded one-half of the lot jointly to William Bruce and David Luckett. In 1796, Bruce deeded his one-fourth interest in the lot to Jacob Holtz. Holtz acquired Luckett's one-fourth interest the following year. Finally, in 1807, Holtz was able to purchase the other half of the lot from Daniel Henop and John W. Henop of Norfolk, Virginia, and Jasper Cope of Baltimore, acting as trustee for the creditors of Philip Henop and Company. Holtz died before he could patent the land, however, and the tract was finally sold to Philemon Cromwell, a Frederick County resident, who patented the land in 1821, thirty-nine years after it had been sold by the state.[71]

Some of the most prominent men in Revolutionary Maryland were among the speculators who purchased land on Monocacy Manor. Army officers included Gen. William Smallwood, a leading military figure during the War for Independence and later three-term governor of the state; Gen. Mordecai Gist, a Baltimore businessman who demonstrated his patriotism by naming his two sons Independent and States; and Gen. Otho Holland Williams. Also among the high-ranking army officers who purchased Monocacy tracts were Col. John Eager Howard, who succeeded Smallwood as governor and who inherited a large estate in Baltimore out of which he donated the land on which the Lexington Market, St. Paul's Cathedral, and Mount Vernon Place are located; Col. Nathaniel Ramsey, the brother of the historian David Ramsey, who was an attorney before the war and one of Smallwood's officers at the battle of Long Island; Col. Moses Rawlings, a resident of Montgomery County who was active in supplying wheat for the army during the war; and Col. Peter Adams, a Caroline County storekeeper. Another prominent speculator was Thomas Johnson, an Annapolis lawyer, delegate to the Continental Congress, general in the army, and first governor of Maryland. James McHenry, a physician who had studied under Dr. Benjamin Rush in Philadelphia, enlisted as a surgeon with the outbreak of war, became an aide to both Washington and Lafayette, and was elected in 1781 to the Maryland State Senate, also purchased land on the manor. McHenry later served as a delegate to the Continental Congress, attended the Constitutional Convention in 1787, and was appointed secretary of war by President Washington in 1796. Merchants who invested in Monocacy land included James Tootell and William Whetcroft of Annapolis and Joseph Dowson of Cambridge in Dorchester County.

Although the list of purchasers of Monocacy Manor tracts includes numerous prominent persons of the late colonial period in Maryland, most were not among the social elite. The factor determining a man's ability to speculate in Monocacy lands was not so much family status or fortune as accessibility to army certificates. High-ranking army officers and storekeepers had the best opportunity to bilk soldiers out of their pay, and as a result, they were the ones in the most advantageous position to profit from the sale of Monocacy Manor.

Most men who purchased land at the sale of Monocacy Manor were solely interested in the speculative value of the property and eventually divested themselves of their holdings, but there were two important exceptions. Gen. Otho Holland Williams not only retained possession of the land he purchased from the state, but he also acquired additional tracts until he owned 923 acres on the manor. Williams never moved to Frederick County, but he did develop and farm his Monocacy land and he established the town of Ceresville on the property. Although not an original purchaser at the state auction, Capt. William Campbell bought land from the largest speculators, eventually amassing a total of fifteen tracts containing 1,674 acres. A resident of Annapolis in the late 1780s, Campbell moved to Frederick County in the early 1790s with his manor tracts forming the basis of his landed estate.[72]

In short, the rampant speculation on Monocacy Manor resulted from legislation that allowed tracts to be purchased with army certificates. Destitute soldiers had no alternative but to assign their pay certificates to army officers or merchants in exchange for much needed clothing, food, and cash, even though what they received was worth only a small fraction of the face value of the certificates. The net result of the state sale was a total dislocation of the tenant population on Monocacy Manor, followed by years of speculative trades and exchanges, culminating in a return of much of the land to Frederick County residents, most of whom had not originally been tenants on the manor.

State confiscation of the proprietary manors resulted in a varying amount of dislocation of the tenant populations. On some manors, especially those on the lower Western Shore that had poor land, few improvements, and indifferent natural resources, many tenants were able to purchase their land at a price they could afford to pay. For these tenants, confiscation may have caused a short-term economic hardship, but by acquiring title to their land they attained freehold status, and even more important, the assurance that they would never again face the prospect of having their homes and improvements sold.

On every manor, however, some tenants were unwilling or unable to purchase their land. Some nonresident tenants refused to buy their lots, but since they owned other land their decision not to purchase at the state sales did not greatly affect their economic condition. But for resident tenants who owned no other land, confiscation posed a serious problem. Tenants on the proprietary manors enjoyed secure tenure on long-terms leases at rents equal to only a fraction of what was charged by private landlords. Even though manor tracts often had poor natural resources and few improvements, many tenants had lived on their lots for decades and they had been able to provide their families with a subsistence by cultivating the land. Tenants who were poor, owned no freehold land, and could not afford to purchase their tracts at the state sales were faced with the unpalatable alternatives of being ejected from their tenements at the expiration of their leases or being forced to pay much higher annual rents if the new owner allowed them to stay on the land.

The most serious threat faced by tenants who desired to purchase their lots at the state sales was having outside investors and speculators bid against them. Bidding competition from outsiders was minimal on the lower Western Shore manors, because the land was poor and improvements on most tenements were of little value. Speculators and investors were much more active at the sales of Gunpowder, Kent, Queen Anne's, and Monocacy manors, with considerable disruption of the tenant populations occurring on the first three and nearly complete dispossession on the last.

At every manor auction speculators and investors were most interested in those lots that had the best resources and improvements. Superior natural resources were essential for enabling a tenant to improve his economic condition, and valuable improvements were tangible evidence that the tenant had invested capital and energy developing his leasehold. Ironically, speculators were most likely to dispossess those tenants who, because of the natural resources on their tenements and their own industriousness, had the best chance of achieving economic mobility by farming their manor lots.

In short, confiscation affected all proprietary tenants, but the results of the state sales differed from one manor to another. When outside bidding pressure was slight, little dislocation of the tenant populations occurred. But when a tract had particularly attractive improvements or resources, or where the terms of sale encouraged speculators, resident tenants were almost always displaced. Because of confiscation some tenants were able to become freeholders who otherwise might never have been able to raise the capital necessary to acquire their land. On the other hand, the state sales enabled some people who had no prior interest in the manors to establish large landed estates at bargain prices and others to reap speculative profits, both of which were done at the expense of tenants who had improved the land and who had derived their livelihood from cultivating the proprietor's soil.

EPILOGUE

The Lords Baltimore reserved manors in their proprietary province of Maryland as a speculative venture. They were successful in attracting hundreds of tenants to the manors, but because of the absentee status of the proprietor and the apathy and mismanagement of provincial officials the manors never became a major source of proprietary revenue. An unintentional result of this lax administration was the growth of stable communities of tenants on each of the manors. The tenants had long-term leases at rents lower than could be obtained from large private landlords, and they were allowed to develop their tracts with practically no interference from proprietary agents. Unlike many tenants on private land who moved after only a year or two in one place, a high percentage of the proprietary tenants remained on the manors their entire lives, and their tracts were inherited by sons or other relations after they died. In most respects, the manor tenants were barely distinguishable from small freeholders, except that the annual rent for manor land—when it was collected—was slightly higher than the quitrent charged on freehold land.

Despite the liberal lease terms, most tenants were very poor. Their poverty was reflected in the small number of them who owned slaves or servants, in the value of personal property recorded in their inventories, and in the small size and poor quality of the dwellings and other improvements on their tenements. Few resident manor tenants were able to accumulate sufficient assets either to improve their own standard of living or to ensure that their children would fare better.

Several factors account for the poverty of the proprietary manor tenants. Most manors had poor soil, which limited the quantity and quality of crops that could be produced on them. Many tenements on the older manors had little or no firewood or trees for fencing left on them, which placed the tenants in a less competitive position with persons who did not have to purchase wood. Furthermore, some leaseholds, especially those on the lower Western Shore manors, had suffered some soil depletion due to decades of cultivation, deforestation, and soil erosion. Finally, the agricultural practices followed by tenants were crude, and at a time when even the most enlightened planters were just beginning to understand the causes of low crop yields and to became concerned about crop rotation, crop alternatives, and proper animal husbandry, tenants inevitably reaped small profits from the soil.

Family size also contributed to tenant poverty. The average tenant family that can be reconstructed included six or more children, all of whom had to be supported by crops grown on the tenement. The necessity of feeding large families forced tenants to devote much of their arable land to consumables, at least until their children were old enough to work in the fields, thereby limiting their production of capital-producing crops. The proceeds from the small cash crops were spent at the local store for goods that could not be grown or manufactured at home, and tenants frequently found that store purchases exceeded their cash income.

Many of the poorest tenants on the proprietary manors were victims of the tobacco staple. By the end of the colonial period, tenants on the Eastern Shore and the upper Western Shore had converted to a diversified crop base, with wheat as the principal cash crop. Wheat was more profitable than tobacco, at least for families without slaves, but tenants in southern Maryland continued to grow tobacco despite smaller returns. Large planters, rather than small producers like the tenants, had to lead the move toward a more diversified crop base. Tenants continued to rely on tobacco because of a traditional attachment to the crop, debts to tobacco factors, and a trade network that was oriented to the marketing of that commodity.

Finally, most tenants owned no extrafamilial laborers, which was both a reflection and a cause of their poverty. The lack of slaves and servants was indicative of the tenants' poverty because the acquisition of bonded labor was an important social and economic imperative in much of Maryland, and, along with land, it formed a major outlet for the investment of surplus capital. The inability of tenants to acquire extrafamilial laborers was a cause of their poverty because surplus capital could be accumulated in agriculture only if the ratio of laborers to dependents was low. The profits from agriculture were small during most of the eighteenth century, regardless of whether wheat or tobacco was the primary cash staple. Profits increased, however, with the scale of the agricultural operation and the concomitant decrease in the number of dependents being supported by the work force. With scores of slave laborers, large planters could produce maximum cash crops, in addition to growing the bulk of the food consumed on their plantations, by forcing every slave to perform his allotted tasks. Tenants who were dependent upon their own families for field labor had to emphasize the production of crops for home consumption, devoting only surplus land and labor to cash crops.

In light of the poverty of most proprietary manor tenants, the high degree of stability of the manor populations might seem incongruous. But manor tenants had few viable alternatives to staying on their tenements. Private leaseholds were much more expensive to rent than proprietary manor land. The soil quality may have been higher on some private leaseholds, but the higher rents charged would have more than offset any increase in the value of crops that could have been produced on them. Freehold land was even more expensive. By the late colonial period, most land in the colony had been patented, and few tenants could pay the prices charged by private landlords to acquire land of their own. The only options open for tenants who hoped to improve their economic condition by moving off the manors was to abandon agriculture completely or to resettle on the distant frontier.

Most proprietary tenants could not change to nonagricultural occupations. Trades and mercantile activities all required skills, education, and capital that the average tenant did not possess. Furthermore, the economy of colonial Maryland was overwhelmingly agricultural, severely limiting the number of job opportunities in other fields.

Migration to the frontier also must have been unacceptable for most tenants. Some tenants did leave the manors for the western sections of Virginia and the Carolinas, but most appear to have been forced to do so because of debt. Moving to the frontier was objectionable for several reasons. First, because of their length of residence on the manors, most tenants had family connections in the neighborhood and leaving would have meant severing family and community ties. Second, the frontier was a dangerous place to live during much of the colonial period, with periodic Indian uprisings augmenting the usual hardships of frontier life. Third, tenants would have had to go very long distances to find land that was inexpensive or free. Large landowners in Maryland and Virginia had engrossed huge tracts of land on the frontier as speculative investments, thereby preempting much of the most accessible and best-quality land. Squatting was possible, but it rarely offered more than a temporary solution to the problem of being landless.

What must be emphasized is that the manor tenants were not members of a transient class. They lived in settled rural neighborhoods, they produced crops for a cash market rather than being strictly subsistence farmers, and they had deep roots that tied them to their homes on the proprietary manors. Resettlement on the frontier would have required that tenants and their families abandon much of what gave meaning to their lives. Geographical mobility has always been relatively easy for the affluent, because money softens the contrasts between old and new environments; for persons who have few worldly goods, friends, family, and familiar surroundings assume a special importance.

The root of the tenants' problem was their inability to accumulate surplus capital from small-scale agriculture. Cash or credit was required for acquiring a freehold in the settled parts of Maryland, and it was also necessary for financing a long move to the frontier and for obtaining land once the frontier had been reached. The fact that most proprietary tenants remained on their leaseholds indicates that they either considered it impossible to alter their situation or that they believed that farming their tenements offered them the best chance for improving their economic condition. If tenants anticipated accumulating sufficient capital through farming their leaseholds to enable them to acquire freeholds or slaves, however, the evidence indicates that most were frustrated in their expectations.

It is possible, on the other hand, that the stability of manor populations was high because tenants did not aspire to become freeholders. Following the decline in tobacco prices in the late seventeenth century and the growth of the number of residents in the colony in the early eighteenth century, tenancy became a permanent condition for an increasing number of Marylanders. By the end of the colonial period, some tenants were second or third generation nonlandowners. The futility of ever achieving economic mobility may have caused many tenants to abandon all hope of acquiring land. But tenancy on a large scale was still a recent phenomenon in Maryland, and the institution had not achieved the mark of respectability that centuries of English experience had given it. The freehold ideal was still a compelling force in Maryland, and most tenants—even those who held beneficial leases from the proprietor— must have longed to become members of the freeholding class. As Johann David Schoepf remarked, "the smallest possession has for every man more charm than the most imposing leasehold."[1]

Regardless of whether tenants felt frustrated at being unable to acquire land of their own, tenancy had become an important institution in Maryland by the end of the colonial period. The proprietor was the largest landlord in the province, but there were many private landlords as well. The 1783 state assessment reveals that about one-half the householders in the older settled counties did not own land. Nearly all these men must have eked out a livelihood by cultivating other men's land, and most private tenants probably had even smaller assets and less chance of achieving economic mobility than did the proprietary tenants.

Although tenancy was firmly established in Maryland by the War for Independence, the institution failed to flourish. The amount of tenancy in the year 1783, the inability of tenants to accumulate capital, and the number of fathers who were unable to acquire land themselves or for their sons, suggest that tenancy should have become a permanent condition for a large segment of the population of Maryland as it had in England. But the trend toward a large, established tenant class in the province was reversed by the War for Independence. Confiscation of the proprietor's estate in Maryland resulted in a massive redistribution of land that had formerly been held by one man, and the same was true of the landed property of wealthy Loyalists, such as the Dulanys. Many tenants were able to purchase land at the state sales of confiscated property, thereby decreasing the number of tenants and increasing the number of small freeholders in the province. But speculators and investors from the middle and upper classes engrossed much of the property confiscated by the state. Confiscation nevertheless served to interrupt the growth of tenancy, because the purchasers of tenanted land could force the tenant to move at the expiration of his lease, either by raising his rent to a prohibitive level or by refusing to let him remain on the property.[2] When his land was purchased by a new owner, the tenant had to look elsewhere, despite strong ties to his neighborhood.

The War for Independence served to halt the growth of tenancy in Maryland in another way. The ranks of privates in the Maryland Continental Line was largely filled by poor whites, principally by recently freed indentured servants and tenant farmers or their sons.[3] Army life was arduous, but it provided the common soldier with the unique experience of traveling far from his home. Exposure to new regions and peoples must have contributed powerfully to breaking down the provincialism of isolated and stable tenant communities. Soldiers were also given warrants for land on the frontier for serving in the war. Many privates sold their warrants to speculators, but some retained theirs to ensure a fresh beginning as landowners in the vast unsettled territory in the west.

Finally, in the decades following the War for Independence an increasing number of tenants concluded that there was little chance for them to ever achieve economic mobility in Maryland. Land remained expensive and tenants continued to receive small surpluses from the crops they could raise. The opening of the West to settlement after the war and the growing number of people motivated to move to the frontier because of land warrants or because of mobility generated by the war undoubtedly encouraged tenants to follow them. In the introduction of his journal, Thomas Bowdle, Jr., a native of Dorchester County, articulated the motives that must have impelled many tenants to leave Maryland after the War for Independence in a search for greater opportunity. Bowdle wrote:

In the year 1799, two families of us hearing good news from a new country in the West of America called Scioto [i.e., the Ohio], began to reflect upon our present situation and viewing circumstances that although we were tolerable good livers, yet had no possessions of our own and seeing that those that possessed the lands in our parts and held slaves, had got the rents of their lands, and the hire of their slaves so high that [it] was most impossible for the poor man to live and also being very severe with those that fell through and not able to make payments in time, and the people being very numerous so that it appears that the rents and hires will never be abated. Upon considerations of these things, and that if they could make out to live tolerable well themselves, they knew that it would be a bad chance for their children. Thus they concluded to carry themselves and their children to a new country in hopes that when they should be taken away, that they should leave their children in a place where they might have a better chance to live.[4]

The Bowdle family was only one of hundreds that decided to move to the west in search of land after the war. As Johann David Schoepf noted, "the people throughout are set upon establishing their children in land-estates which is difficult to manage in the older parts, and hence the incessant migrations to the farther regions."[5]

A great many people who moved west undoubtedly failed to improve their economic condition. They had little capital, and the cost of the move could only have decreased their meager assets. Opportunity was practically nonexistent for tenants who remained in Maryland, however, and as the volume of migration to the west increased, mobility must have at least offered a psychological, if not a realistic, panacea. Westward migration, coupled with increased urbanization and industrialization in the early nineteenth century, provided nonlandowners with a range of alternatives to remaining tenants in Maryland. As a result, tenancy in the last decades of the eighteenth century represented the apex of its development in the province rather than the foundation of a permanent agrarian class whose members extracted a subsistence by tilling land that they did not own.

APPENDIX A

The State Assessment of 1783

The following five tables summarize several categories of data extracted from the 1783 state assessment. The data cover six counties in various sections of the province: Charles and Calvert on the lower Western Shore; Somerset on the lower Eastern Shore; Talbot and Caroline on the Eastern Shore, and Harford on the upper Western Shore. Table 1 shows the size of landholdings of householders in the counties, tables 2 and 3 record the assessed property owned by nonlandowners and landowners, and tables 4 and 5 show the number of slaves owned by nonlandowners and landowners in the six counties. All nonresidents in the counties were eliminated in these tables. Residency was determined by whether a household contained white inhabitants or if property in addition to land was listed. If there were no whites in the household and no property mentioned other than land, it was assumed that the owner was a nonresident. All monetary sums in the tables are expressed in Maryland currency. The 1783 state assessment returns are located at the Maryland Historical Society, Baltimore, Maryland. Photostatic copies and a card index to people and racts of land listed in the assessment are available at the Hall of Records, Annapolis, Maryland.

APPENDIX A

TABLE A-1
Size of Landholdings in Six Maryland Counties, 1783

	Harford County		Caroline County		Charles County	
Acres	householders	percent	householders	percent	householders	pe
0	984	49.87	682	49.42	1,013	5
1–49	123	6.23	42	3.04	46	
50–99	183	9.27	100	7.25	156	
100–199	354	17.92	265	19.20	312	1
200–299	137	6.94	113	8.19	142	
300–399	65	3.29	60	4.35	78	
400–499	38	1.92	43	3.12	31	
500–599	26	1.32	17	1.23	29	
600–699	19	0.96	11	0.80	22	
700–799	6	0.30	11	0.80	14	
800–899	4	0.20	5	0.36	9	
900–999	7	0.35	3	0.22	7	
1000–1499	15	0.76	14	1.01	22	
1500–1999	5	0.25	8	0.58	6	
2000–2999	3	0.15	4	0.29	—	
3000 and above	5	0.25	2	0.14	5	
	1,975	99.98	1,380	100.00	1,892	10

TABLE A-2
Value of Assessed Property of Landless Householders in Six Maryland Counties, 1783

Value (pounds currency)	Harford County		Caroline County		Charles County	
	householders	percent	householders	percent	householders	per
paupers	244	24.77	138	20.23	183	1
10–49	512	51.98	391	57.33	428	4
50–99	131	13.30	93	13.64	161	1
100–149	40	4.06	28	4.11	98	
150–199	15	1.52	10	1.47	49	
200–299	20	2.03	10	1.47	40	
300–399	9	0.91	8	1.17	24	
400–499	7	0.71	2	0.29	13	
500–599	7	0.71	2	0.29	7	
600–699	—	—	—	—	4	
700–799	—	—	—	—	3	
800–899	—	—	—	—	—	
900–999	—	—	—	—	—	
1000 and above	—	—	—	—	3	
	985	99.99	682	100.00	1,013	10

Calvert County		Somerset County		Talbot County	
householders	percent	householders	percent	householders	percent
455	49.84	539	33.27	756	55.59
43	4.71	90	5.56	81	5.96
98	10.73	167	10.31	41	3.01
120	13.14	366	22.59	132	9.71
74	8.11	165	10.19	89	6.54
36	3.94	97	6.00	56	4.12
29	3.18	52	3.21	32	2.35
26	2.85	41	2.53	30	2.21
6	0.66	32	1.98	31	2.28
6	0.66	14	0.86	23	1.69
3	0.33	9	0.56	19	1.40
2	0.22	13	0.80	10	0.74
8	0.88	20	1.23	45	3.31
5	0.55	9	0.56	10	0.74
1	0.11	5	0.31	2	0.15
1	0.11	1	0.06	3	0.22
913	100.02	1,620	100.02	1,360	100.02

Calvert County		Somerset County		Talbot County	
householders	percent	householders	percent	householders	percent
93	20.44	206	38.22	188	24.87
246	54.07	219	40.63	299	39.55
63	13.85	54	10.02	124	16.40
22	4.84	31	5.75	64	8.47
14	3.08	12	2.23	27	3.57
9	1.98	11	2.04	26	3.44
5	1.10	3	0.56	11	1.46
1	0.22	1	0.19	6	0.79
1	0.22	1	0.19	6	0.79
—	—	—	—	2	0.26
—	—	—	—	—	—
—	—	—	—	1	0.13
—	—	1	0.19	1	0.13
1	0.22	—	—	1	0.13
455	100.02	539	100.02	756	99.99

TABLE A-3
Value of Assessed Property of Landed Householders in Six Maryland Counties, 1783

| Value (sterling) | Harford County | | Caroline County | | Charles Cou |
	householders	percent	householders	percent	householders
10–49	53	5.35	48	6.88	21
50–99	147	14.85	146	20.92	93
100–149	152	15.35	130	18.62	72
150–199	105	10.61	91	13.04	73
200–299	134	13.54	77	11.03	112
300–399	98	9.90	59	8.45	79
400–499	49	4.95	39	5.59	69
500–599	42	4.24	17	2.44	50
600–699	37	3.74	15	2.15	65
700–799	27	2.73	13	1.86	34
800–899	18	1.82	15	2.15	32
900–999	14	1.41	13	1.86	16
1000–1099	15	1.52	6	0.86	20
1100–1199	11	1.11	6	0.86	19
1200–1299	12	1.21	—	—	10
1300–1399	11	1.11	3	0.43	15
1400–1499	6	0.61	2	0.29	9
1500–1999	22	2.22	5	0.72	28
2000–2499	5	0.51	2	0.29	23
2500–2999	17	1.72	9	1.29	14
3000 and above	15	1.52	2	0.89	25
	990	100.02	698	100.02	879

TABLE A-4
Slaves Held by Nonlandowning Householders in Six Maryland Counties, 1783

| Number of Slaves | Harford County | | Caroline County | | Charles Count | |
	householders	percent	householders	percent	householders	pe
0	839	85.18	579	84.90	607	5
1	63	6.40	44	6.45	172	1
2	27	2.74	23	3.37	69	
3	8	0.81	12	1.76	38	
4	10	1.02	4	0.59	31	
5	10	1.02	8	1.17	23	
6	14	1.42	2	0.29	22	
7	2	0.20	1	0.15	8	
8	5	0.51	3	0.44	8	
9	4	0.41	—	—	9	
10–14	3	0.30	3	0.44	20	
15–19	—	—	3	0.44	5	
20–24	—	—	—	—	1	
25–29	—	—	—	—	—	
30 and above	—	—	—	—	—	
	985	100.01	682	100.00	1,013	9

Calvert County		Somerset County		Talbot County	
householders	percent	householders	percent	householders	percent
30	6.55	91	8.42	71	11.75
61	13.32	161	14.89	73	12.09
36	7.86	117	10.82	93	15.40
38	8.30	105	9.71	65	10.76
53	11.57	136	12.58	84	13.91
46	10.04	92	8.51	78	12.91
35	7.64	77	7.12	32	5.30
24	5.24	55	5.09	27	4.47
15	3.28	44	4.07	9	1.49
21	4.59	40	3.70	7	1.16
13	2.84	27	2.50	6	0.99
7	1.53	18	1.67	6	0.99
14	3.06	13	1.20	7	1.16
9	1.97	9	0.83	6	0.99
5	1.09	15	1.39	2	0.33
12	2.62	9	0.83	2	0.33
5	1.09	7	0.65	—	—
13	2.84	33	3.05	7	1.16
11	2.40	13	1.20	4	0.66
4	0.87	10	0.93	9	1.49
6	1.31	9	0.83	16	2.65
458	100.01	1,081	99.99	604	99.99

Calvert County		Somerset County		Talbot County	
householders	percent	householders	percent	householders	percent
313	68.79	386	71.61	533	70.50
75	16.48	75	13.91	93	12.30
19	4.18	30	5.57	47	6.22
15	3.30	11	2.04	16	2.12
12	2.64	14	2.60	20	2.65
6	1.32	4	0.74	14	1.85
8	1.76	5	0.93	8	1.06
2	0.44	4	0.74	4	0.53
—	—	3	0.56	8	1.06
1	0.22	1	0.19	3	0.40
3	0.66	5	0.93	6	0.79
—	—	—	—	3	0.40
—	—	—	—	—	—
—	—	—	—	1	0.13
1	0.22	1	0.19	—	—
455	100.01	539	100.01	756	100.01

TABLE A-5
Slaves Held by Landowning Householders in Six Maryland Counties, 1783

Number of Slaves	Harford County		Caroline County		Charles Count	
	householders	percent	householders	percent	householders	pe
0	565	57.07	447	64.04	211	
1	88	8.89	53	7.59	84	
2	57	5.76	42	6.02	59	
3	38	3.84	24	3.44	59	
4	48	4.85	21	3.01	49	
5	37	3.74	13	1.86	38	
6	28	2.83	20	2.87	40	
7	24	2.42	17	2.44	43	
8	18	1.82	11	1.58	44	
9	24	2.42	9	1.29	29	
10–14	37	3.74	20	2.87	112	
15–19	19	1.92	10	1.43	47	
20–24	7	0.71	6	0.86	31	
25–29	3	0.30	1	0.14	13	
30 and above	8	0.81	4	0.57	20	
	990	101.12	698	100.01	879	1

Calvert County		Somerset County		Talbot County	
householders	percent	householders	percent	householders	percent
103	22.49	351	32.47	261	43.21
61	13.32	124	11.47	47	7.78
29	6.33	71	6.57	30	4.97
27	5.90	58	5.37	28	4.64
29	6.33	55	5.09	23	3.81
24	5.24	60	5.55	23	3.81
12	2.62	52	4.81	31	5.13
19	4.15	43	3.98	25	4.14
16	3.49	25	2.31	14	2.32
12	2.62	38	3.52	18	2.98
60	13.10	97	8.97	51	8.44
30	6.55	45	4.16	21	3.48
14	3.06	26	2.41	9	1.49
8	1.75	18	1.67	7	1.16
14	3.06	18	1.67	16	2.65
458	100.01	1,081	100.02	604	100.01

APPENDIX B

The Proprietary Manors

This appendix describes all proprietary manors known to have been in existence in 1767 and 1768. The manors are listed geographically, beginning in St. Mary's County on the lower Western Shore, progressing clockwise up the Western Shore and then down the Eastern Shore. The sources for information are listed at the end of the discussion of each manor.

Lower Western Shore Manors

WEST ST. MARY'S.   Located in south-central St. Mary's County, this manor was originally surveyed in 1642 for Cecilius, second Lord Baltimore, for 2,000 acres. The manor was resurveyed in 1666; its east boundary was the St. Mary's River. In 1768, the manor contained 3,091 acres, 1,720 3/4 acres of which were patented land and 1,370 1/4 acres of which remained leasehold land. See Patents 4:543; Claim of Henry Harford, Public Record Office, A.O. 12/79, f. 127, London (microfilm copy available at the Hall of Records, Annapolis, Maryland); Executive Papers, portfolio 3, folder 19; Plats, division 4, no. 4.

SNOW HILL.   The manor was situated in St. Mary's County across the St. Mary's River from West St. Mary's Manor. The manor was originally surveyed in 1640 for Leonard Calvert, brother of the proprietor and governor of the province, and contained 1,000 acres. Upon resurvey in 1767, the manor was found to contain 926 acres, including the escheat tracts of St. John's and St. Barbara's, which adjoined it. See Patents A.B. and H:93; Executive Papers, portfolio 3, folder 19; Memorandum Book for Snow Hill Manor, n.d. [ca. 1767], Proprietary Papers; Plats, division 4, no. 2.

MILL.   The manor was situated on the western side of the northern branch of the St. George's River in St. Mary's County. The original survey date of this manor is uncertain, although it was probably erected in the 1660s. It was resurveyed for the proprietor in 1755 and found to contain 1,924 acres. In 1768, a survey showed that the manor contained 2,696 acres, 89 acres of which were patented and the remainder held as leasehold land. See Gift Collection, D371 [plat dated 1755]; Plats, division 4, no. 31; Executive Papers, portfolio 3, folder 19; St. Mary's County Unpatented Certificate no. 307.

WOOLSEY.   This manor was originally surveyed for Phillip Calvert in 1664 for 1,900 acres. In 1755, a resurvey of the manor showed that it contained 2,802 acres. In 1768, the manor contained 3,131 3/8 acres, all of which was leasehold land. The manor was located on the east side of the St. George's River, across from Mill Manor, which was on the west side of the river. See Patents 6:276; Gift Collection, D371 [plat dated 1755]; Plats, division 4, no. 44; Executive Papers, portfolio 3, folder 19.

BEAVERDAM.   This manor was situated in the west-central portion of St. Mary's County, adjacent to the western boundaries of the private manors of Delabrooke and Fenwick. The manor was originally surveyed for the proprietor in 1666 and contained 7,180 acres. A resurvey in the 1760s showed 7,680 acres in the manor, 490 1/2 acres of which were patented land and the remainder leasehold land. See A.O. 12/79, f. 127; Executive Papers, portfolio 3, folder 19; Plats, division 4, no. 53.

CHAPTICO. The manor was ⸺riginally surveyed for the proprietor in 1671, but the acreage is not recorded. In 1768, the manor contained 18,546 acres, only 6,551 3/4 acres of which had not been previously patented or sold by the proprietary commissioners in 1767. The manor was situated in the northern part of St. Mary's County, with a small part of the manor lying north of the county line in Charles County. See Patents 16:406; Executive Papers, portfolio 3, folder 19.

CALVERTON. Originally surveyed for the proprietor in 1666 for 6,000 acres, the manor contained 7,230 acres in 1768, 5,359 acres of which were leasehold land. The manor was located inland from the Patuxent River in western Charles County, between Indian Creek on the south and Swanson's Creek on the north. See A.O. 12/79, f. 127; Executive Papers, portfolio 3, folder 19; Plats, division 4, no. 16.

ZACHIAH. Surveyed for the proprietor in 1667, the manor was laid out for 6,000 acres. A resurvey in 1767 showed the manor contained 9,637 acres, 4,230 acres of which were patented land. The manor was located in Charles County on the west side of Zachiah Swamp, at the head of Allen's Fresh Run, a tributary of the Wicomico River. See Patents 10:488; Executive Papers, portfolio 3, folder 19; Plats, division 4, no. 34.

PANGAIAH. This manor, located on the east and west sides of the main tributary of the Port Tobacco River, was originally surveyed for the proprietor in 1667 for 1,200 acres. The boundaries of the manor became hopelessly confused in the early eighteenth century. When the manor was resurveyed in the 1760s, its boundaries were expanded to include a large amount of patented land. In 1768, the manor contained 10,240 1/2 acres, but only 1,451 acres were leasehold land. The manor was located north of present-day Bryan Town. See Patents 10:488; Executive Papers, portfolio 3, folder 19; Calvert to Lord Baltimore, October 26, 1729, Calvert Papers, Number Two, Maryland Historical Society Fund Publication no. 34 (Baltimore, 1894), p. 79.

ANNE ARUNDEL. Originally surveyed for the proprietor in 1669 for 10,000 acres, this manor was resurveyed in 1698 and the acreage increased to 12,634 acres. Upon resurvey in the 1760s, it contained 10,680 7/8 acres. The manor was situated in the southeastern part of Anne Arundel County, with the Patuxent River as its western boundary. It was occasionally called the Ridge Manor. See Patents 16:626; Patents C.D.:54; Executive Papers, portfolio 3, folder 19; Plats, division 3, no. 57.

COLLINGTON. The manor was originally surveyed for the proprietor in 1684 for 1,100 acres. In 1768, the manor contained 1,297 1/4 acres, all of which had been sold by the proprietary commissioners. Located in Prince George's County on a tributary of the Patuxent River, the manor was called Western Branch Manor in the early eighteenth century. See Patents 22:168; Executive Papers, portfolio 3, folder 19; Prince George's County Unpatented Certificate no. 91.

Upper Western Shore Manors

GUNPOWDER. This manor was located in the fork of the Gunpowder River in Baltimore County. It was surveyed for the proprietor in 1683 and contained 7,031 acres. When resurveyed in the 1760s, the manor contained 7,265 1/4 acres. See Patents 22:112; Executive Papers, portfolio 3, folder 19; Plats, division 4, no. 5.

MY LADY'S. This manor was surveyed in 1713 for Lady Baltimore, wife of the proprietor. Upon her death, the manor was devised to her relatives, the Brerewoods. Legal ownership of the manor was a subject of dispute as late as 1768, with both the proprietor and the heirs of the Brerewood family claiming possession. Baltimore's right to the manor was eventually confirmed, and the manor was confiscated by the state as proprietary property. The manor was located on the north side of the main falls of the Gunpowder River, on the west-central boundary of Baltimore County. The Old York Road passed through the manor, and lot 68 is the site of the present-day town of Monkton. See Patents 5:806; Executive Papers, portfolio 3, folder 19; Plats, division 4, no. 7; Executive Papers, portfolio 3, folder 12e.

MONOCACY. The manor was originally surveyed for the proprietor in 1724 for 10,000 acres. The manor, north-northwest of Frederick Town, was bounded on the west by the

Monocacy River. Present-day Woodsborough was established on a lot of the manor. *See* Patents IL B:198; Prince George's County Unpatented Certificate no. 1491-A.

CONEGOCHEAGUE. The manor was originally surveyed for the proprietor in 1734 and contained 10,594 acres. It was resurveyed in 1768 and contained 10,688 1/4 acres. The proprietor gave the resurveyed manor to John Morton Jordan in 1768, thereby terminating its status as a proprietary manor. The manor was located north of the Potomac River west of present-day Hagerstown. In 1768, the manor was in Frederick County, but Washington County now encompasses the area. *See* Patents E.I. 5:580; Patents BC and GS 38:72; Sharpe to Hamersley, October 30, 1768, *Archives of Maryland*, ed. William Hand Browne et al., 72 vols. to date (Baltimore, 1883–), 14:536.

Upper Eastern Shore Manors

SUSQUEHANNAH (New Connaught). First surveyed in 1683 as a private manor for George Talbot, an Irish cousin of the second Lord Baltimore, the manor was laid out for 32,000 acres. The manor, located in Cecil County with the Susquehanna River as its western boundary, extended northward into the present state of Pennsylvania. In 1684, Talbot murdered Christopher Rousby in the province of Virginia. He was eventually captured and executed. Talbot's commission of a capital crime left the status of his property uncertain. Heirs of Talbot, the proprietors of Pennsylvania, and the agents of Lord Baltimore all claimed all or part of the manor and issued leases for tenements on it. Baltimore succeeded in securing his claim to all of the manor south of the Mason-Dixon line by late in the colonial period. *See* Patents 20:366; Plats, division 4, no. 26; Philemon Lloyd to Co-Partners, October 8, 1772, *Calvert Papers, Number Two*, pp. 61–63; Lord Baltimore to Matthew Tilghman Ward, July 19, 1730, *Archives*, 37:580.

NORTH EAST. The manor was surveyed for the proprietor in 1667 for 6,000 acres. It was adjacent to Susquehannah Manor in Cecil County on the North East River. *See* Patents 10:489.

ELK (ELK RIVER). The date of erection is unknown, although it is probable that it was established about the same time as North East Manor (ca. 1667). The manor appears to have been located to the north and east of North East Manor. Its western boundary was probably one of the two main tributaries of the North East River.

KENT. This manor was surveyed for the proprietor in 1675 for 8,000 acres. In 1768, the manor contained the same acreage, but 374 1/4 acres were patented land, and an additional 904 acres of freehold land had recently been sold out of the manor. The manor was situated on the north side of the Chester River in Kent County, beginning at the head of Morgan's Creek. *See* Patents 15:294; Executive Papers, portfolio 3, folder 19.

QUEEN ANNE'S. Surveyed for the proprietor in 1681 and originally called the Manor on Chester River, this manor was laid out for 6,000 acres. It is probable that the manor was originally surveyed in 1666 for the same acreage and then called Talbot's Manor. The manor was situated on the south side of the Chester River in Queen Anne's County. In 1768, the manor still contained 6,000 acres, 936 3/4 of which had been recently sold by the proprietary commissioners. *See* Patents 21:339; Executive Papers, portfolio 3, folder 19; A.O. 12/79, f. 129.

Lower Eastern Shore Manors

WOLCOTE. Originally surveyed in 1674 as "a mannour in Somersett," this manor contained 6,000 acres. It was resurveyed in 1754 for 5,950 acres and given the name Wolcote Manor. The manor was on the south side of the Nanticoke River on Broad Creek. A resurvey in the 1760s showed that all but 200 acres of the manor were in Delaware. *See* Patents 15:388; Executive Papers, portfolio 3, folder 19.

NANTICOKE. When surveyed for the proprietor in 1664, the manor contained 6,000 acres. Bounded by Siccacone Creek on the north-west, the manor was located in Dorchester County on the north side of the Nanticoke River, a short distance from the town of Vienna. *See* Patents 7:444.

WICOMICO. This manor was surveyed in 1674 for the proprietor for 6,000 acres. A plat of the manor made in 1756 shows that the manor contained only 3,957 acres, according to a resurvey of that date. The manor was situated on the dividing line between Somerset and Worcester counties, with the Wicomico River forming its north-west boundary. *See* Patents 15:293; Plats, division, 4, no. 1.

NOTES

Preface

1. Most discussions of tenancy in the Chesapeake Bay region concern Virginia. The Browns include most tenants in the middle rather than the lower class, contending that there was no social stigma attached to being a tenant and that many tenants owned slaves and freeholds. A tenant had ample opportunity for economic mobility and "could climb up the social ladder if he was not already there" (Robert E. and B. Katherine Brown, *Virginia 1705-1786: Democracy or Aristocracy?* [East Lansing, 1964], pp. 23-24, 45-46). Wertenbaker maintains that the easy availability of land kept the number of tenants low in Virginia, at least until the advent of slavery; Thomas J. Wertenbaker, *The Planters of Colonial Virginia* (Princeton, 1922), p. 45. Craven states that there were many tenants in seventeenth-century Virginia, but implies that most soon achieved freehold status; Wesley Frank Craven, *The Southern Colonies in the Seventeenth Century, 1607-1689* (Baton Rouge, 1949), p. 210. *See also* Jackson Turner Main, *The Social Structure of Revolutionary America* (Princeton, 1965), pp. 44-68.

2. The statement is based on my own analysis of the Maryland assessment returns for 1783. Summary data for six sample counties representing different geographical areas in the state are presented in appendix A. The assessment lists are in the Scharf Collection, Maryland Historical Society (hereafter cited as MHS). Unless otherwise noted, all manuscripts cited are located at the Hall of Records, Annapolis, Maryland. For an even higher estimate of the number of adult free white males who were nonlandowners in late colonial Maryland, *see* David Curtis Skaggs, *Roots of Maryland Democracy, 1753-1776* (Westport, Conn., 1973), pp. 40-41.

3. In addition to the works cited below in n. 4, *see* Russell R. Menard, "From Servant to Freeholder: Status Mobility and Property Accumulation in Seventeenth-Century Maryland," *William and Mary Quarterly*, 3rd ser. 30 (1973):37-64 (hereafter cited as *WMQ*).

4. Throughout this study a distinction will be made between the terms "farmer" and "planter," because in the eighteenth century the former usually referred to a person who grew diversified crops and the latter to a person who grew tobacco as a staple; *see* N. F. Cabell, "Some Fragments of an Intended Report on the Post Revolutionary History of Agriculture in Virginia," with notes by E. G. Swem, *WMQ*, 1st ser. 26 (1918):155.

5. In the eighteenth century tenancy in New York developed quite differently than in Maryland, with large landowners engrossing an enormous amount of land and then finding themselves chronically short of tenants to work the soil; *see* Sung Bok Kim, "A New Look at the Great Landlords of Eighteenth-Century New York," *WMQ*, 3rd ser. 27 (1970):581-614. Kim's monograph on New York landlords and tenants, which will be published shortly by the Institute of Early American History and Culture, was not available to this author, but it should prove a basis for useful comparisons on the development of tenancy in colonial America. For tenancy in the Chesapeake Bay region in addition to the sources cited above in n. 1 and n. 4, *see* S. Edward Ayres, "Albemarle County, 1744-1770: An Economic, Political and Social Analysis," *The Magazine of Albemarle County History* 25 (1966-67):36-72; for a discussion of tenancy in the Northern Neck of Virginia, *see* Willard F. Bliss, "The Rise of Tenancy in Virginia," *Virginia Magazine of History and Biography* 58 (1950):427-42 (herafter cited as *VMHB*); Kevin Porter Kelley discovered a high percentage of nonlandowners in the last decade of the seventeenth century in Surry County, Virginia, with tenants accounting for approximately a quarter of the householders ("Economic and Social Development of Seventeenth-Century Surry County, Virginia" [Ph.D. diss., University of Washington, 1972]); the settlement of the Virginia backcountry is examined in Michael L. Nicholls, "Origins of the Virginia Southside, 1703-1753: A Social and

Economic Study" (Ph.D. diss., College of William and Mary, 1972). John Anstey, writing to the Loyalists' Claims Commission on April 20, 1787, noted: ". . . in general, it is worthy of observation, that there is not so great a Disparity in the comparative value of Estates in Maryland, as either in Virginia or New York because the Territory being less extended and interlocked to the North West by Virginia, and the potomac River on the one side; and the pennsylvania Boundaries on the other, [it] has no immeasurable Tracts of *uncultivated* Land, and the Country being proportionally more populous for its size, is comparatively more settled, and the plantations by Consequence more upon a footing of Equality in point of Cultivation. . . ." ("Reports from State Governments, 1787," Loyalist Claims, series 1, Public Record Office, Audit Office 12/94, f. 110, London [microfilm copy available at the Research Department, Colonial Williamsburg Foundation, Williamsburg, Va.]). The difference in the price of land of similar quality in Maryland and Virginia was also noted by Dr. David Stuart in his letter to George Washington, dated November 18, 1791: "The fee-simple prices of land at the distance of ten miles from the [Potomac] river and town of Alexandria, is from twenty shillings to forty per acre, according to quality. It is remarkable that lands in no respect superior on the opposite side of the river in Maryland and equally distance from the river sell currently at four and five pounds per acre. I know not how such a difference is to be accounted for, but from the greater degree of population in proportion to their Country. The same circumstance must, I suppose, account for the lands in Virginia being generally so much cheaper, tho' equal in quality and possessing a milder climate than the land in the Northern States" (Gertrude R. B. Richards, ed., "Dr. David Stuart's Report to President Washington On Agricultural Conditions in Northern Virginia," *VMHB* 61 [1953]:288.

6. *See*, especially, Joan Thirsk, *English Peasant Farming* (London, 1957), and Joan Thirsk, ed., *The Agrarian History of England and Wales* (Cambridge, Eng., 1967), especially chs. 5, 7, and 9. These two studies contain a wealth of detailed information about English rural life and are useful both for the facts they contain and the methodology employed to address the problem of small farmers. *See also* R. H. Tawney, *The Agrarian Problem in the Sixteenth Century* (1912; reprinted, New York, 1967), especially chs. 1–4; W. G. Hoskins, *The Midland Peasant: the Economic and Social History of a Leicestershire Village* (London, 1957); Mildred Campbell, *The English Yeoman under Elizabeth and the Early Stuarts* (New Haven, 1942); Stella Davies, *The Agricultural History of Cheshire 1750–1850* (Manchester, Eng., 1960); L. A. Clarkson, *The Pre-Industrial Economy of England, 1500–1750* (New York, 1972), pp. 62–66, 234; also the informative study of the land system in New France, Richard Colebrook Harris, *The Seigneurial System in Early Canada: A Geographical Study* (Madison, Wis., 1966).

Chapter 1

1. For a discussion of the Maryland charter and the early settlement of the province, *see* Charles M. Andrews, *The Colonial Period of American History*, 4 vols. (New Haven, 1936), 2:282; William Hand Browne, *Maryland: The History of a Palatinate*, rev. ed. (Boston, 1904), pp. 15–20; Charles Albro Barker, *The Background of the Revolution in Maryland* (1940; reprinted, Hamden, Conn., 1967), p. 120; the charter is reprinted in Jack P. Greene, ed., *Settlements to Society: 1584–1763, A Documentary History of American Life*, 2 vols. (New York, 1966), 1:25–28. Proprietary instructions concerning headrights are summarized in Donnell MacClure Owings, "Private Manors: An Edited List," *Maryland Historical Magazine* 33 (1938):309–10.

2. Owings, "Private Manors," p. 307; *see also* Clarence P. Gould, *The Land System in Maryland*, Johns Hopkins Studies in Historical and Political Science, vol. 31 (Baltimore, 1913), p. 9 (hereafter cited as JHSH).

3. Owings, "Private Manors," pp. 308–34. Large tracts of land patented after 1683 were occasionally called "manors," but the owners did not enjoy manorial privileges; *see* Gould, *Land System*, pp. 89–90.

4. Owings, "Private Manors," pp. 309–10.

5. In 1671 a twelve-pence duty on all tobacco exported from the colony was substituted for the quitrents and alienation fines. The tobacco equivalent was continued until 1733 when the proprietor reintroduced the collection of quitrents. *See* Barker, *Background of the*

Revolution, pp. 130–31, 135–36; Beverly W. Bond, *The Quit-Rent System in the American Colonies* (New Haven, 1919), pp. 179–80. As late as 1752, some quitrents were still collected in the form of wheat or other grains on land in St. Mary's County; *see* Calvert to Tasker, May 15, 1752, *Calvert Papers, Number Two*, Maryland Historical Society Fund Publication no. 34 (Baltimore, 1894), p. 143. On March 21, 1735, the proprietor complained that through "Negligence of the Clerks of the Land-Office . . . there were very great Blunders committed as to the Rent Reserved," both by inserting quitrents in patents smaller than usually required and by omitting the word sterling after a rent, thereby enabling land-owners to claim the right to pay quitrents in currency (*see* "Instructions to Benjamin Tasker, esq.," *Archives of Maryland*, ed. William Hand Browne et al., 72 vols. to date [Baltimore, 1883–   ], 39:509 [hereafter cited as *Archives*]).

6. Owings, "Private Manors," p. 310; Gould, *Land System*, pp. 9–10; Sharpe to Baltimore, May 2, 1754, *Archives*, 6:53.

7. Claim of Henry Harford, Public Record Office, Audit Office 12/79, f. 17, London (microfilm copy available at the Hall of Records, Annapolis, Maryland [hereafter cited as A.O. 12/79]).

8. Gould, *Land System*, p. 91.

9. See A.O. 12/79, f. 127, and appendix B.

10. December 14, 1673, *Archives*, 15:31.

11. John Kilty, *The Land-Holder's Assistant, and Land-Office Guide* (Baltimore, 1808), p. 105.

12. A.O. 12/79, f. 127, and appendix B. Small tracts that escheated to the proprietor and were leased as manor land included Abbington and White Plains in Anne Arundel County and St. John's and St. Barbara's in St. Mary's County. Two large private manors that escheated to the proprietor and were thereafter considered proprietary manors were Susquehannah Manor, also known as New Connaught Manor, originally surveyed for George Talbot, and My Lady's Manor, originally surveyed for Lady Baltimore. For further information on the last two manors, *see* appendix B.

13. Kilty, *Land-Holder's Assistant*, p. 236; Sharpe to John Sharpe, May 27, 1756, *Archives*, 6:426; order signed by Benjamin Tasker, July 2, 1739, A.O. 12/79, f. 139; order signed by John Clapham, June 30, 1768, A.O. 12/79, f. 139.

14. Calvert to Tasker, July 9, 1752, *Calvert Papers, Number Two*, pp. 148–49.

15. Gould, *Land System*, pp. 91–92.

16. *Calvert Papers, Number Two*, pp. 148–49.

17. For a discussion of the proprietary sales, *see* chapter 5.

18. *See* "A State of the Sales of His Lordships Mannours," (ca. April 1768), signed by Horatio Sharpe and Daniel Dulany, Executive Papers, portfolio 3, folder 19.

19. Newton D. Mereness states that in the early eighteenth century the proprietary manors had fallen into such a state of disorganization that some "entirely vanished," (*Maryland as a Proprietary Province* [New York, 1901], pp. 53–54). Although no evidence has been found to substantiate Mereness's claim, confusion over the boundaries of some manors did lead to much of the land being patented as freeholds; *see* Calvert to Baltimore, October 26, 1729, *Calvert Papers, Number Two*, p. 79. Mereness may have concluded that some proprietary manors disappeared because several manors were called by more than one name at various points in their history. For example, Wolcote Manor had also been known as Bridgewater Manor and both Queen Anne's Manor and Kent Manor had been called "the Manor on Chester River." The list of manors printed in appendix B includes all manors ever erected for the Calverts that could be discovered. The location of most manors was established by consulting the original patents and certificates of survey. The map at the back of George Johnston's *History of Cecil County, Maryland* (1881; reprinted, Baltimore, 1967) was useful for locating the manors in that county. I was aided in finding the St. Mary's County manors by Russell Menard, who has constructed a tract map for much of that county.

20. *See* appendix B for a more detailed description of the manors and for source citations.

21. "Instructions for the Land Councill," May 5, 1684, *Archives*, 17:259. David Curtis Skaggs notes an increase in the leasing of both private and proprietary land beginning in the 1730s; *see Roots of Maryland Democracy, 1753–1776* (Westport, Conn., 1973), pp. 48–49.

22. Based on data in U.S. Bureau of the Census, *Historical Statistics of the United States*.

Colonial Times to 1957 (Washington, D.C., 1960), pp. 13, 756, the estimated decennial increase in population in Maryland was as follows:

Year	Estimated Population	Decennial Increase (%)	Year	Estimated Population	Decennial Increase (%)
1640	583		1720	66,133	54.72
1650	4,540	672.55	1730	91,113	37.77
1660	8,426	87.07	1740	116,093	27.41
1670	13,226	56.96	1750	141,073	21.51
1680	17,904	35.36	1760	162,267	15.02
1690	24,204	34.18	1770	202,599	24.85
1700	29,604	23.22	1780	245,574	21.16
1710	42,741	44.37	1790	319,728	30.24

For the trend in land prices in the seventeenth century, *see* V. J. Wyckoff, "Land Prices in Seventeenth Century Maryland," *American Economic Review* 28 (1938):82–88. For a discussion of the growing scarcity of vacant land for freeholds and the consequent growth of leaseholding, *see* Gould, *Land System*, pp. 67–81. Land prices in Talbot County between 1663 and 1750 and in Queen Anne's County between 1707 and 1750 are detailed in Paul G. E. Clemens, "From Tobacco to Grain: Economic Development on Maryland's Eastern Shore, 1660–1750" (Ph.D. diss., University of Wisconsin, 1974), appendix I–E. The decreasing availability of land and the resultant rise in tenancy in one Maryland parish is discussed in Carville V. Earle, *The Evolution of A Tidewater Settlement System, All Hallow's Parish, Maryland, 1650–1783*, The University of Chicago Department of Geography Research Paper no. 170 (Chicago, 1975), pp. 183–85, 193–96.

23. The list is in the proprietary accounts for the year 1733, Calvert Papers, no. 914, Maryland Historical Society, Baltimore, Maryland (hereafter cited as MHS).

24. *See*, for example, the information on Gunpowder Manor lots 15, 21, 27, and 30, all of which were leased prior to 1733, in Gaius Marcus Brumbaugh, *Maryland Records, Colonial, Revolutionary, County and Church*, 2 vols. (1915–28; reprinted, Baltimore, 1967), 2:40–41.

25. Calvert to Tasker, July 9, 1752, *Calvert Papers, Number Two*, pp. 148–49; "Memorandum," n.a., n.d., Executive Papers, portfolio 3, folder 19.

26. A list of tenants exists for the year 1731, but it is primarily confined to Kent Manor leaseholders. See "Lord Baltimore's Account Book," Calvert Papers, no. 912, MHS, cited in Gould, *Land System*, p. 92.

27. Baltimore to Lowe, December 5, 1722, *Archives*, 38:432; Baltimore to Lowe, February 25, 1723, ibid., p. 433; Tasker to Baltimore, February 20, 1743, *Calvert Papers, Number Two*, p. 101.

28. Calvert Papers, nos. 914, 922, MHS.

29. See, for example, the instructions from Baltimore to Lowe, December 5, 1722, *Archives*, 38:432.

30. The terms of leasing land on the proprietary manors prior to 1734 are indicated in the following table, which lists all surviving leases that have been discovered. Western Branch was an alternate name for Collington Manor, located in Prince George's County.

Manor	Date of Lease	Tenure	Acres Leased	Consideration Payment (sterling)	Annual Rent (sterling)
Western Branch	1701	3 lives	200	£4	20 s. + 2 capons
Western Branch	1703	3 lives	200	4	20 s. + 2 capons
Kent Manor	1707	3 lives	83	4	8 s. + 2 capons
Kent Manor	1713	3 lives	100	4	10 s. + 1 capon
Queen Anne's	1726	3 lives	100	4	10 s. + 2 capons
Kent Manor	1731	3 lives	100	2	10 s. + 2 capons

SOURCE: Proprietary Leases A–C, Hall of Records, Annapolis, Maryland.

31. For the Kent Manor Lease, *see* n. 30. Aubrey Land estimates that the average non-slaveholding tobacco planter earned only five to fifteen pounds sterling annually during the decade from 1710 to 1719; *see* "The Tobacco Staple and the Planter's Problems: Technology, Labor, and Crops," *Agricultural History* 43 (1969):74.

32. Although the term "developmental leasing" was not used in proprietary records, it is descriptive of the leasing policy the proprietor adopted for his manors. *See*, for example, "Copy of his Lordship's Instructions to the Agent and Receiver General bearing date 30th March, 1753," Executive Papers, portfolio 3, folder 3; Calvert to Tasker, July 9, 1752, *Calvert Papers, Number Two*, pp. 148–49; Proprietary Leases A–C; Sharpe to Calvert, March 31, 1768, *Archives*, 14:479; A.O. 12/79, f. 15; Baltimore to Calvert, entered March 16, 1673, *Archives*, 15:31; Baltimore to Ward, July 19, 1730, ibid., 37:581.

33. The three volumes of Proprietary Leases A–C at the Hall of Records are transcriptions of original documents in the Scharf Collection, MHS.

34. Proprietary Leases A–C.

35. Proprietary Leases C:619–26; Scharf Papers, 23/45, MHS.

36. Proprietary Leases C:474–76, 431–32; Scharf Papers, 23/45, MHS.

37. Proprietary Leases C:9–11, 21–22, 539–41.

38. Baltimore to Ward, July 19, 1730, *Archives*, 37:581. George Washington adhered to the same principles when renting his own land. In instructions to his manager, Battaile Muse, dated March 8, 1786, Washington wrote: "I am desirous you should always keep in view, first, to lease to no person who has Lands of his own adjoining them; and 2ndly, to no one who does not propose to live on the premises. My reasons are these, in the first case my Land will be cut down, worked and destroyed to save his own, whilst the latter will receive all the improvements. In the second case, if the Tenant does not live thereon it will not meet a much better fate, and negro Quarters and Tobacco pens will probably be the best edifices of the Tenement" (*The Writings of George Washington from the Original Manuscript Sources, 1745–1799*, ed. John C. Fitzpatrick, 39 vols. [Washington, D.C., 1931–44], 28:390–91).

39. For example, Proprietary Leases C:338–39, 347–49, 455–57.

40. Ibid., ff. 539–41.

41. Ibid., ff. 9–11, 455–57, 592–94.

42. Ibid., ff. 596–98.

43. Developmental leasing was employed by large landowners throughout the Chesapeake region. The terms offered by most private landlords were not as advantageous as those given by Lord Baltimore, but lower rents were usually charged in exchange for tenants making specified improvements on their leaseholds. The goal of all developmental leasing plans was to turn uncultivated tracts into habitable tenements that could then be rented or sold at a higher price. Tenants, however, were not always cooperative, as evidenced by George Washington's letter to his steward Battaile Muse, dated November 8, 1787: "If the Tenants do not comply with Covenants of their Leases, they cannot expect that I shall sit quietly under it, for the sole motive of leasing the land at the low rents which they give, was in expectation of having improvements made thereon as are mentioned in the leases, if that is not done a great end for which they were leased are defeated" (*Writings of George Washington*, 29:305).

44. The rental rates for land on Anne Arundel Manor are discussed below. Rents on Susquehannah Manor varied, but were frequently double the normal rate, or twenty shillings sterling per 100 acres. The reason for the different rental rates on Susquehannah Manor is that the manor had originally been privately owned and the right to it was a matter of dispute until the 1760s. Tenants on the manor had taken leases from Lord Baltimore's agents, from the proprietors of Pennsylvania, and from heirs of George Talbot, the original owner of the manor. When Baltimore's agents renewed or reissued leases, they usually granted the lease for the same rent that the tenant had previously paid. *See*, for example, Proprietary Leases C:9–11, 21–22, 55–57, and 64–66. Another variation found in some leases was the requirement that the tenant pay capons in addition to the usual monetary rent, a provision common in English leases for centuries. Capons were required of tenants on Queen Anne's Manor and they are mentioned in a few other leases for manor land on the Eastern Shore. Some or all leases for land in St. Mary's and Charles counties

may also have required capons; see ibid., ff. 235–37, 425–27, and 541–43; and Scharf Papers, 23/45, MHS. There is no evidence that the neutered roosters were ever collected, and it is unlikely that any found their way to the proprietor's table.

45. Between 1754 and 1775, Charles Carroll of Annapolis leased his Monocacy Manor estate (a different tract from the proprietary manor of the same name) for 1,000 pounds of tobacco, four shillings sterling, and two capons per year for 100 acres. One thousand pounds of tobacco was worth as much as ten pounds sterling during the years covered by these leases, or from ten to twenty times the amount paid by most proprietary tenants for the same amount of land. Not only did Carroll's tenants pay much higher rents than proprietary tenants, but their leases were less secure. Carroll's leases were usually short-term oral agreements, and he was free to eject a tenant at will. Other large landowners also leased land at rates of at least 1,000 pounds of tobacco per 100 acres. See Charles Carroll of Annapolis Account Book, 1754–1784; Robert Darnall Ledger, 1787–1821; Hollyday Account Book. 1760–1775; Edward Lloyd Memorandum Book, 1768–1772, Lloyd Papers, box 4, all of which are at the MHS. See also Johann David Schoepf, Travels in the Confederation [1783-1784], trans. and ed. Alfred J. Morrison, 2 vols. (1911; reprinted, New York, 1968), 2:39.

46. See, for example, lots 1, 7, 17, "Sale of Mill Manor," September 24–25, 1781, Maryland State Papers (Series F—Confiscated Property), 13/3/1; lots 1, 2, 7, 9, and 20, "Sale of Calverton Manor," October 13, 1781, ibid., 5/1/8; lots 1, 5, 6, 9, 15, 16, 18, 22, 24, 34, 39, 41, 43, 45, 46, 48, 52, 53, 55, 61, 62, 72, and 74, "Sale of Beaverdam Manor," September 13–15, 1781, ibid., 13/5/1.

47. A.O. 12/79, f. 17; Sharpe to Hamersley, March 1767, Archives, 14:381; Proprietary Leases A–C.

48. The Baltimore Reserves differed from the manor reserves, which were tracts of vacant land extending three miles beyond the boundaries of the proprietary manors. The manor reserves were established in the 1730s and later in an effort to prevent encroachment of patented tracts onto the manors. Manor reserves were leased on the same terms as the manors that they adjoined; see A.O. 12/79, ff. 81, 126.

49. "Memorandum," Executive Papers, portfolio 3, folder 19. Pig Point, located a short distance down the Patuxent River from Anne Arundel Manor, was the site of a tobacco inspection station. Anne Arundel tenants must have contributed much of the tobacco that passed through the Pig Point warehouse, and the high quality of the crops produced in the area was attested to by Joshua Johnson, of the Annapolis firm of Wallace, Davidson, and Johnson. Writing to his partners from London in 1773, Johnson stated that he wanted nothing to do with tobacco shipped from the Potomac because of its inferior quality, but he considered tobacco from the Pig Point warehouse to be the best available. See Jacob M. Price, "Joshua Johnson in London, 1771–1775: Credit and Commercial Organization in the British Chesapeake Trade," in Statesmen, Scholars and Merchants: Essays in Eighteenth-Century History presented to Dame Lucy Sutherland, ed. Anne Witeman, J. S. Bromley, and P. G. M. Dickson (Oxford, 1973), p. 172.

50. A.O. 12/79, f. 15.

51. See George Stewart's lease, dated February 6, 1746, Brumbaugh, Maryland Records, 2:17.

52. Sharpe to Calvert, October 20, [1755], Archives, 6:294.

53. Wicomico, Queen Anne's, Kent, My Lady's, Monocacy, Anne Arundel, and Collington manors were all laid out in approximately rectangular shapes. For references to surveys and plats, see appendix B.

54. Sharpe to Baltimore, May 2, 1754, Archives, 6:53.

55. Sharpe to Calvert, February 10, 1754, ibid., p. 38.

56. Sharpe to Baltimore, May 23, 1760, ibid., 9:407–8.

57. For example, there were 264 1/2 acres of vacant land on Gunpowder Manor in 1767, 1,313 3/4 acres on Zachiah Manor in 1768, and 1,870 1/4 acres on Monocacy Manor in 1768; A.O. 12/79, ff. 131, 136–37, 143. A note at the end of the list of vacancies on Monocacy Manor states that only one of the forty-nine vacancies had a source of water, which probably explains why tenants had avoided the tracts; ibid., f. 143.

58. For a good example of how complex lots could become when nearly all of a manor had been leased, see the plat of Beaverdam Manor, n.d., Plats, division 4, no. 53.

59. For a discussion of the confusion resulting from lost boundaries, *see* Sharpe to Calvert, July 30, 1757, *Archives,* 9:62.

60. Jenifer to Duvall, July 25, 1782, Intendants Letter Book 10:133–34; Calvert to Baltimore, October 26, 1729, *Calvert Papers, Number Two,* p. 79.

61. For example, *see* the description of the patented tract "Mitchem Hills" located on Chaptico Manor, "Lands Patented in his Lordship's Manors," n.d., Scharf Papers, MHS.

62. Calvert to Baltimore, October 26, 1729, *Calvert Papers, Number Two,* p. 79.

63. "Lands Patented in his Lordship's Manors," Scharf Papers, MHS.

64. For example, about one-third of Zachiah Manor was taken up by three large patented tracts and lots had to be surveyed from the interstices between them. *See* the plat of Zachiah Manor, 1782, Plats, division 4, no. 34.

65. The description of the quality of soil on the lots surrounding the three Zachiah Manor patented tracts indicates that the patents had been laid out on the most fertile land on the manor; *see* A.O. 12/79, ff. 139–40.

66. Plats, division 4, no. 1.

67. For the proprietor's visit to the colony and the impact it had on provincial affairs, *see* Barker, *Background of the Revolution,* pp. 129–38.

68. For a discussion of proprietary instructions in the eighteenth century, *see* ibid., pp. 121–22.

69. Sharpe to Calvert, July 30, 1757, *Archives,* 9:62.

70. Manor stewards usually received a 10 percent commission on rents they collected in addition to a rent-free tenement. In 1760, the proprietor suggested lowering the stewards' commission to 5 percent, a move opposed by Governor Sharpe; *see* Sharpe to Baltimore, May 23, 1760, ibid., pp. 403–4. Sharpe may have acceded to the proprietor's demand, however, because Jonathan Hall, the steward for Queen Anne's Manor, received only 5 percent of the rents he collected for the year 1767; *see* Executive Papers, portfolio 3, folder 16. Young Parren, steward for the manors in St. Mary's and Charles counties, however, received 10 percent of his receipts in an account dated January 18, 1768; *see* Proprietary Papers (formerly called Executive Papers, box 0).

71. Proprietary Leases A–C. On July 19, 1730, Baltimore wrote to his agent, Matthew Tilghman Ward, that "as to their [the tenants] bringing their Rents on Christmas day, to the Dwelling House of you my Agent, which by their Leases they are to do, You must oblige them, as far as is consistent with reason" (*Archives,* 37:580). In many cases, requiring tenants to deliver their rents to the agent, or even to the manor steward, was not consistent with reason. According to Sharpe, some of the stewards resided so far from the manors they were responible for that they rarely ever saw them; ibid., 9:62.

72. The figure is based on a 10 percent commission on the maximum possible revenue if all the manor land that Parren was responsible for had been leased.

73. Calvert Papers, nos. 927, 932, 935, 939, 943, 955, 956, 960, 977, MHS.

74. The collections from these two manors may have been adversely affected by the French and Indian War, which caused people living on the frontier to abandon their farms. In a letter to Cecilius Calvert dated May 5, 1756, Sharpe wrote: ". . . if we do nothing for the protection of the Frontiers God knows what will be the Consequence, Conegochiegh is already our most Western Settlement & if the Inhabitants of that part of the Country do not stand their Ground & I think there is little Probability of their doing so, I beleive [*sic*] one might foretell without the Spirit of Prophesy that all that part of Frederick County that lies beyond Frederick Town will be abandoned before this time twelve month at farthest" (*Archives,* 6:409).

75. Executive Papers, portfolio 3, folder 19; A.O. 12/79, f. 127; Prince George's County Unpatented Certificates no. 91. Average revenue per annum for the decade from 1752 to 1761 was derived from Calvert Papers, nos. 927, 932, 935, 939, 943, 955, 956, 960, and 977, MHS. The average maximum revenue assumes that all land on the manors was leased at £0.10.0 sterling per 100 acres, except for Anne Arundel Manor where the estimate is based on £5.0.0 sterling per 100 acres, and that the rents were collected. The estimated maximum revenue compares closely with a contemporary estimate of the minimum revenue that the manors should have produced if they had been properly managed; *see* A.O. 12/79, f. 16. The average of £750.0.0 sterling annual income from the manors listed in the

table is 25 percent lower than Barker's figure of about £1,000.0.0 sterling per annum after mid-century, *see Background of the Revolution*, p. 140. Barker failed to consider that every year some stewards failed to turn in rents they had collected. As a result, manor receipts increased markedly some years because one or more stewards were returning several years' receipts. Irregular returns by stewards account for the large annual variations in the amount of manor rents collected. In 1755, for example, only £381.0.9 1/2 sterling was returned, but two years later total receipts amounted to £1,297.0.11 3/4 sterling.

76. See Calvert to Sharpe, June 12, 1755, *Archives*, 6:223; idem, December 23, 1755, ibid., p. 325; Sharpe to Baltimore, May 23, 1760, ibid., 9:407; Barker, *Background of the Revolution*, p. 267.

77. Sharpe to Baltimore, February 9, 1768, *Archives*, 9:465–67; Sharpe to Hamersley, February 11, 1768, ibid., p. 467; Allen to Sharpe, June 6, 1768, ibid., pp. 501–2; Allen to Sharpe, November 29, 1768, ibid., pp. 558–60. For a discussion of Allen's turbulent relationship with the powerful Dulany family, *see* Aubrey C. Land, *The Dulanys of Maryland: A Biographical Study of Daniel Dulany, the Elder (1685–1753) and Daniel Dulany, the Younger (1722–1797)* (Baltimore, 1955), pp. 280–85, 328–29.

78. A.O. 12/79, f. 16.

79. For example, fifteen of the thirty-nine lots on Zachiah Manor had no improvements as late as 1767, ibid., ff. 139–40.

80. For example, see lot 78, Beaverdam Manor, ibid., f. 142, and lot 6, West St. Mary's Manor, in the survey book for West St. Mary's Manor, published in facsimile in Brumbaugh, *Maryland Records*, 2:xi–xvi.

81. Brumbaugh, *Maryland Records*, 2:39.

82. For example, see lots 26 and 27 on Zachiah Manor, A.O. 12/79, f. 140.

83. For evidence of squatters paying rents, *see* Thomas Prather to [John Ross?], May 11, 1762, in folder labeled "Conegocheigh Manor," originally in Loose Papers Concerning British Confiscated Property, but at present not in any collection (hereafter cited as "Conegocheigh Manor" folder). For an example of persons occupying manor land with no lease and without paying rents, *see* the deposition of Joseph Williams, n.d. [1762?], entitled "Williams Application," ibid. See also, lots 47, 52, and 55 on Beaverdam Manor, which were inhabited by tenants who apparently were paying rents although the leases on their lots had expired and had not been renewed; Brumbaugh, *Maryland Records*, 2:67–68.

84. Kent County Unpatented Certificates, no. 121.

85. For example, *see* Henry Downes to Clement Holliday, June 10, 1782, Executive Papers, box 34; James G. Heron to William Pinkney, March 30, 1792, British Confiscated Property Papers, folder no. 57.

86. The account of rents collected in 1757 is from "Monocacy Mannor, A List of Persons that live on," Scharf Papers, MHS. Leases on the manor issued prior to 1758 were for three lives, but after that date for only twenty-one years. Thirty-seven three-life leases were still in force on Monocacy Manor in 1782, "Sales on Monocacy Manor," British Confiscated Property Papers, folder no. 66. Some of the twenty-one year leases were probably renewals on three-life leases, which would have increased both the number of lots and the acreage leased on the manor in 1757.

87. "Christmas, 1765, Totals for the manors in St. Mary's County, Young Parran, Steward," in Proprietary Papers. Proprietary leaseholders were not unique in their inability to pay their annual rents. For a discussion of arrears owed by tenants on private estates in the Northern Neck of Virginia, *see* Willard F. Bliss, "The Rise of Tenancy in Virginia," *VMHB* 58(1950):433–36.

88. A.O. 12/79, f. 16.

89. Instructions from Baltimore to Sharpe, dated December 20 and 27, 1760, Executive Papers, portfolio 3, folder 5.

90. *See* lots 2, 5, 7, 9, and 10, "West St. Mary's Manor, Survey Book," in Brumbaugh, *Maryland Records*, 2:xi–xvi.

91. *See,* for example, "A List of Rents, Arrears & Alienation Fines Received from the Sundry Tenants on his Lordships Manors of Mill, Woosley [*sic*]," 1767, Proprietary Papers.

92. Baltimore to Ward, July 19, 1730, *Archives*, 37:580–81; Baltimore to Ward, January 29, 1730, ibid., p. 582; Calvert to Tasker, May 15, 1752, *Calvert Papers, Number Two*, pp.

148–49; "Copy of his Lordship's Instructions to the Agent and Receiver General bearing date 30th of March, 1753 . . . ," Executive Papers, portfolio 3, folder 3.

93. Donnell MacClure Owings, *His Lordship's Patronage, Offices of Profit in Colonial Maryland* (Baltimore, 1953), pp. 121–22. The administration of Governor Sharpe can be especially well documented because of his voluminous correspondence, which has been printed in *Archives*, vols. 6, 9, 14, and 31. A different assessment of Governor Sharpe was provided by Jonathan Boucher, the noted Anglican minister, tutor, and Tory, who termed Sharpe "a well-meaning but weak man, and much under the influence of a Mr. Ridout, his Secretary" (*Reminiscences of an American Loyalist, 1738–1789*, ed. Jonathan Bouchier [Boston and New York, 1925], p. 54).

94. May 14, 1755, *Archives*, 6:206–7.

95. Sharpe to Calvert, November 29, 1753, ibid., 6:12–15.

96. Calvert to Sharpe, March 23, 1754, ibid., 6:40–42.

97. Sharpe to Calvert, October 20, [1755], ibid., p. 295.

98. Sharpe to Baltimore, February 4, 1757, ibid., p. 522. Copies of three of these plats are still extant. The Wicomico Manor plat is fairly detailed, including the bounds of every leasehold and the location of the river and roads on the manor, Plats, division 4, no. 1. The plats of Woolsey and Mill Manors include only the boundaries of the manors with no indication about the location of leaseholds, Gift Collection, D 371, nos. 14, 171.

99. Sharpe to Baltimore, February 4, 1757, *Archives*, 6:522.

100. Ibid.

101. Plats of some manors may never have been executed. None had been returned for Monocacy, North East, Elk, and Wicomico manors by April 1768, and there is no evidence that they were made after that date; *see* "A State of the Sales of His Lordship's Mannours," Executive Papers, portfolio 3, folder 19.

102. Sharpe to Baltimore, February 4, 1757, *Archives*, 6:522.

103. Sharpe to Calvert, July 30, 1757, ibid., 9:62.

104. Ibid., pp. 62–63.

105. Ibid.

106. December 26, 1757, ibid., p. 116.

107. Sharpe to Baltimore, May 23, 1760, ibid., 9:403.

108. Lloyd purchased the land for the Revenue Office in the summer of 1763, but construction did not begin for another three years; *see* Sharpe to Calvert, September, 1763, ibid., 14:117; Sharpe to Baltimore, October 22, 1766, ibid., p. 336.

109. Sharpe to Calvert, February 10, 1754, ibid., 6:38; Sharpe to Calvert, June 6, 1754, ibid., p. 71.

110. *See* the lease for lot 65 issued to Peter Hertzog, dated September 29, 1759, Brumbaugh, *Maryland Records*, 2:56.

111. Prather to Ross, June 23, 1762, "Conegocheigh Manor" folder. In one case, Governor Sharpe received a petition asking that a lease be issued under the old terms and he was inclined to grant the request. Sharpe wrote to Calvert on November 13, 1764, that in regard to a petition "of Mrs. Harrison on behalf of her Son and Infant I can only say that it was I apprehend in a great measure owing to Mr. Harrison's own Dilitoriness that he did not obtain a Lease on Lives for the Land mentioned in the Petition before His Lordships prohibition to granting Mannour Leases for a longer Term than Twenty one years was received & published here, but at the same time as the then Steward of the Mannor seems to have been to blame also, & Mr. Harrison who was a Person of the most upright behaviour & in every respect a worthy good Man has left his Widow (a Woman of great Merit) & a young Family in Distress or at least poorly provided for, I should be glad if His Lordship would shew her some favour by ordering a Lease be granted to the Orphan on the old Conditions with this exception that instead of the Terms being for three Lives it may be only for a certain Number of years" (*Archives*, 14:183).

112. Exceptions can be found, but in general all leases issued after 1760 were for twenty-one years at double the old rents; *see* Brumbaugh, *Maryland Records*, 2:4–78.

113. January 16, 1765, *Archives*, 14:189–93. The manors designated for sale were Pancaya (Pangaiah), Beaverdam, Mill, Woolsey, and Bridgewater (Wolcote). In addition, all uncultivated and untenanted reserved lands around the manors were to be sold. The manors and reserves contained a total of 28,530 acres.

114. Sharpe to Calvert, July 10, 1765, ibid., pp. 202-4.

115. Ibid., 32:134-40; Sharpe to Calvert, July 10, 1765, ibid., 14:202-4.

116. Gould states that "the spendthrift proprietor never let the interests of posterity interfere with the interests of the present" (*Land System*, p. 100). Frederick, Lord Baltimore, traveled extensively, and considered himself both enlightened and literate. Following his tour of the Mideast, Baltimore published *A Tour to the East in the Years 1763 and 1764. With Remarks on the City of Constantinople and the Turks. Also select Pieces of Oriental Wit, Poetry and Wisdom* (London, 1767), and in 1769 and 1771 books of poetry written by him were published in Venice. Undoubtedly much to his chagrin, none of Baltimore's own publications equalled the popularity of *The Trial of Frederick Calvert . . . for the Rape on the Body of Sarah Woodcock*, issued in 1768 in London, Dublin, and Edinburgh, which recounted in detail the trial at which Baltimore was acquitted of the alleged indiscretion.

117. Gould, *Land System*, pp. 99–100; Dulany's letter is printed in *Calvert Papers, Number Two*, pp. 242-43.

118. *Calvert Papers, Number Two*, pp. 148–49.

119. For the annual revenue from the manors, *see* table 1-3. The gross proprietary revenue in each year is derived from Barker, *Background of the Revolution*, table II, p. 380.

120. Rents due for the manors in Charles and St. Mary's counties had risen from an estimated maximum of £176.0.0 sterling in the 1750s to an actual amount due of £220.16.5 sterling in 1766, undoubtedly because of the doubling of rents on new and renewed leases; *see* table 1-3 and "A List of His Lordships Mannours in Charles and St. Mary's Co.," Proprietary Papers.

121. Dulany to Calvert, September 10, 1764, *Calvert Papers, Number Two*, pp. 243-44.

Chapter 2

1. For the dates of survey, size, and location of the sample manors, *see* chapter 1 and appendix B.

2. A.O. 12/79, f. 155; Gauis Marcus Brumbaugh, *Maryland Records, Colonial, Revolutionary, County and Church*, 2 vols. (1915–28; reprinted, Baltimore, 1967), 2:4–14, 25–33, 39–43, 63–73.

3. In 1768, 1,870 1/4 of a total of 9,231 1/2 acres of leasehold land on Monocacy Manor were vacant; *see* Brumbaugh, *Maryland Records*, 2:60.

4. No abstract of leases for Queen Anne's Manor has been located. The data in table 3-1 are based on the holdings of tenants on the manor in 1767 when the proprietary survey was made; *see* A.O. 12/79, f. 129.

5. Kinship usually had to be assumed on the basis of common surnames. In many instances, the exact relationship between two or more tenants with the same last name could be determined from probate records, family genealogies, or information contained in three-life leases. When the kinship of two persons with the same surname was doubtful, they were counted as belonging to separate families.

6. It is difficult to determine how frequently leaseholders died without close kin, because such persons usually did not leave wills. One who did was Anthony Cameron, a leaseholder on Kent Manor who died in 1751. He devised his tenement to a friend who was also a tenant on the manor; *see* Kent County Original Wills, no. 239.

7. *See*, for example, the inventory of Abraham Parker, tenant on Calverton Manor, Charles County Inventories B 1:236; inventory of Richard Vincent, leaseholder on Zachiah Manor, Charles County Inventories 5:277. Throughout this chapter, unless specifically noted, all sums are given in Maryland currency. Although the exchange rate fluctuated during the colonial period, after the French and Indian War 1.0 pound sterling was generally worth 1.67 pounds Maryland currency.

8. Brumbaugh, *Maryland Records*, 2:4–73.

9. The poverty of leaseholders who migrated from the manors must be assumed because there is no way to determine where they settled or how large an estate they took with them. On the other hand, no tenant who migrated is known to have held freehold land or slaves in addition to his manor tenement, the standard measures of wealth in the Chesapeake Bay region during the eighteenth century.

10. "Deposition of Mary Sparkes of Queen Anne's County, taken March 17, 1756,"

attached to the lease for the Queen Anne's Manor tenement leased to Benjamin Riddle, in folder labeled, "Riddle, Benjamin, Queen Anne's County, Lease to," Scharf Papers, MHS.

11. For example, Robert Hart, a resident of Cecil County, acquired lot 39 on Kent Manor, probably as a speculative investment because the lot was never improved; see A.O. 12/79, f. 130. George Plater purchased lots 1 and 13 on Beaverdam Manor. Both tracts were well developed, but Plater was one of the largest landowners in the county and did not cultivate the tracts himself; see Brumbaugh, *Maryland Records*, 2:63; A.O. 12/79, f. 141. Philip Key, another wealthy St. Mary's County freeholder, acquired manor property, probably for speculation or subleasing; see lot 37, Chaptico Manor, Brumbaugh, *Maryland Records*, 2:71; see also A.O. 12/79, f. 136.

12. For a discussion of tobacco and maize cultivation, see chapter 4.

13. The following is based on an analysis of the descriptions of natural resources on the manors found in A.O. 12/79, ff. 129–43.

14. The meaning of the word "broken" when used to describe a condition of the soil is ambiguous. The term clearly implies a topographic feature that rendered the soil surface uneven, but the width and depth of the cuts and ravines could vary. The most probable cause for a broken soil surface was water erosion.

15. For a discussion of soil wastage in relationship to the size of landholdings and the amount of deforestation, see A.R. Hall, *Early Erosion-Control Practices in Virginia*, U.S. Department of Agriculture Miscellaneous Publication no. 256 (Washington, D.C., 1938), pp. 6–7.

16. The underrepresentation of the poor in colonial Maryland probate records varied over time and from one county to another. In general, the poorest whites were more likely to have their estates inventoried in the seventeenth and early eighteenth centuries than they were at the end of the colonial period. The conclusion that the poor are greatly underrepresented in the probate records filed after the mid-eighteenth century is based on my own work with Talbot County inventories and an unpublished report prepared by Lois Green Carr of the St. Mary's City Commission. For general comments on the failure of some people, especially the poorer members of the community living outside population centers, to register vital events, see James H. Cassedy, *Demography in Early America: Beginnings of the Statistical Mind, 1600–1800* (Cambridge, Mass., 1969), pp. 36–37.

17. The courthouse fire of 1831 destroyed all the original probate papers, post-Revolutionary administration accounts to 1798, and inventories to 1795; see Morris L. Radoff, Gust Skordas, and Phebe R. Jacobsen, *The Courthouses and Records of Maryland. Part Two: The Records* (Annapolis, Md., 1963), p. 157.

18. St. Mary's County Debt Book, 1767, f. 29.

19. Calverton Manor was located much farther from the Charles County Courthouse at Port Tobacco than was Zachiah Manor, which may account for the smaller number of probate records from tenants on the former than from tenants on the latter.

20. Estate size is defined as the total value of the inventory in current money, less the value of manor land if included, plus any additional inventories and assets added in the accounts of the estate. The inventory was made by two court-appointed citizens, usually with the aid of a relative of the deceased and one or more of the creditors of the estate. The inventory consisted of an itemized list and the value of all personal property belonging to the deceased. The account was a report submitted by the executor or administrator of an estate to the county court listing the value of the inventory, all money received from debts due to the estate, and all other income accruing to the estate, such as the value of crops harvested. Usually more than one account was submitted before an estate was finally settled. The difference between the inventory, debts collected, and other money added to the estate, and the charges against the estate was the balance, or net worth, of the estate. If total assets exceeded total debts, the balance was distributed to the heirs of the deceased; if the estate had a negative balance, the estate was usually sold and as many of the debts paid in full or in part as was possible.

21. Charles County Inventories 5:277–79.

22. Accounts 63:202–4; ibid., 69:247–48.

23. For a discussion of the amount of crops that could be produced on an acre of land, see chapter 4.

24. Accounts 69:247–48; for a discussion of the relationship between the number of tenants compared to laborers in tenant households and the effect this ratio had on impeding capital accumulation, *see* Allan Kulikoff, "Tobacco and Slaves: Population, Economy and Society in Eighteenth-Century Prince George's County, Maryland" (Ph.D. diss., Brandeis University, 1976), pp. 158–61.

25. *See,* for example, Wills 27:117; Kent County Inventories 10:141.

26. Inventories 80:193.

27. Wills 37:375; Inventories 104:111.

28. Kent County Inventories 10:45, 141.

29. Kent County Original Inventories, box 21, no. 54; Inventories 92:92, 99; ibid., 97:154.

30. Kent County Inventories 10:208; ibid., 9:194; ibid., 10:63.

31. Brumbaugh, *Maryland Records,* 2:39–41.

32. Baltimore County Debt Book, 1768, ff. 24, 28; Wills 30:862; Baltimore County Wills 4:394.

33. Baltimore County Deeds T.R. no. C:489; Baltimore County Original Wills, box 15, no. 35; Baltimore County Original Inventories, box 23, no. 70.

34. Brumbaugh, *Maryland Records,* 2:51–60. For the non-English migration into the Monocacy River Valley, *see* Charles Albro Barker, *The Background of the Revolution in Maryland* (1940; reprinted, Hamden, Conn., 1967), pp. 8–10; Dieter Cunz, *The Maryland Germans: A History* (Princeton, 1948), pp. 47–93; and William Eddis, *Letters from America,* ed. Aubrey C. Land (Cambridge, Mass., 1969), pp. 50–52.

35. The slaveowners were Charles Hedge, Jr., Casper Devilbess (Devilbiss), and George Devilbess (Devilbiss), and only the last resided on the manor; *see* Frederick County Inventories C no. 3:65; ibid., p. 680; Frederick County Wills G.M. no. 3:159.

36. The statement is based on an analysis of debt book entries and wills for all tenants in St. Mary's, Charles, and Frederick counties.

37. Brumbaugh, *Maryland Records,* 2:51; Frederick County Debt Book, 1768, f. 14.

38. Brumbaugh, *Maryland Records,* 2:58; A.O. 12/79, f. 142; Frederick County Wills A no. 1:58; Frederick County Inventories A no. 1:196.

39. Brumbaugh, *Maryland Records,* 2:55; Frederick County Inventories C no. 3:328.

40. Leaseholders or lives on leases who left the manor were Handell Hann (Henn), Solomon Douther, Christian Rodebaugh, and John Hann (Henn); *see* Brumbaugh, *Maryland Records,* 2:51–56.

Chapter 3

1. Among the standard works on colonial Tidewater architecture are Henry Chandlee Forman, *Early Manor and Plantation Houses of Maryland* (Easton, Md., 1934); idem, *The Architecture of the Old South: The Medieval Style* (Cambridge, Mass., 1948); idem, *Tidewater Maryland Architecture and Gardens* (New York, 1956); Thomas Tileston Waterman, *The Dwellings of Colonial America* (Chapel Hill, 1950); idem, *The Mansions of Virginia, 1706–1776* (Chapel Hill, 1945); J. M. Hammond, *Colonial Mansions of Maryland and Delaware* (Philadelphia, 1914); Sidney Fiske Kimball, *Domestic Architecture of the American Colonies and of the Early Republic* (New York, 1927); Hugh Morrison, *Early American Architecture from the First Colonial Settlements to the National Period* (New York, 1952); and Katherine Scarborough, *Homes of the Cavaliers* (Cambridge, Md., 1969). The architectural features of a great many eighteenth-century Maryland houses, including numerous smaller structures, are discussed in Edward C. Papenfuse, Gregory A. Stiverson, Susan A. Collins, and Lois Green Carr, *Maryland: A New Guide to the Old Line State* (Baltimore, 1976).

2. Thomas Jefferson, *Notes on the State of Virginia,* ed. William Peden (Chapel Hill, 1955), p. 152.

3. Benjamin Henry Latrobe, *The Journal of Latrobe* (New York, 1905), p. 23; *see also* Johann David Schoepf, *Travels in the Confederation [1783–1784],* trans. and ed. Alfred J. Morrison, 2 vols. (New York, 1968), 2:32–33.

4. The average dimensions are derived from the mean lengths and widths recorded for each dwelling on the manor.

5. "Valuation of the Estate of Elizabeth Plater, orphan of Col. George Plater," St. Mary's County Valuations and Indentures, 1780–1808, ff. 159–60.

6. John Ferdinand Dalziel Smyth, *A Tour in the United States of America*, 2 vols. (1784; reprinted, New York, 1968), 1:49.

7. Forman, *Architecture of the Old South*, pp. 16–17; Harold R. Shurtleff, *The Log Cabin Myth: A Study of the Early Dwellings of the English Colonists in North America* (Cambridge, Mass., 1939), pp. 16–20; Morrison, *Early American Architecture*, pp. 22–34, 136, 138–40, 157–58.

8. Forman, *Architecture of the Old South*, p. 20; Shurtleff, *Log Cabin Myth*, photograph opposite p. 184; Henry Glassie, *Pattern in the Material Folk Culture of the Eastern United States* (Philadelphia, 1968), pp. 113–14; C. A. Weslager, *The Log Cabin in America: From Pioneer Days to the Present* (New Brunswick, N.J., 1969), p. 92.

9. A.O. 12/79, f. 133. The extent to which Maxwell was unusual compared to other tenants is revealed by his inventory, which included fifty-one slaves, a gold watch, a spinnet, a *"chamera observo* and some views," and "9 heads of the antients," Charles County Inventories A.F. 7:346.

10. Lot 5, A.O. 12/79, f. 133.

11. "Travel Diary of Bishop and Mrs. Reichel and their Company from Lititz to Salem in the Wachau (Wachovia) From May 22, to June 15, 1780," in Newton D. Mereness, ed., *Travels in the American Colonies* (New York, 1916), p. 590.

12. Only one dwelling on the sample manors was described as being two stories high. The structure was a two-story log tavern on Monocacy Manor; *see* lot 63, A.O. 12/79, f. 142.

13. Julia Cherry Spruill, *Women's Life and Work in the Southern Colonies* (1938; reprinted, New York, 1972), p. 22.

14. John Beale Bordley, *Essay and Notes on Husbandry and Rural Affairs*, 2nd ed. (Philadelphia, 1801), pp. 184–85.

15. Landon Carter stored unshucked corn in tobacco houses; *see The Diary of Colonel Landon Carter of Sabine Hall, 1752–1778*, ed. Jack P. Greene, 2 vols. (Charlottesville, Va. 1965), 1:354.

16. Bordley, *Essay and Notes*, pp. 141, 169, 184–85; Harry J. Carman, ed., *American Husbandry* (New York, 1939), p. 197; Lewis Cecil Gray, *History of Agriculture in the Southern United States to 1860*, 2 vols. (1933; reprinted, Gloucester, Mass., 1958), 1:145–47, 200–2, 204–8.

17. A.O. 12/79, ff. 141–42.

18. Edward Kimber, describing the houses at Snow Hill, St. Mary's County, noted: "Some have their foundations in the Ground, others are built on Puncheons or Logs, a Foot or two from the Earth, which is more airy, and a Defence against the Vermin" ("Observations in Several Voyages and Travels in America," *WMQ*, 1st ser. 15 [1907]: 153). The "posted" dwellings described by the manor surveyor were probably frame buildings set on posts, such as those Kimber saw at Snow Hill.

19. Weslager, *Log Cabin*, pp. 135–205; Shurtleff, *Log Cabin Myth*, pp. 163–85.

20. Gaius Marcus Brumbaugh, *Maryland Records, Colonial, Revolutionary, County and Church*, 2 vols. (1915–28; reprinted, Baltimore, 1967), 2:39–41; A.O. 12/79, f. 131.

21. For a description of the various types of log construction, *see* Shurtleff, *Log Cabin Myth*, pp. 11, 171–72, 175; Weslager, *Log Cabin*, pp. 8–19.

22. A.O. 12/79, f. 132.

23. *Travels in North America in the Years 1780, 1781 and 1782 by the Marquis de Chastellux*, trans. and ed. Howard C. Rice, Jr., 2 vols. (Chapel Hill, 1963), 2:438; Fred Shelley, ed., "The Journal of Ebenezer Hazard in Virginia, 1777," *VMHB* 62 (1954):414.

24. Bordley, *Essay and Notes*, pp. 182–83.

Chapter 4

1. The standard treatment of agriculture in the Chesapeake Bay region is Lewis Cecil Gray, *History of Agriculture in the Southern United States to 1860*, 2 vols. (1933; reprinted, Gloucester, Mass., 1958), especially 1: chs. 2, 7. *See also* Avery Odelle Craven, *Soil Exhaustion as a Factor in the Agricultural History of Virginia and Maryland, 1606–1860* (1926; re-

printed, Gloucester, Mass., 1965); Arthur Pierce Middleton, *Tobacco Coast: A Maritime History of Chesapeake Bay in the Colonial Era* (Newport News, Va., 1953), pp. 156–77.

2. *See* especially, Aubrey C. Land, "Economic Behavior in a Planting Society: The Eighteenth-Century Chesapeake," *Journal of Southern History* 33 (1967):469–85.

3. *See* private leases cited above, ch. 1, no. 45; *see also* Willard F. Bliss, "The Rise of Tenancy in Virginia," *VMHB* 58 (1950):430; Rodney C. Loehr, "Self-Sufficiency on the Farm," *Agricultural History* 26 (1952):37–41.

4. John Beale Bordley, *Essay and Notes on Husbandry and Rural Affairs*, 2nd ed. (Philadelphia, 1801), pp. 134–35.

5. James T. Lemon, "Urbanization and the Development of Eighteenth-Century Southeastern Pennsylvania and Adjacent Delaware," *WMQ*, 3rd ser. 24 (1967):502–7; Charles Albro Barker, *The Background of the Revolution in Maryland* (1940; reprinted, Hamden, Conn., 1967), p. 98; Clarence P. Gould, *Money and Transportation in Maryland: 1720–1765*, JHSH, ser. 33 (Baltimore, 1915), pp. 13–14. For a recent analysis of diversification on the Eastern Shore, *see* Paul G. E. Clemens, "From Tobacco to Grain: Economic Development on Maryland's Eastern Shore, 1660–1750" (Ph.D. diss., University of Wisconsin, 1974), pp. 100–34.

6. Gould, *Money and Transportation*, pp. 125–28; "Sundry Purchasers of Kent Manor to the Intendant," Intendants Letter Book 10:147; John F. Walzer, "Colonial Philadelphia and Its Backcountry," *Winterthur Portfolio* 7 (Charlottesville, Va., 1972), pp. 169–70.

7. Middleton, *Tobacco Coast*, pp. 180–82; Barker, *Background of the Revolution*, pp. 98, 109–10; Edward C. Papenfuse, Jr., "Economic Analysis and Loyalist Strategy During the American Revolution: Robert Alexander's Remarks on the Economy of the Penninsula or Eastern Shore of Maryland," *Maryland Historical Magazine* 68 (1973): 173–95.

8. William Strickland, *Journal of a Tour in the United States of America, 1794–1795*, ed. J. E. Strickland (New York, 1971), p. 223.

9. Barker, *Background of the Revolution*, p. 12; lot 9, A.O. 12/79, f. 142.

10. John Mitchell argued in *The Present State of Great Britain and North America* (1767; reprinted, New York, 1970), p. 136, that between forty and fifty acres per laborer were needed when tobacco was the staple crop. Mitchell's treatise was a polemic against imperial restrictions on western settlement, however, so his figures were probably exaggerated in order to give credence to his argument that the region east of the mountains was rapidly filling up. It was necessary to rest tobacco fields every few years, and they usually had to lie fallow for about twenty years before they could be replanted with tobacco; *see* Papenfuse, "Planter Behavior," p. 304. Assuming that tobacco could be grown three years in succession before the land had to be fallowed for twenty years, only twenty-four acres were necessary for the average tenant without slaves or servants, because most could not plant more than three acres in the crop. Three acres was considered the maximum acreage that could be tended by an adult slave who worked full-time in the fields; *see* Richard Parkinson, *A Tour in America, in 1798, 1799, and 1800. Exhibiting Sketches of Society and Manners, and a Particular Account of the American System of Agriculture, with its Recent Improvements*, 2 vols. (London, 1805), 2:413.

11. Edward C. Papenfuse, Jr., "Planter Behavior and Economic Opportunity in a Staple Economy," *Agricultural History* 46 (1972):305–6.

12. Middleton, *Tobacco Coast*, 107–9; Jacob M. Price, "The Rise of Glasgow in the Chesapeake Tobacco Trade, 1707–1775," *WMQ*, 3rd ser. 11 (1954):179–99.

13. *See* Gregory A. Stiverson, "Gentlemen of Industry, Skill, and Application: Plantation Management in Eighteenth-Century Virginia" (unpub. research report, Research Department, Colonial Williamsburg Foundation, Williamsburg, Va., 1975), pp. 97–98, 114–15.

14. Gray, *History of Agriculture*, 1:215–18.

15. Bordley, *Essay and Notes*, pp. 134–35.

16. Middleton, *Tobacco Coast*, pp. 125–32; Papenfuse, "Planter Behavior," pp. 307–11; Gray, *History of Agriculture*, 1:268–76.

17. Bordley, *Essay and Notes*, pp. 184–85; A.O. 12/79, ff. 131–43; Papenfuse, "Planter Behavior," pp. 303–6.

18. William Eddis, *Letters from America*, ed. Aubrey C. Land (Cambridge, Mass., 1969),

p. 67. *See also* Bordley, *Essay and Notes,* p. 39; Johann David Schoepf, *Travels in the Confederation* [*1783-1784*], 2 vols. (1911; reprinted, New York, 1968), 1:36; "Pehr Kalm's Description of Maize, How It is Planted and Cultivated in North America, Together with the Many Uses of This Crop Plant," ed. and trans. Esther L. Larsen, *Agricultural History* 9 (1935):98–117.

19. *The Diary of Colonel Landon Carter of Sabine Hall, 1752-1778,* ed. Jack P. Greene, 2 vols. (Charlottesville, Va., 1965), 2:679–80; *The Journal of John Harrower: An Indentured Servant in the Colony of Virginia, 1773-1776,* ed. Edward Miles Riley (Williamsburg, Va., 1963), pp. 52–53; John Ferdinand Dalziel Smyth, *A Tour in the United States of America,* 2 vols. (1784, reprinted, New York, 1968), 2:123; Parkinson, *Tour,* 2:595–96; John Beale Bordley, *A Summary View of the Courses of Crops, In the Husbandry of England and Maryland* (Philadelphia, 1784), pp. 4, 16–18.

20. William Tatham, *An Historical and Practical Essay on the Culture and Commerce of Tobacco* (London, 1800), pp. 17–18.

21. Papenfuse, "Planter Behavior," pp. 305–6.

22. Schoepf, *Travels,* 2:37. Landon Carter counted the number of kernels in a pint of corn on two occasions. In 1766 he arrived at a figure of 800 kernels in a pint, or 51,200 per bushel, and in 1772 he counted 860 kernels per pint, or 55,040 in a bushel (*Diary,* 1:296; 2:678). The calculation of the number of hills that could be planted with two bushels of seed assumes that four kernels were planted in each hill, the figure mentioned by Schoepf, *Travels,* 2:37.

23. For a discussion of the prudent overplanting of maize, *see* Gregory A. Stiverson, "Early American Farming: A Comment," *Agricultural History* 50 (1976):38–40.

24. William Strickland, *Observations on the Agriculture of the United States* (1801; reprinted in facsimile in *Journal of a Tour,* ed. J. E. Strickland, p. 43); Parkinson, *Tour,* 1:200; Francois Alexandre La Rochefoucauld Liancourt, *Travels Through the United States of North America, The Country of the Iroquois, and Upper Canada, in the Years 1795, 1796, and 1797; With an Authentic Account of Lower Canada. By the Duke de la Rochefoucault Liancourt,* 4 vols. (London, 1799), 3:142.

25. Bordley, *Essay and Notes,* pp. 14–17, 36; Strickland, *Observations,* 42–43.

26. Gaius Marcus Brumbaugh, *Maryland Records, Colonial, Revolutionary, County and Church,* 2 vols. (1915–28; reprinted, Baltimore, 1967), 2:4–74; A.O. 12/79, f. 129; Papenfuse, "Planter Behavior," pp. 303–5.

27. Among the more important sources for crop yields in the Chesapeake Bay region during the eighteenth century are Bordley, *Summary View;* idem, *Essay and Notes;* R. O. Bausman and J. A. Munroe, eds., "James Tilton's Notes on the Agriculture of Delaware in 1788," *Agricultural History* 20 (1946):183–84; Mitchell, *Present State,* p. 140; "Estimate of the Cost of Mrs. French's Land... ," [1790?], in *The Writings of George Washington from the Original Manuscript Sources,* ed. John C. Fitzpatrick, 39 vols. (Washington, D.C., 1931–44) 31:188–89; Gertrude R. B. Richards, ed., "Dr. Stuart's Report to President Washington on Agricultural Conditions in Northern Virginia," *VMHB* 61 (1953):287; A. G. Bradley, ed., *The Journal of Nicholas Cresswell, 1774–1777,* 2nd ed. (New York, 1928), p. 25. Cf. James T. Lemon, *The Best Poor Man's Country: A Geographical Study of Early Southeastern Pennsylvania* (Baltimore, 1972), p. 154; and Harry Roy Merrens, *Colonial North Carolina in the Eighteenth Century* (Chapel Hill, 1964), p. 234.

28. Harry J. Carman, ed., *American Husbandry* (New York, 1939), p. 197; Richards, ed., "Dr. David Stuart's Report," p. 287; Bordley, *Essay and Notes,* pp. 141, 182, 185; Craven, *Soil Exhaustion,* p. 33.

29. Gray, *History of Agriculture,* 1:169–70; Bordley, *Essay and Notes,* pp. 39, 542.

30. Bordley, *Essay and Notes,* p. 269.

31. Ibid., pp. 245, 247.

32. Ibid., p. 245; Bausman and Monroe, eds., "James Tilton's Notes," p. 183. Treading remained the dominant method of threshing wheat until well into the nineteenth century. In a letter written March 30, 1816, Nicholas Ridgeley of Dover, Delaware, stated that "eight tenths, if not more, of all the wheat which is carried to Brandywine, Philadelphia or Baltimore, from this penninsula, is trodden out by horses, and will continue to be so, until some cheaper and better plan can be invented" (*Memoirs of the Philadelphia Society for Promoting Agriculture,* 6 vols. to date [Philadelphia, 1808-], 4:29).

33. Gray, *History of Agriculture*, 1:170–71.

34. Bordley, *Essay and Notes*, p. 269.

35. Thomas Jefferson confirmed that these figures represented a practical maximum and minimum for the production of tobacco and wheat respectively. He wrote: "We find it easier to make an hundred bushels of wheat than a thousand weight of tobacco, and they are worth more when made" (*Notes on the State of Virginia*, ed. William Peden [Chapel Hill, 1955], p. 168).

36. Middleton, *Tobacco Coast*, 107–9. By comparing the price of wheat in Philadelphia to that of Virginia tobacco in Holland, Clemens established that "wheat prices increased relative to tobacco prices in the late 1740's and the early 1750's and again in the early 1760's" ("From Tobacco to Grain," p. 130 and table 9); *see also* the table for wheat prices, 1710–1775, and the table for tobacco prices, 1711–1775, in Allan Kulikoff, "Tobacco and Slaves: Population, Economy and Society in Eighteenth-Century Prince George's County, Maryland" (Ph.D. diss., Brandeis University, 1976), pp. 497–500, 501–4.

37. Papenfuse, "Planter Behavior," pp. 307–10.

38. A similar relationship between tenants and storekeepers existed in Virginia. In 1759, Robert Bristow asked his steward, Mr. Lashbrooks, if his tenants could not pay their annual rents to him in money rather than in tobacco. Lashbrooks replied, "The Tenants in Common are as much in Debt to the Merch[an]ts as their whole Crop comes too, in which case he never pays money & as their rent is frequently paid thro the Credit they have with the [Merchants] they must submit to his Choice." Questions and answers enclosed with letters dated 14 and 24 March 1759, Robert Bristow Letter Book, Loyalist Claims, Public Record Office, A.O. 13/84, London (microfilm copy available at the Research Department, Colonial Williamsburg Foundation, Williamsburg, Va.)

39. Bordley, *Essay and Notes*, p. 301.

40. The growth of a native merchant marine in the first half of the eighteenth century was also important, because it greatly expanded the ability of farmers to market foodstuffs in the West Indies; *see* Middleton, *Tobacco Coast*, pp. 180–86.

41. In 1733, over 60.0 percent of the households in Talbot County on the Eastern Shore owned no slaves; fifty years later the percentage had dropped to 48.2 percent. The largest expansion in slaveholding was among small planters. In the earlier year only 24.1 percent of landowners with less than 200 acres owned a slave, but in the latter year 44.7 percent were slave owners. Figures compiled from Talbot County Debt Books; Talbot County Tax List, 1733, MHS, and the State Assessment of 1783, Scharf Papers, MHS.

42. In 1783, slaves comprised 44.7 percent of the population of Charles County on the lower Western Shore and only 23.4 percent of the population of Baltimore County; *see* "Summary of the 1783 Assessment," Scharf Collection, MHS. For slaveholders on Gunpowder Manor, *see* above, table 2–13.

43. This estimate is based on an analysis of the arable land in Talbot County in 1783, State Assessment of 1783, MHS.

44. This assumes that the wheat, maize, fallow, and pasture fields were approximately the same size; *see* Parkinson, *Tour*, 1:200.

Chapter 5

1. For the first order to sell the manors, *see* Baltimore to Sharpe, January 16, 1765, *Archives*, 14:189–93; for Sharpe's response and the difficulties the order created, *see* Sharpe to Calvert, July 10, 1765, ibid., pp. 202–5; the second sale order is in ibid., 32:134–40; *see also* Hamersley to Sharpe, February 23, 1766, ibid., 14:266–67; Charles Albro Barker, *The Background of the Revolution in Maryland* (1940; reprinted, Hamden, Conn., 1967), pp. 264–66. Writing in August 1766 to his employers, Farell and Jones, Bristol tobacco merchants, the Virginian John Wayles commented on Jordan's arrival in the colonies: "Mr John Morton Jerdon [*sic*] & his very Pretty wife Arrived here in May. He is in the Character of Lord Baltimores Agent & is empowered with others to sell his Lordships Manners [*sic*] & Uncultivated Lands in Maryland, for which he says he is to receive ten thousand pounds besides Expences. his Retinue is little inferior to any Lords" (John M. Hemphill, II, ed., "John Wayles Rates his Neighbours," *VMHB* 66 [1958]:305.).

2. January 16, 1765, *Archives*, 14:189–93.

3. Ibid., 32:134–40.

4. A.O. 12/79, f. 154.

5. Sharpe to Baltimore, May 29, 1766, *Archives*, 14:309–10. The advertisement, also dated May 29, 1766, appeared in the *Maryland Gazette* issue of the same date. The advertisement was repeated weekly until the issue of July 3, in which the place of sale was specified as the house of Jonathan Rawlings, "Near West-River."

6. An advertisement in the *Maryland Gazette* for July 10, 1766, announced that the sale of Anne Arundel Manor had been postponed "to a future Day." For the claims against Baltimore's right to Anne Arundel Manor, *see* Baltimore to Sharpe, November 6, 1766, *Archives*, 14:340; Hamersley to Sharpe, November 8, 1766, ibid., p. 343.

7. Executive Papers, portfolio 3, folder 19.

8. Sharpe to Baltimore, March 31, 1768, *Archives*, 14:477–79; Sharpe to Hamersley, April 1, 1768, ibid., p. 485.

9. Sharpe to Baltimore, March 31, 1768, ibid., 477–78. As late as October 4, 1771, Arnold Elzey was ordered to resurvey tenements on Wicomico Manor for those tenants who wished to purchase their tracts; *see* Proprietary Papers. Only a single sale after 1771 has been discovered, however, that being to John Greenwood for a portion of the reserved lands surrounding Kent Manor, which he purchased in June 1774; *see* Kent County Patented Certificates no. 233.

10. March 31, 1768, *Archives*, 14:477–78.

11. "Memorandum," Executive Papers, portfolio 3, folder 19.

12. Sharpe to Baltimore, October 29, 1767, *Archives*, 14:424.

13. Sharpe to Baltimore, March, 1767, ibid., p. 375.

14. A.O. 12/79, f. 127.

15. Ibid., f. 154.

16. No lists of purchasers at the proprietary sales have been discovered. Purchasers can be determined from the survey certificates issued for lots that were sold and from the individual manor lists in the Maryland State Papers (Series F–Confiscated Property).

17. Kent County Original Wills, no. 432; ibid., no. 171; Kent County Inventories 9:68, 174; Kent County Accounts 8:67, 517; ibid., 8:69; Kent County Original Wills, no. 187; Kent County Inventories 10:305; Kent County Accounts 9:242; for the marketing routes for wheat grown on the manor, *see* "Sundry Purchasers of Kent Manor to the Intendant," August 7, 1782, Intendants Letter Book 10:146–47.

18. Sharpe to Baltimore, November 24, 1767, *Archives*, 14:436.

19. Ibid. The fact that not a single lot on Monocacy Manor was sold seems to contradict the statement that wheat-growing tenants were better able to purchase land at the proprietary sales. Actually, there is no evidence that the commissioners ever attempted to sell Monocacy Manor, although their reason for not doing so is unknown. Therefore, tenants on Monocacy Manor may have been financially able to purchase their tenements, but they were not given the opportunity to bid on their lots.

20. Sharpe to Baltimore, October 29, 1767, *Archives*, 14:424; Sharpe to Baltimore, November 24, 1767, ibid., p. 436.

21. On August 13, 1767, Hamersley wrote to Sharpe: "The sense of people here Corresponds entirely with your Excellency's opinion, that the subsisting Leases are a great Discouragement to the Sale of the Manors, and the Mischief is greater as there seems to be no remedy to it, and yet I should think the Tenants would be glad to Buy their respective Interests, or, If not, that others would be glad to buy them, together with the reversions expectant upon their Leases" (ibid., p. 417).

22. Sharpe to Baltimore, October 22, 1766, ibid., p. 335.

23. For example, *see* Sharpe to Hamersley, July 27, 1767, ibid., p. 411; Sharpe to Baltimore, September 3, 1767, ibid., p. 420.

24. Sharpe to Baltimore, October 22, 1766, ibid., pp. 335–36.

25. *See* especially "A Senator," *Maryland Gazette*, February 11, 1780; the controversy over confiscation is dealt with at length in Richard Arthur Overfield, "The Loyalists of Maryland During the American Revolution" (Ph.D. diss., University of Maryland, 1968), pp. 324–79; *see also* Philip A. Crowl, *Maryland During and After the Revolution: A Political and*

Economic Study, JHSH 61 (Baltimore, 1943), pp. 41–42; Ronald Hoffman, *A Spirit of Dissension: Economics, Politics, and the Revolution in Maryland* (Baltimore, 1973), pp. 259–62.

26. Crowl, *Maryland During and After the Revolution,* pp. 42–45; John Kilty, *The Land-Holder's Assistant, and Land-Office Guide* (Baltimore, 1808), pp. 333–42; Edward C. Papenfuse, *In Pursuit of Profit: The Annapolis Merchants in the Era of the American Revolution* (Baltimore, 1975), p. 99.

27. Overfield, "Loyalists of Maryland," pp. 324–79; Crowl, *Maryland During and After the Revolution,* pp. 42–44.

28. William Kilty, *The Laws of Maryland,* 7 vols. (Annapolis, 1799–1818), 1:June 1780, ch. XXIV; October 1780, ch. XXXVIII, ch. LI; May 1781, ch. XXIII, ch. XXXIII; November 1781, ch. XX, ch. XXVIII, ch. XXXI; April 1782, ch. III; November 1782, ch. XXIV, ch. XXXIII.

29. *See* Wallace Brown, *The King's Friends: The Composition and Motives of the American Loyalist Claimants* (Providence, R.I., 1966), p. 165. Throughout this chapter, unless specifically noted, all sums are given in Maryland currency.

30. Confiscated Property—Accounts, n.d., Scharf Collection, MHS.

31. A.O. 12/79, ff. 8–9. Harford received no compensation from Maryland, but he was ultimately granted £90,000 sterling by the British government; *see* J. Thomas Scharf, *History of Maryland From the Earliest Period to the Present Day,* 3 vols. (1879; reprinted, Hatboro, Pa., 1967), 2:394.

32. Confiscated Property—Accounts, MHS.

33. For the terms of sale, *see* Kilty, *Laws,* 1:October 1780, ch. XXXVIII; May 1781, ch. XXIII; November 1781, ch. XX, ch. XXXI.

34. Ibid., October 1780, ch. XLIV.

35. *See,* for example, Commissioners to Major Jenifer, February 27, 1781, Maryland State Papers (Series A), 34/1; Letter no. 2, February 28, 1781, Commissioners' Ledger and Journal of Confiscated British Property, ff. 4–5. Paca never attended a meeting of the commissioners of confiscated property. He tendered his resignation soon after their first meeting, and on May 2, 1781, Nathaniel Ramsey was appointed to serve in his place. Uriah Forrest resigned on July 13, 1781, and Gabriel Duvall, previously clerk for the commissioners, was selected as his replacement. Hollyday, Ramsey, and Duvall were in charge of the state sales in late 1781 and 1782, at which time the bulk of the property confiscated by the state was sold. *See* the Proceedings of the Commissioners of Confiscated British Property, 1781–82, ff. 1, 3, 89–90, 235.

36. Commissioners' Ledger, March 3, 1781, f. 3; May 29, 1781, ff. 66–68.

37. The commissioners had access to at least one of the proprietary plats that had been executed prior to the proprietary sales of the manors in the 1760s, because Beaverdam Manor lots were sold on the basis of Jonathan Abell's 1768 survey of that manor; *see* Thomas Spalding, Jr., Bond to State, Executive Papers, box 35. One problem with using the proprietary plats was that they were frequently inaccurate; *see* Thomas McPherson to Gabriel Duvall, April 3, 1782, Maryland State Papers (Series A), 34/41.

38. Lots were considered to be more valuable if the lease had expired than if lives or years encumbered the tract. When one or more of the persons on a three-life lease had moved from the state, the purchaser was responsible for locating them and determining if all were dead before he could assume full title to his purchase; *see* Chancery Records 22:480–87.

39. On at least two manors, tenants without valid leases were allowed to stay on their tracts for a short period after the sale, presumably to permit them to make other living arrangements; *see* Commissioners' Ledger, ff. 155–56.

40. Journal of the Proceedings of the Commissioners of Confiscated British Property, 1781, f. 123.

41. For contemporary accounts of the sales, see the depositions in *John Cartwright re. Richard Carnes* vs. *State of Maryland,* Chancery Records 33:289–302; also, the depositions in *John Davidson* vs. *the Attorney General on behalf of the State of Maryland,* ibid., 22:480–87.

42. Kilty, *Laws,* 1:May 1781, ch. XXIII; November 1781, ch. XX, ch. XXI. Throughout the eighteenth century the term "specie" had two distinct meanings. The word could refer to gold and silver in the form of coin or bullion, or to the legally established exchange rate

at which a particular type of money could be converted into gold or silver. The confiscation acts specified that payment be in specie because there were several types of currency in circulation at the time, and the exchange rate of each to a gold or silver equivalent varied. The paper currency known as red money—one of several currency emissions authorized by the state to support wartime spending—was issued by the state in compliance with an act of the General Assembly of May 10, 1781.

43. "Smallwood's Essay on Speculation," Maryland State Papers (Series F—Confiscated Property), 17/4/1; Edward C. Papenfuse, Jr. and Gregory A. Stiverson, "General Smallwood's Recruits: The Peacetime Career of the Revolutionary War Private," *WMQ*, 3rd ser., 30 (1973):127–28. A packet of depreciation certificates redeemed by William Campbell, one of the largest purchasers of land on Monocacy Manor, can be found in the Scharf Collection, MHS. Campbell acquired the certificates, worth £925.11.7 face value, from eight soldiers, six of whom were privates, one a sergeant, and one of unspecified rank.

44. *See,* for example, April 9, 1781, Commissioners' Ledger, ff. 31–32; Kilty, *Laws,* 1:November 1781, ch. XXXI.

45. Crowl, *Maryland During and After the Revolution,* p. 46.

46. Chancery Records 33:289–302.

47. Chew to Daniel of St. Thomas Jenifer, Scharf Collection, MHS.

48. Ridout Papers, D 371.

49. Intendants Letter Book 10, ff. 146–47; for additional evidence concerning the problem of people paying for land purchased at the state sales, *see* J. Parnham to Gabriel Duvall, May 14, 1782, Maryland State Papers (Series A), 34/47.

50. The undated petition is in Maryland State Papers (Series F—Confiscated Property), 4/1/7.

51. For examples of forfeitures, see lots 29, 55, and 63, Monocacy Manor, Sale Book of British Confiscated Property, 1781–1785, f. 53; the patenting of manor tracts sold by the state can be traced in Return Book for Reserved Lands, 1786–1824.

52. Assignments are most frequently found in the packets of patented and unpatented certificates of survey, either on a separate slip of paper or on the back of the certificate itself.

53. Sale Book, 1781–1785; Return Book for Reserved Lands.

54. Throughout this discussion the term "patentee" will designate both persons who actually patented their land and those persons who failed to patent their tracts but enjoyed quiet possession of the land.

55. Sale of Beaverdam Manor, September 13–15, 1781, Maryland State Papers (Series F—Confiscated Property), 13/5/1.

56. Sale Book, 1781–1785, f. 12. Hanson Briscoe and Joseph Shamwell testified in October 1792 that Samuel Higgs and his securities had moved out of the state and had "not left any property behind them & that they were extremely indigent when they removed from this state. . . ." Higgs and his securities had fled to the Carolinas, and the sheriff had sold all the fence logs and timber on Higgs's lot to pay back taxes. For the correspondence concerning Higgs's forfeiture, *see* Maryland State Papers (Series F—Confiscated Property), 13/4/1–13/4/5.

57. Chancery Records 33:289–302.

58. Sale Book, 1781–1785; Return Book of Reserved Lands; Charles County Patented Certificates nos. 924 and 1121; Charles County Land Records I.B. no. 2, p. 137.

59. Sale Book, 1781–1785.

60. *See* David C. Skaggs and Richard K. MacMaster, "Post-Revolutionary Letters of Alexander Hamilton," *Maryland Historical Magazine* 43 (1968):22–25. Latimer died in 1805 deeply in debt, with his creditors acquiring all of his speculative tracts; *see* Chancery Records 66: 703.

61. Sale Book, 1781–1785, f. 21

62. Kent County Patented Certificates no. 554.

63. Prices are recorded for sixteen lots, ranging from £1.10.6 to £2.17.6 per acre. The most frequently occurring price was £2.0.6 per acre; *see* Sale Book, 1781–1785, f. 32.

64. Chancery Records 49:336.

65. Sale Book, 1781–1785, f. 32. The date and place for the auction of Gunpowder Manor was announced in the *Maryland Gazette* on August 8, 1782.

66. Gen. William Smallwood reported to General Washington on July 30, 1782, that there was "base speculation made on the officers' and soldiers' certificates for pay and depreciation, which, through mere necessity, they were obliged in many instances, to part with at a twentieth part of their value. . ." (Thomas Balch, ed., *Papers Relating Chiefly to the Maryland Line During the Revolution* [Philadelphia, 1857], p. 189).

67. Maryland State Papers (Series F—Confiscated Property), 7/1/2; Journal of the Proceedings of the Commissioners of Confiscated British Property, 1781, f. 41.

68. Frederick County Land Records W.R. 11:470–71; Frederick County Patented Certificates no. 5233.

69. For example, *see* Frederick County Patented Certificates nos. 2502–47, 2502–22–24, 2502–48, and 2502–35.

70. The change in ownership of Monocacy tracts is apparent from the 1798 county assessment; *see* District no. 2, Israel's Creek and Manor hundreds, Frederick County Assessment for 1798.

71. Frederick County Patented Certificates no. 2502–25.

72. Sale Book, 1781–1785; biographical information is from a variety of sources, including official records, especially the Chancery Records and Revolutionary War Papers; *see also* Frank F. White, Jr., *The Governors of Maryland, 1777–1970*, Hall of Records Commission, Publication no. 15 (Annapolis, Md., 1970); T. J. C. Williams, *History of Frederick County Maryland*, 2 vols. (1910; reprinted, Baltimore, 1967); Cary Howard, "John Eager Howard: Patriot and Public Servant," *Maryland Historical Magazine* 42 (1967):300–17; W. F. Brand, *A Sketch of the Life and Character of Nathaniel Ramsay*, Maryland Historical Society Fund Publication no. 24 (Baltimore, 1887); Scharf, *History of Maryland;* and *Calendar of the General Otho Holland Williams Papers in the Maryland Historical Society* (Baltimore, 1940), items 917, 997.

Epilogue

1. Johann David Schoepf, *Travels in the Confederation [1783–1784]*, 2 vols. (1911, reprinted, New York, 1968), 2:32.

2. Tenants occasionally refused to leave their homes, even though their land had been sold as confiscated property. Henry Downes, the purchaser of a lot at the state sale of confiscated property in Caroline County, wrote on June 10, 1782 to Clement Hollyday, one of the commissioners for the sale of confiscated property, complaining that when he went to take possession of the land the resident tenant, "tho' he claims no other right than possession, refused to give it up or pay any acknowledgement." Downes demanded that Hollyday see that the tenant was ejected from the premises. *See* Maryland State Papers (Series A), 34/52.

3. Edward C. Papenfuse, Jr. and Gregory A. Stiverson, "General Smallwood's Recruits: The Peacetime Career of the Revolutionary War Private," *WMQ*, 3rd ser., 30 (1973): 127–28.

4. Portion of a typescript of the Journal of Thomas Bowdle, Jr.

5. Schoepf, *Travels*, 2:36.

ESSAY ON SOURCES

The genesis of this volume was a paper I researched and wrote my first year in the Early American History Seminar at the Johns Hopkins University. That paper—a comparison of wealth, primarily in terms of landownership and slaveownership, of heads of households in Talbot County in 1733 and 1783—revealed one quite unexpected bit of information: nonlandowners comprised nearly 54 percent of the heads of households in 1733, and in 1783 an even slightly higher percentage of householders were in that category. Furthermore, even a cursory examination of names on the two tax lists indicated that some men who had been in their early twenties in 1733 had been unable over the course of half a century to secure title to land, and the sons of many others were nonlandowners in 1783. Because the opportunities for employment outside of agriculture were limited in eighteenth-century Talbot County, most of the men identified as nonlandowners on the 1733 and 1783 tax lists, I concluded, must have tilled soil owned by other men. Furthermore, it appeared that tenancy had become a permanent condition for many families in that county by 1783.

Identifying changes in wealth, landholding patterns, and slaveownership was the purpose of this first research paper, and those topics dominated most of the text. My interests then shifted, however, to nonlandowners, and especially to the possibility that, as had occurred in England centuries earlier, a sizable portion of families in Maryland were prevented from ever acquiring sufficient capital to purchase land of their own. The standard works on economic and social history that mentioned tenants in the Chesapeake colonies, such as Robert E. Brown and B. Katherine Brown, *Virginia, 1705–1786: Democracy or Aristocracy?* (East Lansing, Mich., 1964); Thomas J. Wertenbaker, *The Planters of Colonial Virginia* (Princeton, 1922); Wesley Frank Craven, *The Southern Colonies in the Seventeenth Century, 1607–1689* (Baton Rouge, 1949); and Jackson Turner Main, *The Social Structure of Revolutionary America* (Princeton, 1965), all stated or implied that tenants had little difficulty acquiring the capital necessary to secure a freehold. Willard F. Bliss, on the other hand, had described the Northern Neck of Virginia as being heavily populated with tenants in his "The Rise of Tenancy in Virginia" (*Virginia Magazine of History and Biography* 58 [1950]: 427–42 [hereafter cited as *VMHB*]), due primarily to the engrossment of land by large property owners.

The next few months were devoted to analyzing five other counties in different geographical areas of Maryland that were also listed on the 1783 assessment to determine whether the high rate of nonlandowners in Talbot County was an aberration. It proved not to be. The number of poor people in Maryland in 1783 was enormous, with nonlandowners accounting for half or more of the householders in all the sample counties, except in Somerset on the lower Eastern Shore. Furthermore, of these nonlandowners, the percentage who were paupers (defined in the law as householders with less than £10 of assessable property) and nonlandowners with less than £50 of taxable property accounted for from 60 to 90 percent of the householders in the nonlandowning class. Because few personal articles were exempted from taxation in the assessment of 1783, it seemed unlikely that the vast majority of the nonlandowners with less than £50 of taxable property would ever be able to acquire land.

This group of poor whites—specifically those who formed the largest segment of it, tenants who farmed land owned by other men—became the subject of my Ph.D. dissertation. At first I hoped to do a comparative study of tenants on the proprietary manors, tenants on manors owned by the Jesuits, and tenants who leased land from private landlords. A search through the private records of large planters at the Maryland Historical Society in Baltimore (hereafter cited as MHS) produced some records relating to tenants

175

on private estates, especially the Charles Carroll of Annapolis Account Book, 1754-1784; the Robert Darnall Ledger, 1787-1821; the Hollyday Account Book, 1760-1777; and the Edward Lloyd Memorandum Book, 1768-1772, in the Lloyd Papers, box 4; but the total number of leases was insufficient to include them in my study. The Jesuit records, if they exist, could not be found.

I was thus left with only the tenants on Lord Baltimore's manors, but the records relating to some of the proprietor's manors were so rich that comparing these tenants to other classes of tenants would not have been possible, given the time limitations I had imposed upon myself for completing the dissertation. The most important collections utilized were: Proprietary Leases A–C, Hall of Records (unless otherwise noted, all subsequent records referred to are at the Hall of Records, Annapolis, Maryland); transcripts of original leases to proprietary tenants in the Scharf Collection (MHS); Calvert Papers (MHS), which contain a wealth of information on the revenue the proprietor received from the manors, as well as a vast amount of additional related material; *Calvert Papers, Number Two*, Maryland Historical Society Fund Publication no. 34 (Baltimore, 1894), which contains material that complements the unpublished Calvert Papers; Executive Papers, portfolio 3, which has instructions from the proprietor concerning the manors; *Archives of Maryland*, edited by William Hand Browne et al., 72 vols. to date (Baltimore, 1883–), especially valuable for the volumes containing the correspondence of Governor Horatio Sharpe with the proprietor and the proprietor's secretaries; the lists of leaseholds on the various proprietary manors in the Scharf Collection (MHS), created in 1767-68, prior to the proprietary sales of the manors, which are printed, with some errors, in Gaius Marcus Brumbaugh, *Maryland Records, Colonial, Revolutionary, County and Church*, 2 vols. (1915-28; reprinted, Baltimore, 1967); the Claim of Henry Harford, Public Record Office, Audit Office 12/79, London (microfilm copy available at the Hall of Records), which contains some information concerning the reasons the proprietors established their manors in Maryland, lists of manor tracts and the improvements on them, and Harford's estimate of the amount of money he lost by the state's confiscation of his property during the War for Independence; British Confiscated Property Papers, which deal primarily with the proprietary sales of the manors after 1767; Plats, which show manor boundaries and the lines of individual tenements within them; Gift Collection, which contains two additional manor plats; "Conegocheigh Manor," a folder originally in a collection called Loose Papers Concerning British Confiscated Property, but which, since the collection was reworked a few years ago, has disappeared (as an administrator of the Hall of Records, I must hasten to add that it will one day be found!); and Maryland State Papers (Series A) and (Series F—Confiscated Property), which detail the state's confiscation and sale of the proprietary manors.

After digesting the information concerning the management of the proprietary manors and the tenants who lived on them, I produced a 620-page dissertation entitled "Landless Husbandmen. Tenants on the Maryland Proprietary Manors in the Eighteenth Century: An Economic Study" (Ph.D. dissertation, Johns Hopkins University, 1973). I mention this because of the 220 pages of appendixes in the dissertation, only the two shortest of which are reproduced in this volume. The other tables in the appendixes indicate, tract by tract, the natural resources and types of improvements on the sample proprietary manors in 1767-68 and the name of the original leaseholder, the tenant in possession of the tract in 1767-58, the purchaser of the lot at the proprietary or state sale of the tract, and the ultimate patentee of the property. A copy of the dissertation is available at the Hall of Records and it has been microfilmed by University Microfilms.

Even before finishing the dissertation, I had accepted a three-year research appointment with the Colonial Williamsburg Foundation to study large-scale plantation management in eighteenth-century Virginia. There I found a plethora of account books and private rental agreements from large landowners—precisely the type of material lacking for my originally intended comparison of tenants on private estates and proprietary manors in Maryland. The Virginia sources confirmed that developmental leasing was intended only as a short-term arrangement whereby a landlord would provide tenants with beneficial lease terms in exchange for specified improvements that would permit the landlord to sell or rent the tenement at a much higher rate at the expiration of the lease. I was also able to find an abundance of supporting evidence for statements I had made in the dissertation about dwellings and other improvements constructed by tenants, the kinds of agricultural methods employed by planters in all wealth categories, and the perceived need—at least by the more enlightened planters—to break away from maize and tobacco as their principal crops.

Thus, when I returned to the manuscript that ultimately resulted in this volume I was able to add a great deal of information, which is mostly to be found in the notes, and at the same time pare down the number of pages in the final version of the text. This was made possible because it was no longer necessary to be speculative about many of the topics discussed in my original dissertation (speculating, or hedging, is essential in a dissertation, because the professors who conduct the final orals before granting a Ph.D. degree delight in discovering a weakly supported, or better yet, totally unsupported, statement, and both speculating and hedging require many pages; a simple statement of fact does not). In addition, during my three-year hiatus researching the Virginia elite, other historians had produced publications or dissertations that directly bore on tenants, or at least on people at the lower end of the economic spectrum. James T. Lemon had published *The Best Poor Man's Country: A Geographical Study of Early Southeastern Pennsylvania* (Baltimore, 1972), in which he argued that, as his title implies, life was quite good for all classes of Pennsylvanians in the colonial period and that, contrary to earlier statements by historians, the influx of Germans into Pennsylvania had not caused an improvement in agricultural practices. Sung Bok Kim had demonstrated, in "A New Look at the Great Landlords of Eighteenth-Century New York" (*William and Mary Quarterly*, 3rd ser., 27[1970]:581–614 [hereafter cited as *WMQ*]), that the great landlords in that colony had enormous difficulty finding tenants, again suggesting that America actually was "the best poor man's country."

During the same period of time, however, works appeared that tended to support my conclusion that at least in Maryland tenancy had become an increasingly permanent condition for an ever larger portion of the population during the course of the eighteenth century. Dr. Lois Green Carr and her researchers, employed by the St. Mary's City Commission, began to publish some of their findings, such as the article Dr. Carr co-authored with Russell R. Menard and P.M.G. Harris, "Opportunity and Inequality: The Distribution of Wealth on the Lower Western Shore of Maryland, 1638–1705," *MHM* 69 (1974):169–84. Other pertinent works had also been written, including: Paul G. E. Clemens, "From Tobacco to Grain: Economic Development on Maryland's Eastern Shore, 1660–1750" (Ph.D. dissertation, University of Wisconsin, 1974); Carville V. Earle, *The Evolution of a Tidewater Settlement System, All Hallow's Parish, Maryland, 1650–1783*, The University of Chicago Department of Geography Research Paper no. 170 (Chicago, 1975), in which he demonstrates that as the amount of vacant land in the parish declined the number of tenants rose; David Curtis Skaggs, *Roots of Maryland Democracy, 1753–1776* (Westport, Conn., 1973), in which he argues that the number of tenants in Maryland was even higher than I had said; and Kevin Porter Kelley, who in his "Economic and Social Development of Seventeenth-Century Surry County, Virginia" (Ph.D. dissertation, University of Washington, 1972), found that tenancy had already become prevalent in one of the first-settled counties of Virginia by the end of the seventeenth century.

In addition to the works cited above, this volume depended heavily on several printed and manuscript sources to develop the essential understanding of how the land system in Maryland operated, particularly with reference to the proprietary manors, and to determine how the proprietor, and later the state government, approached the problem of managing and then selling the manors. Charles Albro Barker's *The Background of the Revolution in Maryland* (1940; reprinted, Hamden, Conn., 1967) is an absolutely essential source for any student of colonial Maryland history, and Clarence P. Gould's *The Land System in Maryland*, Johns Hopkins Studies in History and Political Science (hereafter cited as JHSH), vol. 31 (Baltimore, 1913), is equally indispensable. Donnell MacClure Owings's two publications, *His Lordship's Patronage, Offices of Profit in Colonial Maryland* (Baltimore, 1953) and "Private Manors: An Edited List," *MHM* 33 (1938):307–34, contain much useful information, and John Kilty's *The Land-Holder's Assistant, and Land-Office Guide* (Baltimore, 1808) proved extremely useful, because as Clerk of the Land Office Kilty had access to records that, in many cases, have disappeared. Arthur Pierce Middleton's *Tobacco Coast: A Maritime History of Chesapeake Bay in the Colonial Era* (Newport News, Va., 1953) is a gold mine of information that unfortunately has been too long out of print.

With respect to the most important sources consulted for each chapter of the book, the majority of those for Chapter One have been noted above concerning the records, printed or in manuscript, relating to the efforts of the successive Lords Baltimore to manage their manors in Maryland. An interesting article detailing Governor Sharpe's problem with incompetent officials appointed by Frederick, sixth Lord Baltimore, however, is James Haw's "The Patronage Follies: Bennet Allen, John Morton Jordan, and the Fall of Horatio Sharpe," *MHM* 71(1976):135–50. While Haw's argument that Sharpe's dismissal from office was largely due to the great influence Allen and Jordan had with the proprietor is not entirely convincing, it does cast a reasonable doubt on the general assumption that Sharpe was replaced by Lord Baltimore's brother-in-law, Robert Eden, for reasons other than simple nepotism.

The examination of tenants on the eight sample manors in Chapter Two relied heavily on wills, inventories, accounts, and final distributions, either in the original, or in volumes from the Prerogative Court or individual county court series. With specific reference to the Germans on Monocacy Manor, Dieter Cunz, *The Maryland Germans: A History* (Princeton, 1948), was particularly helpful.

The bulk of the information on tenant dwellings and other improvements discussed in Chapter Three came, as previously noted, from Henry Harford's claim for compensation for property confiscated by Maryland during the War for Independence. For a general history of colonial Maryland architecture one need go no further than *The Architecture of the Old South: The Medieval Style* (Cambridge, Mass., 1948); *Early Manor and Plantation Houses of Maryland* (Easton, Md., 1943); and *Tidewater Maryland Architecture and Gardens* (New York, 1956), all by Henry Chandlee Forman, although Thomas Tileston Waterman's *The Dwellings of Colonial America* (Chapel Hill, N.C., 1950) was also helpful in the background research for the chapter. Hugh Morrison's *Early American Architecture from the First Colonial Settlements to the National Period* (New York, 1952) was especially useful in describing how both frame and log structures were built. In describing the kinds of frame dwellings tenants on the lower Western shore inhabited, I was especially fortunate to discover the "Valuation of the Estate of Elizabeth Plater, orphan of Col. George Plater," St. Mary's County Valuations and Indentures, 1780–1808, ff. 159–60. The appearance of log structures on a few of the lower Western Shore and Eastern Shore manors, the large number of them on Gunpowder Manor, and their preponderance on Monocacy Manor was one of the most intriguing discoveries in the lists of improvements contained in Harford's claim for compensation for property sequestered from him by the state. To gain an understanding of how log structures were built and when and where log construction was used in colonial America, I found Harold R. Shurtleff, *The Log Cabin Myth: A Study of the Early Dwellings of the English Colonists in North America* (Cambridge, Mass., 1939), and C. A. Weslager, *The Log Cabin in America: From Pioneer Days to the Present* (New Brunswick, N.J., 1969), of most use, although Henry Glassie, *Pattern in the Material Folk Culture of the Eastern United States* (Philadelphia, 1968), was also helpful, especially with respect to log barns. Thomas Jefferson, in his *Notes on the State of Virginia*, edited by William Peden (Chapel Hill, N.C., 1955), also has some interesting comments on the differences between frame and log dwellings in terms of both comfort and durability. A good comparative view of the dwellings of the poor in eighteenth-century England can be derived by consulting G. F. Fussell and Constance Goodman, "The Housing of the Rural Population in the Eighteenth Century," *Economic History* 2 (1930):63–90.

Writing the chapter on tenant agriculture, Chapter Four, was the most difficult, because at the time I began research on it there was very little information published on cultivation methods, field patterns, crop yields, and how the practices of small producers differed from large planters who owned slave laborers. This astonishing lack of historical research—most colonial Americans, at least in the south, did make their living from agriculture—is slowly being rectified, but the emphasis of most historians is still on the effects of alterations in the transportation and marketing of tobacco and other commodities, the impact of diversification on previously staple-producing areas, and similar economic topics. Few seem to care about the fleece weight of eighteenth-century sheep or the slaughter weight of beef or pork; marle and creek muck seem unworthy of consideration, and yet planters in the eighteenth century considered these matters of importance, and George Washington even ordered a hippopotamus dredge to mine the muck-rich Potomac River. The fact that maize yields were so low that planters with large numbers of

slaves had to devote hundreds of acres to its cultivation concerned the slaveowners themselves, but the problem has been considered by few of the numerous historians studying
eighteenth-century slavery. Perhaps at some point in the next half-century I will have time
to revise the 500-odd pages of manuscript that I condensed into "Gentlemen of Industry,
Skill, and Application: Plantation Management in Eighteenth-Century Virginia" (unpublished research report, Research Department, Colonial Williamsburg Foundation, 1975).
Then, at least some of the information I needed for writing the chapter on agriculture will
be more readily accessible to others.

The standard treatment of agriculture in the south is Lewis Cecil Gray's *History of
Agriculture in the Southern United States to 1860*, 2 vols. (1933; reprinted, Gloucester, Mass.,
1958), and it still remains a useful source. Avery Odelle Craven's *Soil Exhaustion as a Factor
in the Agricultural History of Virginia and Maryland, 1606–1860* (1926; reprinted, Gloucester,
Mass., 1965) overstates the debilitating effects of the plant, but it cannot be ignored by a
student of the agricultural history of the Chesapeake Bay region. My need to know more
about German farming practices led me to Richard H. Shryock's "British Versus German
Traditions in Colonial Agriculture," *Mississippi Valley Historical Review* 21 (1939):39–54.
Rodney C. Loehr's "Self-Sufficiency on the Farm," *Agricultural History* 26 (1952):37–41
(hereafter cited as *Ag. H.*), and his "The Influence of English Agriculture on American
Agriculture, 1775–1825," *Ag. H.* 11 (1937):3–15, both provided pertinent information on
colonial American agriculture. A. G. McCall's "The Development of Soil Science," *Ag. H.* 5
(1931):43–56, provides a brief discussion on that topic, but John Taylor's *Arator: Being a
Series of Agricultural Essays, Practical and Political*, 3rd ed. (Baltimore, 1817), proved much
more rewarding, because of his extensive discussions of experiments he had conducted
with various fertilizers to improve the quality of the soil. Allen Walker Read's "The Comments of British Travelers on Early American Terms Relating to Agriculture," *Ag. H.* 7
(1933):99–109, might interest those who do not know what a "worm fence" is or cannot
comprehend what is meant when a planter notes that he spent the day "laying by" his
cornfield.

Agricultural diversification figured prominently in the chapter on agriculture, and I
benefited most from Paul G. E. Clemens, "From Tobacco to Grain: Economic Development on Maryland's Eastern Shore, 1660–1750" (Ph.D. dissertation, University of Wisconsin, 1974), and Clarence P. Gould, *Money and Transportation in Maryland: 1720–1765*,
JHSH (Baltimore, 1915). The ability of farmers to market their grain crops more easily as
the trading network of Philadelphia expanded is examined in James T. Lemon's "Urbanization and the Development of Eighteenth-Century Southeastern Pennsylvania and Adjacent Delaware," *WMQ*, 3rd ser., 24 (1967):502–42, and the movement away from tobacco
in Tidewater Virginia is discussed in W. A. Low, "The Farmer in Post-Revolutionary
America, 1783–1789," *Ag. H.* 25 (1951):122–27. Agricultural diversification is but one of
the fascinating topics dealt with in Brooke Hindle's elegantly written treatise, *The Pursuit of
Science in Revolutionary America, 1735–1789* (Chapel Hill, N.C. 1956).

The economic aspects of agriculture in Maryland and surrounding regions are treated in
a variety of recent works. Their number, in fact, is so large that I will list only the most
important, and those without further comment: Paul G. E. Clemens's "From Tobacco to
Grain" and Carville V. Earle's *The Evolution of a Tidewater Settlement System*, both cited above;
Allan Kulikoff, "Tobacco and Slaves: Population, Economy and Society in Eighteenth-
Century Prince George's County, Maryland" (Ph.D. dissertation, Brandeis University,
1976); Edward C. Papenfuse, Jr., "Planter Behavior and Economic Opportunity in a Staple
Economy," *Ag. H.* 46 (1972):297–311; Aubrey C. Land, "Economic Behavior in a Planting
Society: The Eighteenth-Century Chesapeake," *Journal of Southern History* 33 (1967):469–
85; Jacob M. Price, "The Rise of Glasgow in the Chesapeake Tobacco Trade, 1707–1775,"
WMQ, 3rd ser., 11 (1954):179–99; David Klingaman, "Food Surpluses and Deficits in the
American Colonies, 1768–1772," *Journal of Economic History* 31 (1971):553–69; and Russell
R. Menard, "From Servant to Freeholder: Status Mobility and Property Accumulation in
Seventeenth-Century Maryland," *WMQ*, 3rd ser., 30 (1973):37–64.

My major problem with writing the chapter on agriculture was, as stated above, the
dearth of information on methods of crop cultivation and crop yields. Some of the sources
I used to derive what I believe are realistic figures on these topics are found in notes in my
"Early American Farming: A Comment," *Ag. H.* 50 (1976):37–44. An indispensable source

on all aspects of husbandry in Maryland is John Beale Bordley's *Essay and Notes on Husbandry and Rural Affairs,* 2nd ed. (Philadelphia, 1801), and his *A Summary View of the Courses of Crops, in the Husbandry of England and Maryland* (Philadelphia, 1784), although a much slimmer volume, contains some valuable information not contained in his magnum opus. The *Diary of Colonel Landon Carter of Sabine Hall, 1752–1778,* edited by Jack P. Greene, 2 vols. (Charlottesville, Va., 1965), is a treasure trove of agricultural minutiae that provides exactly the kind of specific information needed to construct average yields for a variety of crops. The same is true of the published works of George Washington (*The Writings of George Washington from the Original Manuscript Sources, 1745–1799,* edited by John C. Fitzpatrick, 39 vols. [Washington, D.C., 1931–44], and *The Diaries of George Washington, 1748–1799,* edited by John C. Fitzpatrick, 4 vols. [Boston and New York, 1925]), because Washington, if we had not insisted on making him commander-in-chief of the army during the War for Independence and then elected him to two, allegedly unwanted, terms as president, would today be remembered principally as one of the outstanding agricultural innovators of his time. Some especially pertinent information can be gleaned from *Thomas Jefferson's Farm Book,* edited by Edwin Morris Betts (Princeton, 1953) and, to a lesser extent, from *Thomas Jefferson's Garden Book, 1766–1824,* edited by Edwin Morris Betts (Philadelphia, 1944).

Although many of the sources cited above deal in part with tobacco, several works should be singled out because of their special importance to the study of this crop plant. William Tatham's *An Historical and Practical Essay on the Culture and Commerce of Tobacco* (London, 1800) is particularly important, because it was written by a Virginian intimately associated with the cultivation of the plant. Aubrey C. Land's "The Tobacco Staple and the Planter's Problems: Technology, Labor, and Crops," *Ag. H.* 43 (1969): 69–81, contains a good deal of economic information, but he does discuss in some detail the tools used to cultivate tobacco and why the use of slave labor may have impeded the adoption of more sophisticated methods of crop cultivation. Paul G. E. Clemens's "The Operation of an Eighteenth-Century Tobacco Plantation," *Ag. H.* 49 (1975):517–31, is again largely an economic piece, but his comparison of profits that could be made from tobacco does discuss the special difficulties in cultivating the plant imposed upon tenants. Russell R. Menard's price series for tobacco ("A Note on Chesapeake Tobacco Prices, 1618–1660," *VMHB* 84 [1976]: 401–10, and "Farm Prices of Maryland Tobacco, 1659–1710," *MHM* 68 [1973]: 80–85) have relevance to this volume in that they establish that tobacco became the dominant staple in the Chesapeake Bay region because it brought extremely high prices in the early decades of production in the colonies. A somewhat curious, but in other ways useful, treatise on tobacco is " 'A National Property.' Richard Claiborne's Tobacco Treatise for Poland," edited by Davis Curtis Carroll, *WMQ,* 3rd ser., 21 (1964):93–117.

Another source of information on crops of all types cultivated in the Chesapeake Bay region are the letter books kept by eighteenth-century residents of the area. The most useful of these is R. O. Bausman and J. A. Munroe, eds., "James Tilton's Notes on the Agriculture of Delaware in 1788," *Ag. H.* 20 (1946):176–87, which were originally composed as an answer to queries sent by a Frenchman, the Abbé Alexandre Henri Tessier. A tutor hired by Robert Carter, of Nomini Hall, Virginia, kept a diary of the daily activities on Carter's plantation, including numerous notations concerning agriculture. His observations were later published as the *Journal & Letters of Philip Vickers Fithian, 1773–1774: A Plantation Tutor of the Old Dominion,* edited by Hunter Dickinson Farish, new edition (Williamsburg, Va., 1957). Another tutor who kept a journal that contains considerable material of interest to the agricultural historian was John Harrower, who came to the colony from Scotland in 1773 as an indentured servant after being ruined in business by the Panic of 1772. His notes, edited by Edward Miles Riley, appeared in print as *The Journal of John Harrower: An Indentured Servant in the Colony of Virginia, 1773–1776* (Williamsburg, Va., 1963). *The Journal of Nicholas Cresswell, 1774–1777,* edited by A. G. Bradley, 2nd edition (New York, 1928), is also worth perusing for agricultural information, and William Eddis's *Letters from America,* edited by Aubrey C. Land (Cambridge, Mass., 1969), contains a few pertinent facts.

Travel accounts of foreigners who paid brief visits to America must be used with extreme caution, because in many cases the reason they first appeared in print is that the author expected to profit from writing the book. In terms of agricultural information they can be a very rich source, however, and if the researcher carefully compares them, the intentional or unintentional biases can be detected and good evidence for cultivation patterns and crop yields can be secured. The two most valuable travel accounts for the research on this volume were Richard Parkinson, *A Tour in America in 1798, 1799, and 1800. Exhibiting Sketches of Society and Manners, and a Particular Account of the American System of Agriculture, with Its Recent Improvements,* 2 vols. (London, 1805), and Johann David Schoepf, *Travels in the Confederation [1783-1784],* translated and edited by Alfred J. Morrison, 2 vols. (New York, 1968). "Virginia in 1732: The Travel Journal of William Hugh Grove," edited by Gregory A. Stiverson and Patrick H. Butler III, *VMHB* 85 (1977):18-44, is largely devoted to a description of the flora and fauna of Virginia, but Grove does have numerous references relating to crops and their cultivation. Grove is an especially good source because not only was he a very well-educated and unbiased observer, but he also spent most of his stay in the colony on a single plantation, rather than traveling from place to place. William Strickland's *Journal of a Tour in the United States of America, 1794-1797,* edited by J. E. Strickland, and his *Observations on the Agriculture of the United States of America,* printed in facsimile with the first title (New York, 1971), both contain a vast amount of information on agriculture. Two other travel accounts that should be consulted are John Ferdinand Dalziel Smyth, *A Tour in the United States of America,* 2 vols. (1784; reprinted, New York, 1968), and Alexandre La Rochefoucauld Liancourt, *Travels Through the United States of North America . . . ,* 4 vols. (London, 1799).

Of lesser importance to the study of crops and cultivation patterns in the Chesapeake Bay region, but still worth reviewing are: Carl Raymond Woodward, *Ploughs and Politicks. Charles Read of New Jersey and His Notes on Agriculture, 1715-1774* (New Brunswick, N.J., 1941); the charming comments of Janet Schaw in the *Journal of a Lady of Quality; Being the Narrative of a Journey from Scotland to the West Indies, North Carolina, and Portugal, in the years 1774 to 1776,* edited by Evangeline Walker Andrews and Charles McLean Andrews (New Haven, Conn., 1923); and the horrendous, but often witty and occasionally pertinent, versification of Anne Ritson in her *A Poetical Picture of America* (1809; reprinted, Norfolk, Va., 1810). *Gentleman's Progress. The Itinerarium of Dr. Alexander Hamilton, 1744,* edited and with an introduction by Carl Bridenbaugh (Chapel Hill, N.C., 1948), only briefly mentions diversified agriculture in Cecil County, but I highly recommend it in any case because of Hamilton's charm and droll sense of humor.

One final title that deserves a special paragraph of its own is "Pehr Kalm's Description of Maize, How It Is Planted and Cultivated in North America, Together with the Many Uses of This Crop Plant," edited and translated by Esther L. Larsen (*Ag. H.* 9[1935]:98-117). The importance of maize, not only to the tenants on the proprietary manors, but to everyone, rich and poor, in eighteenth-century Maryland, makes this essay by the famed Swedish botanist who visited America in 1748 essential reading for any student of American agriculture.

The primary sources used in the discussion of the proprietor's attempt to sell his manor lands in Maryland, which is discussed at the beginning of Chapter Five, have been listed above. The three secondary sources most useful for tracing the background of the state's decision to confiscate what remained of the proprietor's property in the state are Philip A. Crowl, *Maryland During and After the Revolution: A Political and Economic Study,* JHSH (Baltimore, 1943); Richard Arthur Overfield, "The Loyalists of Maryland During the American Revolution" (Ph.D. dissertation, University of Maryland, 1968); and Ronald Hoffman, *A Spirit of Dissension: Economics, Politics, and the Revolution in Maryland* (Baltimore, 1973).

The laws passed by the state, divesting the proprietor of his lands in Maryland, can be found in William Kilty, *The Laws of Maryland,* 7 vols. (Annapolis, Md., 1799-1818). The mechanics of how the state actually went about sequestering Harford's assets and selling his manor lands can be traced in the following records or record series: Confiscated Property—Accounts; Commissioner's Ledger and Journal of Confiscated British Property; Proceedings of the Commissioners of Confiscated British Property, 1781-82; Intendants Letter Book 10; and Return Book for Reserved Lands, 1786-1824. Announcements of the impending sale of the various manors were inserted in the *Maryland Gazette* and the *Maryland Journal and Baltimore Advertiser.*

The commissioners appointed to sell the proprietor's manors attempted to secure copies of the plats Governor Sharpe had prepared prior to the proprietary sale of the manors in the late 1760s. Some material relating to this can be found in Maryland State Papers (Series A). Tracing what happened to individual tenements sold by the state can be accomplished by examining the Unpatented Certificates of Survey, Patented Certificates of Survey, and Land Record series. The Sale Book of British Confiscated Property, 1781–1785, is especially useful for identifying forfeitures that occurred on tracts sold at the state sale of the manors, and the Chancery Records series contain several cases that detail how the manor sales were conducted and illuminate controversies that arose over specific tracts sold on several manors.

The speculation in army certificates that figured so prominently in the state sale of Monocacy Manor tracts can be fleshed out in records in State Papers (Series F—Confiscated Property) and in the Scharf Collection (MHS). Further information on speculation can be found in Edward C. Papenfuse, Jr., and Gregory A. Stiverson, "General Smallwood's Recruits: The Peacetime Career of the Revolutionary War Private," *WMQ*, 3rd ser., 30(1973):117–32.

INDEX

Abbington, 156 n. 12; proprietary sale of, 107
Adams, George, 133
Adams, Martin, 54
Adams, Peter, 133
Agricultural diversification, 87, 90–91; impediments to, on the lower Western Shore, 100–102; importance of trade networks and, 100–101; slavery as an impediment to, 101–2
Alienation fines, nonpayment of, by tenants, 21
Allen, Bennett, 19
Anderson, Edward, 129
Annapolis, proprietary lands reserved around, 3
Anne Arundel Manor, 6, 8; cost of leasing land on, 14; description of, 151; developmental leasing on, 13–14; proprietary sale of, 107–8; quality of soil on, 13
Anstey, John, 20

Baker, Charles, 53
Baltimore, Lady (wife of Charles, third Lord Baltimore), 7
Baltimore, proprietary lands reserved around, 3
Baltimore Reserved Lands. *See* Baltimore Reserves
Baltimore Reserves, 7; terms for leasing land on, 13; value of land on, 105, 107
Barns, 69, 73–76, 80–81
Beaverdam Manor, 5, 28, 45; description of, 150; dwellings and other improvements on, 57, 59–60, 62–71; economic status of tenants on, 44–45; effects of state sales of, 125, 127; natural resources on, 41, 44; price of tracts sold at state sale of, 127; proprietary sales of land on, 108
Biggs, John, 54
Black, James, 109, 130
Bordley, John Beale: on cultivation of tobacco, 93; on cultivation of wheat, 87, 100; opinion of, on poor whites, 84; on treading wheat with horses, 97
Bowdle, Thomas, Jr., on the disadvantages of being a tenant, 141–42
Brerewood family, 7

Briscoe, Hanson, 127
Briscoe, Isaac, 109
Brooke, Henry, 51
Brown, Henry, 109
Brown, James. *See* James Brown and Company
Bruce, William, 133

Cabin roof, definition of, 79–80
Calvert, Cecilius, second Lord Baltimore, 3
Calvert, Cecilius (secretary), 5, 22–23
Calvert, Charles, fifth Lord Baltimore, 15; policy of, on leasing manors, 9–10; visit of, to Maryland, 8, 10, 17
Calvert, Charles (governor), 3
Calvert, Charles, third Lord Baltimore, 2–3
Calvert, Frederick, sixth Lord Baltimore, 7, 15, 19, 21–22, 117; death of, 107; decision of, to sell the proprietary manors, 25–27, 104–5, 110
Calvert family, 1–3, 5
Calverton Manor, 6, 28; crops grown by tenants on, 87; description of, 151; dwellings and other improvements on, 59–60, 62–71; economic status of tenants on, 44–45; effect of state sales of, 129; natural resources on, 43
Campbell, William, 134
Capons, proprietary leases requiring, 158–59 n. 44
Carnes, Richard, 118, 127–28
Carroll, Charles, of Carrollton, opinion of, on confiscation of British property, 111
Cartwright, John, 118
Caution money, definition of, 2
Ceresville, 134
Chamberlain, John, 53, 76
Chaptico Manor, 6, 28; description of, 151; dwellings and other improvements on, 59–60, 62–71; effect of state sales of land on, 127–28; natural resources on, 43; proprietary sales of land on, 108
Chastellux, François-Jean de Beauvoir, Chevalier de, on poor whites, 83–84
Chew, Samuel, on taxes, 119
Chimneys: description of wooden, 62; on detached kitchens, 65; on tenant dwellings, 62–63, 73, 76, 79

183

THE JOHNS HOPKINS UNIVERSITY PRESS

This book was compsed in VIP Baskerville text and display type by The Composing Room of Michigan from a design by Susan Bishop. It was printed on 55-lb. Bookmark paper and bound in Holloston Roxite cloth by Publication Press, Inc.

Library of Congress Cataloging in Publication Data

Stiverson, Gregory A.
  Poverty in a land of plenty.

  (Maryland bicentennial studies)
  Includes bibliographical references and index.
    1. Farm tenancy—Maryland—History. I. Title. II. Series.
HD1511.U5S74   333.5'3'09752   77-4554
ISBN 0-8018-1966-0